INTELLECTUAL
PRIVILEGE

INTELLECTUAL PRIVILEGE

Copyright, Common Law, and the Common Good

TOM W. BELL

MERCATUS CENTER
George Mason University

Founders' © 2014 by Tom W. Bell (see opposite for more information)

Mercatus Center at George Mason University
3434 Washington Boulevard, 4th Floor
Arlington, VA 22201

Library of Congress Cataloging-in-Publication Data

Bell, Tom W.
 Intellectual privilege : copyright, common law, and the common good /
Tom W. Bell.
    pages cm
 ISBN 978-0-9892193-8-9 (pbk.) -- ISBN 978-0-9892193-9-6 (e-book
(kindle))
1. Copyright--United States. I. Title.
 KF2994.B45 2014
 346.7304'82--dc23
                            2014005816

Printed in USA

COPYRIGHT NOTE

Not long ago, in "Five Reforms for Copyright" (chapter 7 of *Copyright Unbalanced: From Incentive to Excess*, published by the Mercatus Center at George Mason University in 2012), I suggested that the United States should return to the kind of copyright the Founders supported: the one they created in their 1790 Copyright Act. The Founders' copyright had a term of only fourteen years with the option to renew for another fourteen. It conditioned copyright on the satisfaction of strict statutory formalities and covered only maps, charts, and books. The Founders' copyright protected only against unauthorized reproductions and offered only two remedies—statutory damages and the destruction of infringing works.

This book follows through on that policy advice. The Mercatus Center and I agreed to publish it under terms chosen to recreate the legal effect of the Founders' 1790 Copyright Act. For example, the book's copyright will expire in 2042 (if not before), and you should feel free to make a movie or other derivative work at any time. How do we plan to achieve this effect? The book's publication contract includes the following provisions, under the heading "Copyright":

1. That the copyright term, rights, and remedies ("Privileges") in the Book will extend only so far as would have been allowed by the U.S. Copyright Act of 1790, as of its enactment. With regard to all other copyright Privileges, [the Mercatus Center and Tom W. Bell] make a Creative Commons CC0 1.0 Public Domain Dedication, waiving all copyright and related or neighboring Privileges with respect to the Book to the fullest possible extent.

2. The Mercatus Center will make good faith efforts to comply with the formalities of the 1790 Copyright Act or, if current government policies make that impossible, to approximate the effect of those formalities through other means.

3. Prof. Bell and the Mercatus Center intend third parties to rely on this Agreement to limit the copyright Privileges in the Book. To encourage that reliance, Publisher will include in the Book prominent notice of these copyright terms.

I dedicate this book to my mother, Helen Cunningham, a now-retired librarian whose love of learning I have been privileged and quite right to copy. (You get the next one, Dad!)

CONTENTS

COPYRIGHT ON THE THIRD HAND

T wo views dominate the debate over copyright policy. The view from the left tends to question all restraints on expression, whether they arise from censorship, copyright, or the common law, and regards property rights as far from sacrosanct. From the right, in contrast, copyright looks like any other sort of property, which as such demands the same respect afforded to tangible property like land, buildings, and tools. Each viewpoint reveals important truths: copyright impinges on freedoms of expression, even while its exclusive rights stimulate the creation of new works. Both viewpoints, however, fail to perceive copyright's most distinguishing feature: its origin as a statutory privilege distinctly different from, and less justified than, the rights Americans enjoy thanks to the common law.

These pages build on that insight to offer a third view of copyright, one that does not quite fit the traditional left-right divide. You might think of it as a (not *the*) libertarian view, given that reasonable libertarians will disagree with many of this book's finer points and some of its major ones. Regardless of how you label this approach, though, it offers fresh answers to unresolved questions about the best way forward for copyright law and policy.

1. LEFT, RIGHT, AND FORWARD

Like most commentators, I largely agree that copyright represents not so much a form of property as a mere tool of policy, one designed to "promote the Progress of Science and useful Arts," as the Constitution puts it.[1] I thus refer to copyright not as a form of intellectual *property* but rather a form of intellectual *privilege*. So understood, copyright's justification relies entirely on whether it provides a "necessary and proper" means to "promote the general Welfare, and secure the Blessings of Liberty."[2]

As a creature of statute, copyright represents a notable exception to our natural and common-law rights. My friends on the left too often fail to make that distinction, instead classifying copyright as one of the many manifestations of state power that parade under the name of "property" and that they would subordinate to freedom of expression, security from want, distributional fairness, popular will, or other values. I instead hold that the common law, because it largely instantiates our natural rights, merits special regard. Hence my complaint against copyright: it violates the natural and common-law rights that we would otherwise enjoy to freely use our voices, pens, and presses. Hence also the argument I make to my friends on the right: copyright does not merit as much respect as tangible forms of property; as a statutory privilege to violate other, more fundamental rights, copyright instead merits critical scrutiny.

That critique of copyright hardly renders it unjustified per se. We can in theory excuse apparent violations of natural and common-law rights, such as the takings effectuated by taxation or the restraints imposed by antitrust law, as the costs of obtaining a greater good. So we might in theory justify copyright, too. But even then copyright would rank as a necessary evil at best. And even then, its status would rely on the contingencies of fact. If, for instance, as argued below, technological and social developments tend to render copyright unnecessary, it will someday rank as simply an evil. Perhaps, in some areas and in some respects, that day has already come. Regardless, we all have an interest in ensuring that copyright stays within its proper bounds. I thus offer here not an attack on copyright, but rather an appreciation of its noble goals, a frank account of its recent excesses, and some friendly advice about how to once more put copyright in the service of the general welfare.

2. ON ONE MORE HAND

On the one hand, we can disparage both copyright and common-law mechanisms for protecting expressive works. On the other hand, we can exalt copyright as a form of property more powerful than any conflicting common-law right. If we limit ourselves to those two hands, however, we embrace a false dichotomy. Conceptually, at least, we can best grasp copyright policy "on the third hand," recognizing that it cries out for justification because it violates common-law rights, and justifying it—if we can—only as a necessary and proper mechanism for promoting the public good.

This third view suggests a great deal about both how current copyright policies malfunction and how to fix them. The insights of this distinctly libertarian view of copyright include:

- A picture of copyright's relation to other forms of intellectual privilege/property;

- A bird's-eye view of the common law;

- An economic model for maximizing copyright's social benefits;

- A history of the non-natural, statutory origins of copyright;

- Reasons for respecting others' copyrights;

- An understanding of copyright as a type of statutory privilege, not property;

- The indelicate imbalancing of copyright policy;

- Fared use as a welcome relief from the misty boundaries of fair use;

- Using copyright's misuse defense to open an exit to the common law;

- Why and how to deregulate access to original expressive works;

- The benefits of *un*copyright and an open copyright system; and

- An account of why we will outgrow the need for copyright.

More generally, this perspective opens the prospect of moving beyond copyright's statutory privileges to once more rely on the common law to promote the common good.

I do not want to claim too much for this book's originality, however. The approach taken here finds its most direct precedents in the work of Thomas Jefferson, Tom G. Palmer, Timothy Sandefur, and other thinkers sensitive to the conflict between natural rights and copyrights. To these influences I add institutional analyses inspired by the likes of Friedrich A. Hayek, who explained spontaneous orders, and of the public choice school, which ably explains the incentives that influence lawmakers' behavior (and, sometimes, misbehavior). Randy E. Barnett has helped me to appreciate the source and importance of natural rights, while Richard A. Epstein and Bruno Leoni have taught me to appreciate the power and elegance of the common law's few simple rules. Economics can teach us a great deal about the function, proper limits, and probable future of copyright; William M. Landes and Richard A. Posner, among others, have influenced me on that front. Though this book aims to construct a new theory of copyright, therefore, it builds on solid foundations.

This book does not offer a comprehensive explanation of the libertarian approach to such fundamental questions as the significance of natural rights, the problems of political failure, and the relative fairness and efficiency of common-law rules. Readers who find the book's discussion of such points too brief should refer to the scholarship amply cited throughout. Readers entirely new to libertarian theory may find its moderation a pleasant surprise. This book nowhere calls for radically rewriting the Copyright Act, monetizing all exchanges of expressive works, or kicking artists to the curb.

The libertarian view of copyright offered here ends up confirming many opinions so popular as to verge on banal—that the Copyright Act pursues noble aims, that we can thank the gift economy for many expressive works, and that great artists merit respect, for instance. The same viewpoint also suggests original criticisms of, fixes to, and predictions about copyright policy. This says something about the virtues of libertarian theory. These pages do not go very far beyond that sort of proof-in-the-pudding to explain or justify libertarian theory, however, leaving that for other works.

3. STRUCTURE OF THE BOOK

Part I of the book describes copyright from a freedom-friendly, natural rights–respecting point of view, a vantage that offers many fresh and telling observations. Chapter 1 provides a quick introduction to copyright, describing its fundamental nature, its constitutional roots, its statutory enactment, and its relation to other legal entities. Chapter 2 turns to copyright policy, explaining the market failure that copyrights aim to cure and evaluating how well they work. Chapter 3 measures copyright against natural rights theory, unveiling a strong case for regarding copyright as an unnatural statutory privilege.

That skeptical take on copyrights does not mean they merit *no* respect. As chapter 4 explains, many moral considerations weigh against infringement. It does mean, though, that we should distinguish copyrights from natural and common-law rights. Chapter 5 describes copyright as an intellectual privilege, one that entitles its holder to restrict others' enjoyment of their natural and common-law rights.

Part I's libertarian perspective on copyright ends with a slightly sinister portrait. In contrast to the many courts and commentators who claim that copyright policy strikes a delicate balance between public and private interests, chapter 6 argues that copyright policy, even at its best, puts those forces into an *in*delicate *im*balance: "indelicate" because issued from the rough-and-tumble of political processes; "imbalance" because, even if they wanted to, policymakers could not fine-tune copyright to maximize social utility. Lawmakers do not demand the sort of numbers that delicately balancing copyright would require—numbers that, at any rate, do not exist.

Everyone can agree that copyright has not achieved perfection. Part II suggests several ways to improve copyright, all with the goal of promoting the public welfare more efficiently and treating natural and common-law rights with more respect. Chapter 7 explains why the fair use defense will shrink as licensing opportunities grow, and why we should welcome broader participation in markets for expressive works. Copyright holders might combine their statutory rights with technologically souped-up common-law rights to claim too much control over expressive works, but, as chapter 8 suggests, the misuse defense offers a ready cure for that scenario. Chapter 9 explains how we can open an escape hatch to a better world, one where the common law supplants copyright in promoting the authorship of original expressive works.

Part III describes a world free of copyrights and yet rich in consent and originality. Chapter 10 explains how uncopyright and ardent amateurs can overcome the supposed market failure that justifies copyright. Chapter 11 offers an economic analysis suggesting that as markets for expressive works grow, the need for copyright shrinks. Together, these chapters describe a future world in which the common law does a better job of promoting the general welfare, and progress in the useful arts and sciences, than copyright has ever done.

4. THE LIMITS OF LABELS

Although I describe the approach to copyright policy set forth in these pages as a libertarian one, I do not claim it as the libertarian one. Friends of liberty do not always agree about copyright. Many famous ones—such as Ayn Rand, Herbert Spencer, and Lysander Spooner—have ardently defended copyrights as both just and prudent. Others, such as Thomas Jefferson and (much more recently) Tom G. Palmer, have cast a skeptical eye on copyrights, seeing them as statutory inventions that violate customary, natural, and common-law rights. For reasons that I hope to make clear, I find the second approach more convincing.

I intend my references to left- and right-wing views only to help identify, rather than to pigeonhole, general points of view. Even someone who generally favors economic regulation over social regulation might voice support for stronger copyrights, just as even a free-market social conservative might argue for a broader fair use defense. Legal academics, in particular, often fail to fit four-square within traditional political stereotypes. Still, it often proves useful to distinguish among left-wing, right-wing, and libertarian views of copyright, because each of those categories marks out a particular relationship between respect for copyrights and respect for natural and common-law rights.

PART I

COPYRIGHT TODAY

What is copyright? The following introductory chapters explore its many aspects from several different points of view. Overall, they reveal copyright as a public policy tool justifiable in theory but of dubious value in practice.

Chapter 1 offers an introduction to copyright law and the common law, and to how the two relate. Chapter 2 provides a stripped-down description of copyright policy, built around the standard economic model of copyright. Chapter 3 covers the philosophical foundations of copyright, with a particular focus on the question of whether copyrights qualify as natural property rights or mere statutory privileges.

Questions about copyright's role in ordinary everyday life—whether or not to make a mix CD for a friend, for instance—are addressed in chapter 4. Chapter 5 reviews the language of copyright, arguing in favor of describing it not as a form of property but as a statutory privilege. Chapter 6 delves into the politics of copyright law, suggesting that public choice effects overwhelm the edicts of good public policy. The lesson, in sum, is that the United States needs less copyright and more freedom.

CHAPTER 1

WHAT IS COPYRIGHT?

W ho cares about copyright? It hardly seems a matter of life or death whether, for instance, ringtones qualify as public per-formances.[1] Still, copyright policy strongly shapes where we find our amusements, what we learn from others, and how we express ourselves.[2] Matters of life or death those are not. Neither, though, are they mere trifles.

This chapter offers a brief survey of copyright, providing readers unfamiliar with copyright with a useful background for the more specialized chapters that follow. Even old hands can find some fresh insights here, though. The chapter begins by reverse-engineering copyright's deep structure, explaining it as a statutory privilege to violate common-law rights. The chapter then traces copyright's constitutional limitations and reviews its enactment in statutory and case law. Next comes a portrait of copyright's relationship to patents, trademarks, and other types of IP (an acronym you can read as "intellectual privilege" or "intellectual property" as you see fit). The chapter concludes by drawing a contrast between copyright's complicated statutory privilege and the few simple rules of the common law.

1. COPYRIGHT: A STATUTORY PRIVILEGE TO VIOLATE COMMON-LAW RIGHTS

Copyright represents a unique and powerful legal privilege, one that allows copyright holders to restrict a wide range of unauthorized uses of expressive works. The author of a book might for instance refuse anyone else the right to copy, make a new version of, or publicly read or display the book. Few authors would flatly forbid such things, of course; there is no money to be had in that. Instead, authors and other copyright holders typically allow access to their works upon the satisfaction of certain conditions—including, most notably, payment. Copyright thus creates both a legal power to censor and an economic incentive to speak, an uneasy but unavoidable conflict that Neil Netanel, a professor at University of California, Los Angeles, School of Law, has aptly described as "copyright's paradox."[3]

Copyright's paradox reaches beyond mere speech, however. Although often described as a form of property, copyright relies for its very existence on *violating* property rights—the traditional common-law rights that each of us presumably enjoys in such tangible things as our printing presses, guitars, and throats. A copyright holder's statutory privileges do not come out of thin air, after all; they derive from others' property rights in tangible goods. A copyright holder's exclusive right to reproduce a work, for instance, limits what printers can do with their presses. Copyright's public performance right restrains wayward guitars, while the exclusive right to create derivative works would throttle any throat that dared to reinterpret a song. In effect, copyright redistributes common-law rights from we the people to authors and their assigns.

Copyright therefore violates *common-law* property in the name of *intellectual* property. That—rather than its apparent conflict with the First Amendment—marks copyright's most fundamental paradox. Common-law property rights largely encompass and embody our freedoms of expression. A conscientious regard for the rights of publishers to peaceably enjoy their paper and presses, for instance, and of readers to buy such books and newspapers as they alone see fit, poses a formidable bar to state censorship.[4] Copyright, because it conflicts not just with our freedoms of expression but also with our rights to our persons and property, stands revealed as a threat to common-law rights. That is not to condemn copyright as necessarily unjustified, of course. Our common-law rights suffer many infringements in the name of the general welfare—taxes, for instance. Nonetheless, that insight marks copyright as suspect.

Well-informed and well-meaning people disagree about copyright. Some regard it as a natural right, while others regard it as wholly unjustified. We can thus hardly rely on received wisdom to inform us about the fundamentals of copyright. Instead, we can only say that theories about

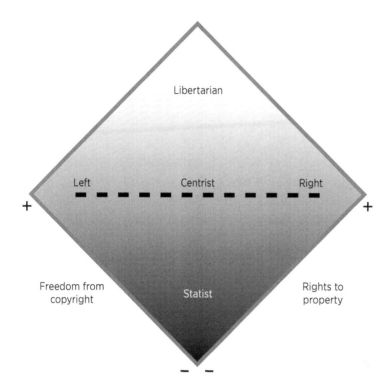

Figure 1. Political Views of Copyright

copyright fall into several broad types, each corresponding to a general political philosophy. Figure 1, above, illustrates.

The left tends to look askance at copyrights, subordinating them along with traditional property rights to such fundamental values as freedom of expression, distributional fairness, or security from want. The right, in contrast, tends to conflate property rights and copyrights, demanding respect for both. Those political labels gloss over some subtle distinctions and nonconforming examples, of course; "left" and "right" do not serve as exact and complete definitions. Nonetheless, they offer recognizable and useful simplifications.

In copyright theory as in general, the conflict between left-wing and right-wing views tends to make the most noise and attract the most attention. Notably, however, those perspectives mark only two corners of the map in figure 1. In the middle sits the sober centrism that currently reigns in judicial and academic treatments of copyright. According to that view, federal lawmakers have discretion to pursue copyright's constitutional mandate howsoever they see fit, so long as they do not change "the traditional contours of copyright protection," thereby triggering a First Amendment analysis.[5] Content to rely on the Constitution to justify copyright, that centrist view need not commit to any particular theory of property.

The bottom corner of figure 1 maps out the statist legal positivist view that copyright ranks as but one of many judicially recognized claims, all of them equally valid as creations of state power.[6] Common-law rights merit no special regard according to that view, and natural rights do not exist. Rights, whether they cover works of authorship, plots of land, or printing presses, issue only from the state.[7] That hardly gives copyrights a free pass, though; they must satisfy the same criteria that properly regulate all government action, such as promoting the general welfare, implementing the Constitution, or fulfilling the will of the people. Statist legal positivists do not, however, look askance at copyright as an apparent violation of other, more important values. They look at copyrights as at least as justified as any form of property right and possibly, by dint of their origins in positive (i.e., statutory) law, more justified than contradictory common-law rights.

This book explores the fourth fundamental view of copyright, the one perched in the upper quadrant of figure 1. That libertarian view smiles on property as not merely a tool of wise public policy, nor just a respected pillar of the common law, but as a fundamental human right. Copyright, because it relies on state power and infringes natural and common-law rights, commits at least an apparent injustice.

Are copyright's apparent violations of our natural and common-law rights excusable? This book tackles the question from both economic and philosophical standpoints. In sum, although the United States could in theory enjoy an optimal level of copyright, legislative processes tend in practice to oversupply it. We should instead try to rely on common-law mechanisms to reward original expressions.

Before we turn to those observations, however, let us address copyright's legal justification as a power enumerated in the US Constitution and codified in the Copyright Act. The next two sections take up those topics, each in turn. The first argues that copyright of some sort—though not necessarily of the present sort—has a solid footing in the Constitution's text. The second section tours the major landmarks of the Copyright Act, as well as some of its curiosities and horrors.

2. COPYRIGHT'S CONSTITUTIONAL LIMITATIONS

Because the Constitution expressly authorizes federal lawmakers to create special statutory privileges for authors, copyright enjoys a stronger foundation under US law than a great many government programs. As the Constitution says, "The Congress shall have Power . . . To promote the Progress of Science and useful Arts, by securing for limited Times to Authors . . . the exclusive Right to their . . . Writings."[8] Although it never uses the word, the Constitution plainly authorizes the sort of legal device we have come to call "copyright." To stay within the constitutional language that would justify it, however, copyrights must promote the progress of certain things—science and useful arts—via certain means: i.e., rights granted to authors, to their writings, for limited times.

In an attempt to implement that constitutional mandate, the Copyright Act adds a great many more qualifications and complications to copyright law. These are covered in some detail below. First, though, let us discuss the four constitutional limitations on copyright: it must promote progress, it rests in authorship, it applies to writings, and it lasts for limited times. In theory these could sharply curtail federal power. In practice they do not.

Copyright Must Promote Progress

The Constitution evidently acquiesces to copyrights not for their own sake but rather for purely practical reasons: to promote progress. What sort of progress? Here, even concerning the first words of the copyright clause, interpretations clash. Far from resolving the matter, the Supreme Court has offhandedly read the clause first one way, then another, and then yet another, leaving serious consideration to commentators.[9]

In full, the relevant constitutional clause enumerates a power "To promote the Progress of Science and useful Arts, by securing for limited

Times to Authors and Inventors the exclusive Right to their respective Writings and Discoveries."[10] Some authorities argue that "respective" imposes on the clause a comprehensively parallel construction, one under which copyright need only promote "the Progress of Science" to fulfill its mandate.[11] According to that view, patent law, the other subject of the relevant constitutional clause, aims only at promoting useful arts.[12]

Other commentators favor a reading that would have copyright promote the progress of both science and useful arts.[13] According to that view, "respective" imposes a parallel construction not on the clause's justificatory preamble but rather on "Authors and Inventors." To put it another way, the clause splits into two tracks only after "Times"—a word that obviously applies to both copyrights and patents. What good grammar here requires, moreover, traditional canons of statutory interpretation would likewise counsel: a reading of the copyright clause most likely to protect common-law rights from statutory encroachments.

What would copyright look like if lawmakers took the constitutional text seriously, requiring that copyright promote the progress of both science and useful arts? We would then have to look askance at the current practice of affording copyright protection to such purely artistic creations as songs, plays, novels, paintings, and sculptures. Even construing "science" broadly enough to cover all the *humane* sciences—a reading that copyright scholar and law professor Malla Pollack defends as a plausible original meaning of the term[14]—copyright law today focuses far more on expressive arts than on "useful" ones.

Taking "Science and useful Arts" seriously would thus radically narrow the proper scope of copyright. The first Copyright Act, enacted in 1790 by some of the same people who wrote and ratified the Constitution, covered only maps, charts, and books.[15] Permitting copyrights in the first two types of works plainly promoted both science and useful arts. The Founders probably regarded books, too, primarily as tools rather than diversions. In 1790 novels had yet to rise to prominence. The first American novel, William Hill Brown's *The Power of Sympathy*, had appeared only the year before, and even it aimed at practical ends, promising "to Expose the fatal consequences of SEDUCTION."[16] Judging from the titles in libraries and on sale, fiction made up only a small portion of the books available in late-eighteenth-century America.[17] The 1790 Copyright Act moreover excluded such purely artistic expressions as songs, plays, paintings, and sculptures—even though its drafters undoubtedly knew of and appreciated those sorts of works.

It appears, then, that "To promote the Progress of Science and useful Arts" originally meant that copyrights had to serve practical ends rather than merely expressive ones. But originalists should not rely solely on that constitutional limitation on copyright's scope. Given that "science" now connotes a more technical and specialized endeavor than it did in the eighteenth century, the plain, present, public meaning of the Constitution likewise counsels against extending copyright protection to purely artistic works.[18] Whether we give the Constitution's text its original meaning or its current one, therefore, copyright should cover little more than maps, charts, nonfiction books, illustrations, documentaries, computer programs, and architecture. Most songs, plays, fictional books, paintings, sculptures, dances, movies, and other artistic works should fail to qualify for copyright protection according to that view, because they fail to promote the progress of both science and useful arts.[19]

However rigorously logical, that argument against the constitutionality of almost all modern copyright law will probably generate more grins than agreement. Courts and commentators have hitherto hardly bothered to distinguish between "Science and useful Arts";[20] still less have they taken those words to limit federal power. Here as elsewhere, acquiescence to long-accepted practices has dulled us to the Constitution's bracingly straightforward words. We should read them anew and reflect that the founding generation evidently did not think that granting statutory privileges to such purely artistic creations as romantic operas or pretty pictures would promote the progress of both science and useful arts. Most honest laypeople today would, if presented with the Constitution's plain language rather than the convoluted arguments of judges, lawyers, and legal academics, probably come to the same conclusion about pop songs, blockbuster movies, and the like.

This is certainly not to say that purely expressive works lack value. They promote such cherished ends as beauty, truth, and entertainment. The Constitution requires that copyright promote something else, however—"the Progress of Science and useful Arts"—and a great many works now covered by copyright cannot plausibly claim to do both.

Though much more could be said about this parsimonious reading of the copyright clause, it here serves primarily to illustrate by way of contrast the generosity of the Supreme Court's interpretation of the clause. In the 2003 case *Eldred v. Ashcroft*, the court addressed the constitutionality of the Sonny Bono Copyright Term Extension Act, which extended US copyright terms not just for new works but for extant ones. The petitioners challenged the act as incapable of promoting progress "because it does not stimulate the creation of new works but merely adds value to works already created."[21] The court rebutted that argument, citing the fact that lawmakers had passed retroactive term extensions many times before, and reasoning that "Congress could rationally seek to 'promote . . . Progress' by including in every copyright statute an express guarantee that authors would receive the benefit of any later legislative extension of the copyright term."[22]

Eldred thus viewed prior retroactive copyright extensions, because they gave contemporary authors a reasonable expectation of further such extensions, as a basis for judging the latest one constitutional. The same argument could not have saved the first retroactive copyright extension, of course, the beneficiaries of which had no similar history to rely on, but it evidently did not face a constitutional challenge. A wag might say that *Eldred* turned a law that was unconstitutional when *first* passed into a defense of the constitutionality of *later* such laws, all based on the all-too-reasonable expectation that lawmakers would repeat the wrong. In truth, though, the justices probably never considered whether a retroactive copyright term extension could violate the Constitution, given that the *Eldred* court deferentially asked only whether the Sonny Bono Copyright Term Extension Act qualified as "a rational exercise of the legislative authority conferred by the Copyright Clause."[23] By thus announcing that it would enforce the "promote . . . Progress" term under the "rational basis" test—a test that asks only whether lawmakers could have had some reason for their actions—the *Eldred* court effectively said that it would pay no heed to the Constitution's demand that copyright law promote progress.[24]

Copyright Rests in Authorship

Copyright today covers a wide variety of works, including books, songs, movies, paintings, computer programs, and other original creations that convey authorship. In theory, even something as mundane as a casual doodle qualifies for copyright protection. As the Supreme Court explained in *Feist Publications, Inc. v. Rural Telephone Service Co.*, when it comes to satisfying copyright's authorship requirement, "The vast majority of works make the grade quite easily, as they possess some creative spark, 'no matter how crude, humble or obvious' it might be."[25] Only a "narrow category of works in which the creative spark is utterly lacking or so trivial as to be virtually nonexistent,"[26] such as the alphabetical listing of names at issue in *Feist*, will show too little authorship to qualify for copyright protection.

Copyright Applies to Writings

Considering all the works protected by copyright, US law evidently takes "Writings" in the Constitution to cover far more than mere words on paper. It does, however, require recordation of an author's expression. Copyright can inhere only in a *fixed* work—one preserved, as the act says, "in a tangible medium of expression . . . by or under the authority of the author, [rendering it] sufficiently permanent or stable to permit it to be perceived, reproduced or otherwise communicated for a period of more than transitory duration."[27] Books, phonorecords, paintings, sculptures, DVDs, buildings, and works in many other mediums qualify as "writings" under this standard; only such expressions as an unrecorded extemporaneous dance or a jazz improvisation remain unfixed and thus uncopyrightable.

Copyright Lasts for Limited Times

The Constitution requires only that copyrights last for "limited times"; it does not require that they last for a relatively brief time or for any particular time at all. To judge from the analysis in *Eldred*, moreover, federal lawmakers can change copyright terms—even the terms for already-existing works—largely as they alone see fit.[28] According to that view, "limited times" does little more than forbid nominally immortal copyrights. It does not forbid lawmakers from giving copyright extraordinarily long terms—say, a million years—or from repeatedly extending copyright terms so as to assure that they endure indefinitely. Given that "limited times" has no practical impact on copyright, we may well wonder why the Founders saw fit to include the phrase. Most likely, they meant to signal that copyrights represent not natural rights, which exist independently of lawmakers' whims, but rather statutory privileges, the scope of which depend entirely on legislated definitions.

3. THE COPYRIGHT ACT

What the Constitution defines in just one clause of twenty-seven words,[29] the Copyright Act covers in nine chapters, eighty-six sections, and over 78,000 words.[30] Obviously, I cannot hope to cover all that material in detail. Instead, this section discusses some of the most important and interesting provisions relating to copyright formation, term, exclusive rights, infringement, defenses, and remedies. That tour finds both solid good sense and twisted rules of dubious provenance in the Copyright Act's provisions. The section concludes with a bestiary of legal creatures, such as moral rights and copyright management systems, related to but distinct from US copyright law proper.

Subject Matter

The Copyright Act expressly recognizes several categories of expressive works, including literary works; musical works (along with any accompanying words); dramatic works (along with any accompanying music); pantomimes and choreographic works; pictorial, graphic, and sculptural works; motion pictures and other audiovisual works; sound recordings; and architectural works.[31] Computer software, though having significant economic importance as a separate category of work, does not appear in that statutory list but qualifies for copyright protection as a type of literary work, a category comprising all non-audiovisual works preserved in words, numbers, or other symbols.[32]

Copyright could in theory extend to works of authorship preserved in smells, tastes, or textures. Those media can, after all, record original expressions in much the same way that words, sounds, and pictures do. But the Copyright Act does not list perfumes, flavors, or textures within the scope of its coverage, nor does the Copyright Office offer any forms for registering such works[33]—and US courts have yet to demand otherwise.[34] These limits on copyright represent not just good law, but good policy. The problems of determining infringement alone counsel against expanding copyright coverage to such things as perfumes and flavors, because Americans suffer no obvious, persistent, and painful shortage of original works. Who among us, after all, bemoans the market's failure to supply, say, new varieties of air fresheners or packaged snacks at a low price?

The Copyright Act expressly disclaims restricting access to any "idea, procedure, process, system, method of operation, concept, principle, or discovery," a provision that helps preserve a fairly clean line between copyrightable works and patentable ones. *Lotus v. Borland*, for instance, explained that a computer program's command menu hierarchy could not be copyrighted because it "serves as the method by which the program is operated and controlled."[35] Similarly, courts have repeatedly protected stock scenarios and motifs—*scenes à faire*, in jurisprudential lingo—from suffering capture within copyright's exclusive rights.[36] The balcony scene, one-point perspective, blues chord progressions, and other creative building blocks thus remain free for all authors to use and reuse. Courts have created the merger doctrine to help ensure that nobody wins a copyright on an idea by way of copyrighting the only way of expressing it. The court in *Baker v. Selden*, for instance, having held that a method of accounting could not be copyrighted, also denied copyrights in the paperwork necessary for putting that method into use.[37]

As a further safeguard, this time against anyone using copyrights to secure the functional equivalent of a patent, the Copyright Act provides that if a "pictorial, graphic, or sculptural work" serves as a "useful article"— an artfully designed cork remover, for instance—the work qualifies for copyright "only to the extent that [the] design incorporates pictorial, graphic, or sculptural features that can be identified separately from, and are incapable of existing independently of, the utilitarian aspects of the article."[38] If a form cannot be peeled away from its functions, in other words, it cannot qualify for copyright. The designs of clothes, furniture, automobile bodies, and uninhabited architectural structures such as bridges or plazas have thus developed without the benefit of US copyright law.[39] And yet develop they have. Can anyone plausibly claim, after all, that Americans suffer a horrible deficiency in original dresses or sports cars? Here, as with perfumes, tastes, and textures, there are telling examples of industries that do not appear to have suffered for want of copyright's privileges.[40] Perhaps, as will be discussed more fully in chapter 9, that real-world experiment can teach us something about the need for copyrights in such things as books, songs, and computer programs.

Other sections of the Copyright Act forbid copyrights in works of the federal government[41] and in infringing works.[42] The former limit ensures that the public, as the ultimate patrons of the US federal government, preserves free access to its original expressions. The latter ensures that only original works enjoy copyright's privileges, and that only a copyright's holder enjoys the right to create derivative works.

Formation

As enacted, copyright subsists in an original work of authorship from its fixation in a tangible medium of expression.[43] More precisely, copy*rights* arise from the moment of a work's fixation. To enjoy copyright *remedies*—the ability to bring suit in federal court for infringement—copyright holders generally must register their works with the US Copyright Office.[44] That poses far less of a burden than getting a patent, however, and arguably even less than getting a driver's license, since registration forms typically run only a few pages,[45] get only a cursory review by the Copyright Office,[46] and demand payment of less than $100.[47]

The Copyright Act imposes no deadline on registration, so that an author can register a copyright at any time from the work's creation until its term expires.[48] The act encourages registration for authors likely to seek federal enforcement of copyright's privileges, however. If an author waits more than three months after first publishing a work to register it, and the author suffers infringement before registering, the act denies the remedies of statutory damages or attorneys' fees. If a work's author registers it within three months of first publication, in contrast, the act affords those and the rest of its remedies retroactively, to the date after publication and before registration, when infringement happened.[49] Especially eager authors—at least, ones who prepare certain works for commercial distribution—can even preregister their works.[50]

Although the requirements of authorship and fixation derive from the Constitution's text, the requirement of originality evidently does not. Patents, which arise from the same clause as copyrights, demand "novelty" from inventors. The difference between those words? Copyright's "original" means "new to the author," whereas patent's "novel" means "new to the world." In theory, authors who unwittingly mimic each other can hold copyrights in parallel. As Judge Learned Hand famously put it, "If by some magic a man who had never known it were to compose anew Keats's *Ode on a Grecian Urn,* he would be an 'author,' and, if he copyrighted it, others might not copy that poem, though they might of course copy Keats's."[51] In practice, Judge Hand's somewhat metaphysical scenario remains little more than that—metaphysical—because courts take marked similarities between two works as evidence that the later author copied the earlier one.

The act no longer requires authors to satisfy exacting statutory formalities in order to claim copyrights. Instead, simply fixing a work in a tangible medium suffices to secure its copyright. Using a copyright notice—a statement such as "© [year] by [author]"—does little more than negate the defense of innocent infringement, a defense that otherwise might limit actual or statutory damages.[52] Beyond that, though, the Copyright Act distributes its privileges very liberally, sweeping within its domain everything from software operating systems to graffiti tags, and from summer blockbuster movies to doodles in the margin of class notes. Scholars such as Christopher Sprigman, William M. Landes, Richard A. Posner, and Lawrence Lessig have ably criticized this laxity, and suggested instead that lawmakers reinstitute various copyright renewal requirements.[53] For now, though, US law makes copyright formation cheap and easy for authors.

Duration

The Copyright Act limits the standard copyright term for works created since 1978 to "the life of the author and 70 years after the author's death."[54]

Complications arise in the case of joint works, which are protected for the lifespan of the last surviving author plus 70 years; anonymous and pseudonymous works, which are protected for the lesser of the first publication of the work plus 95 years or the date of its creation plus 120 years; and works made for hire, which receive the same term as anonymous or pseudonymous ones.[55] Subtleties likewise abound in the rules covering works created before 1978.[56]

The duration of copyright has changed repeatedly over the decades, but the changes have always brought longer terms. The 1790 Copyright Act set the term as fourteen years, with an option to renew for another fourteen.[57] Subsequent acts repeatedly extended the term, not just for forthcoming works but also retroactively for existing ones. (Chapter 6 explains this phenomenon in public-choice terms, and figure 11 illustrates it as a steadily rising staircase.)

Exclusive Rights

Copyright rights resemble, but hardly mirror, property rights. The Copyright Act gives every author exclusive copying, adaptation, and publication rights, but it subjects those rights to a great many more limitations than the common law imposes on property rights in tangible things. Suffice it to say that copyright does not mirror tangible property, which is subject to a relatively simple rule for ownership's duration: a person can own moveable and real property for as long as it physically exists.

Structurally speaking, section 106 of the act giveth, and sections 107–22 taketh away. Tucked between those provisions, section 106A offers quasi-copyright rights to certain visual artists, a statutory afterthought discussed below along with statutory inventions. Other provisions in the act provide for the alienation—by sale, license, mortgage, and so forth—of copyright rights. Here, too, copyrights bear a family resemblance to the property rights honored in the common law.

Section 106 of the Copyright Act offers a fairly simple, though curiously circumscribed, list of rights. It enumerates six exclusive rights enjoyed by copyright holders. The first three rights—the right to make copies, the right to prepare derivative versions, and the right to distribute copies to the public—apply to all sorts of works. The fourth exclusive right listed in section 106, the right to perform the work publicly, applies only to dynamic works, such as songs and movies (but, notably, not to sound recordings). The fifth exclusive right, in contrast—the exclusive right to publicly display a work—applies only to visual works, such as paintings and sculptures. Lastly, section 106(6) gives those who create sound recordings the exclusive right "to perform the copyrighted work by means of a digital audio transmission."[58]

Section 106(6) does not wholly patch a notable lacuna in the act: the absence of any exclusive right to publicly perform sound recordings in any medium.[59] That means, for example, that a broadcast radio station need not ask the permission of record companies before playing their CDs on the air.

Why don't sound recordings fall under the public performance right in section 106(4)? In 1972, when sound recordings first received copyright protection under US law, lawmakers assuaged concerns about the costs imposed by the newly created statutory privilege by limiting it to less than the full panoply of exclusive rights.[60] The political maneuvering has continued since then; lawmakers have heard repeated pleas for broader sound-recording rights.[61] Lobbying has thus far garnered only section 106(6)'s digital audio transmission right, but not an all-purpose exclusive right to publicly perform sound recordings.

Has denying the holders of sound recordings a public performance right caused a market failure? Not evidently. Americans enjoy varied and cheap access to recorded music. Record companies may not make as much money as they would like to make, of course, but who does? The Constitution assigns to copyright the goal not of enriching any particular copyright holder but rather of promoting the progress of science and useful arts. On that measure, it seems fair to say that, regardless of whether the United States suffers a shortage of wealthy record companies, it does not suffer a shortage of recorded music.

Sections 107–22 of the Copyright Act impose many wide-ranging limitations on the exclusive rights set forth in section 106. The most famous of these limitations, fair use, provides a powerful but inexact defense against infringement claims. The fair use defense depends on four statutory factors: the nature of the use, the nature of the allegedly infringed work, the amount of the work used, and the effect of the use on the market for the infringed work.[62]

The first-sale doctrine, together with similar doctrines in section 109, allows the lawful owner of a particular, material copy of a work to dispose of it largely free of interference from the copyright holder.[63] Thus, for instance, a reader can (arguably) highlight a book without creating an unauthorized, and thus infringing, derivative work.[64] Still other provisions limit copyright's exclusive rights by imposing compulsory licenses on certain uses of certain works—the equivalent, in real property terms, of forcing a landowner to admit all paying customers.[65]

The provisions of sections 107–22 range from subtle generalities to nearly impenetrable thickets of fine detail, which taken as a whole bar copyright holders from the powerful exclusivity enjoyed by fee-simple owners of real or moveable property. Granted, copyright rights can be transferred in whole or in part, by gift, sale, operation of law, or other means of conveyance.[66] In that, copyrights function similarly to property rights generally. As legal scholars Ronald A. Cass and Keith N. Hylton ably explain, copyright's property-like features rank among its best features.[67] Nevertheless, copyright holders cannot claim alienation rights as robust as those enjoyed by the owners of tangible property. In that, copyright veers from the property model, leaving some authors (individuals who create their own works rather than those who hire others to create) holding something short of the power to assign all copyright's privileges to another party.

Because copyright shortchanges authors in terms of property rights, publishers stand on shaky ground. Those to whom an author and holder of a copyright tries to transfer rights cannot claim possession with anything like the security enjoyed by those who take title to tangible property. Limitations on the power of alienation appear in several sections of the act, all of which allow authors (or certain members of their estates) to take back copyright rights freely given to others.[68] Those exercising the termination power need not compensate losing transferees; indeed, they cannot even credibly commit to do so, given that the act refuses to countenance the enforceability of any agreement limiting termination.[69]

Although designed to protect authors from deals that seem unfairly disadvantageous in retrospect, the termination power most likely hurts the very authors who most need help, particularly those who might prefer to cash out the full value of their copyright rights. It also most helps the authors who suffer the least disadvantages—those who have become so successful that they can renegotiate on more favorable terms bargains made earlier in their careers. In that, the alienability of copyright rights looks not only much weaker than the alienability of tangible property, where the law respects the finality of transfers of title,[70] but also much less wise.

Infringement

Copyright infringement occurs when someone violates one of a copyright holder's exclusive privileges.[71] The copyright holder can then invoke the Copyright Act's enforcement mechanisms to make the infringer cease and pay.[72] At that level of generality, copyright infringement resembles the tort law wrong of trespass to real property. Liability in tort for trespass follows fairly clear lines—often, ones literally marked on the ground.[73] The 1790 Copyright Act likewise stuck to fairly well-defined boundaries, forbidding only the unauthorized duplication of entire works. Copyright has since expanded to vague borders, covering not just simple piracy now but also reinterpretations, longish quotations, and even unintentional borrowings of parts of a work. The courts struggle to define the proper boundaries of authors' expressions, leaving Americans wondering about what does and what does not infringe.

Run-of-the-mill piracy cases, where the defendant has made and sold many near-exact copies of the plaintiff's work, present obvious cases of infringement. Much of copyright's case law, however, deals with more subtle forms of infringement, as when a play's broad themes echo those of an earlier production,[74] or when a sketch deliberately mimics the style and subject matter developed by a particular artist.[75] Such cases do not present clear-cut violations of copyright's exclusive rights. The parties cannot agree whether one of copyright's borders has suffered a "trespass"—a sort of ignorance that seldom persists in real property law—so they litigate.

Courts asked to resolve those hard cases agree on infringement's general elements. A plaintiff alleging copyright infringement must establish both that the defendant *copied* the infringed work, an inquiry that further devolves into the elements of "proof of access" and "similarity," and that the defendant engaged in the *improper appropriation* of the work.[76] Courts also appear to agree that expert opinion—the views of a musicologist or art critic, for instance—can help decide the question of the amount of similarity required to show copying,[77] whereas lay opinion should decide the question of the amount of similarity—"substantial similarity"—required to establish improper appropriation.[78] Beyond this, however, the exact contours of infringement grow blurry.

For one thing, federal circuits do not agree on how proofs of access and striking similarity combine to establish the copying element of infringement. Some say the copyright plaintiff must always offer independent evidence of access;[79] others say that showing striking similarities between the infringed and infringing works can suffice to prove copying.[80] Furthermore, tests of infringement vary from medium to medium. In copyright cases concerning rights to computer software, courts often apply the "abstraction, filtration, comparison" test first set forth in *Computer Associates International, Inc. v. Altai, Inc.*[81] Music infringement cases evidently call for a different sort of analysis and cases concerning visual art for still another.[82] And what of a movie that builds on a song, or a poem about a book?

Courts have added indirect, or "secondary," liability to the panoply of legal tools that the act gives copyright holders, allowing them to sue even defendants only remotely connected to a direct infringer. As legal scholars Douglas Lichtman and William M. Landes observe, that judicial innovation probably represents wise public policy if the federal government wants to empower copyright holders to stop a significant percentage of mass infringements.[83] On the other hand, secondary liability has given copyright holders a power not evident in the Copyright Act,[84] expanding and blurring their statutory privileges. At present, after several Supreme Court judgments on the question, it appears that secondary liability for copyright infringement can arise in either of two ways. The first is upon a demonstration that the defendant committed *vicarious* infringement, by having the right and ability to prevent the infringement and by directly benefiting from the infringement. The second is by *contributory* infringement, by both aiding and abetting the primary infringement and by having had knowledge of it[85] (except that, in the latter case, the "substantial non-infringing uses" defense from *Sony Corp. v. Universal City Studios, Inc.*[86] does not foreclose proof that the defendant induced infringement).[87] Such rules, regardless of whether they on net improve copyright policy, cannot help but expand the scope of infringement in far-reaching yet ill-defined ways.

Though copyright infringement eludes precise definition, it happens with startling frequency—as will be shown in chapter 4. Some of that disturbing result is attributable to the extraordinarily broad scope of copyright infringement, the topic of this subsection, and the rest to the extraordinarily powerful remedies that copyright law brings to bear against infringement, the topic of the following subsection.

Remedies

The Copyright Act offers many and powerful remedies for infringement. It authorizes courts to levy injunctions against all manner of infringements, such as by ordering a defendant to stop reproducing or publicly distributing an allegedly infringing work.[88] For monetary relief, a copyright holder can choose between *actual* damages (caused by lost sales, for instance), together with any profits unjustly earned by the infringing party (but only insofar as that measure does not duplicate the award of actual damages), or *statutory* damages (set by the court, depending on various factors, between $200 and $150,000 per work infringed).[89] The act also allows for awards of costs and attorneys' fees.[90]

Other remedies apply only in special cases. Copyright holders can invoke the federal government's help in barring the import or export of infringing works, for instance.[91] Private litigants can also subpoena digital service providers to disclose the identity of an alleged infringer.[92] Certain defendants—proprietors of bars or restaurants, typically—may be liable for treble damages if they try to exonerate themselves with a legal claim that they "did not have reasonable grounds to believe" would actually exempt their public performance or display of a plaintiff's work.[93]

Recent amendments to the Copyright Act increase the power and scope of the remedies for infringement, subjecting infringing works and the articles used to make them to the civil asset forfeiture rules already wreaking havoc on property rights under the guise of the Drug War.[94] The act has long provided similar remedies in cases of criminal infringement.[95] Its criminal sanctions include fines and jail time for activities ranging from large-scale commercial piracy to loaning a friend a DVD of a movie soon to appear in theaters.[96]

Statutory Rights Related to Copyright

In addition to its namesake right, which covers expressive works, the Copyright Act also creates rights in artistic reputations,[97] in copyright management and protection systems,[98] and in boat hulls.[99] Because each of these three legislative innovations represents a statutory privilege that is outside the scope of common-law rights, each proves susceptible to criticism on the same grounds that criticism is levied against copyright. None, however, represents anything properly called "copyright."

The first of these rights vests in the authors of fine visual arts, rather than in copyright holders. Unlike copyrights, authors' rights (often mislabeled "moral rights" due to a mistranslation of *droits morales*) cannot be transferred; a visual artist can only waive them, at most.[100] Authors' rights allegedly protect the reputations of fine artists by empowering them to claim or disclaim authorship in given works and to prevent changes to their works in ways that might harm their artistic legacies.[101] Copyright, in contrast, aims at preventing a market failure in the supply of fixed expressive works.

The second paracopyright privilege restricts access to and use of the means of protecting copyrighted works, rather the works themselves. It appears in chapter 12 of the Copyright Act, and aims at protecting the digital management systems that themselves protect copyrights. Section 1201 throws various legal barriers in front of those who would circumvent technological measures controlling access to copyrighted works, such as the code that hinders computer users from making copies of DVDs, while section 1202 prohibits tinkering with information attached to a work, such things as the identity of its copyright holder or the terms of its use. Violating those provisions may trigger civil or criminal remedies.[102] Notably, a defendant can violate these digital management system privileges completely independently of any copyright infringement. These are not copyrights.

The third paracopyright privilege creates exclusive rights in a particular sort of useful design—one that, strictly speaking, falls entirely outside the scope of copyright. Chapter 13 of the Copyright Act paints with a broad brush, claiming that "the designer or owner of an original design of a useful article which makes the article attractive or distinctive" may enjoy the chapter's exclusive rights.[103] Thanks to a bit of legislative legerdemain, however, those provisions apply only to "a vessel hull or deck, including a plug or mold, which in normal use has an intrinsic utilitarian function that is not merely to portray the appearance of the article or to convey information."[104] That language, carefully chosen to fill a gap left in the act's definition of copyrightable works,[105] marks chapter 13's protections for ship designs as quite distinct from the sort of statutory privileges that concern the rest of this book.

4. COPYRIGHT'S FAMILY RELATIONS

All copyrighted works originate as ideas, born when authors choose how to express themselves. The slightest exercise of discretion will suffice; just about anything more original than an alphabetical listing of names can qualify as copyrightable.[106] Having crossed that low hurdle, it remains only for an author to fix the expression in a tangible medium for more than a transitory duration. The author must, in other words, record his or her authorship. After thereby fixing the work—in words, music, pictures, computer code, architecture, or almost any expressive medium—the author enjoys powerful legal rights grace of the federal Copyright Act.[107] Copyright thus inheres both in doodles and in multimillion-dollar movies, in works ranging in creativity from formulaic news blurbs to shockingly novel paintings.

These fundamental features of copyright mark it as a distinct legal species. Though laypeople often confuse copyrights with patents, trademarks, and other intangible goods, each of these related types of IP corresponds to a unique combination of subject matter and supporting law. Figure 2 maps the location of copyright and other legal rights within IP's world.

Figure 2 maps several legal dimensions. The left vertical scale divides IP into two fundamentally different categories. IP above the horizontal divide, such a trademark, has value only insofar as it helps to identify other things of value. Below the divide falls intrinsically valuable subject matter. Above, trademark helps consumers identify what they buy;

below, copyrights and patents give consumers things worth buying. The right vertical scale shows the source of a legal restriction. Toward the middle lies state common law, farther out lies state statutory law, and at the extremes lie federal statutory law. Unfair competition straddles all three categories, for instance, whereas copyright depends entirely on federal statutory law. The bottom horizontal scale indicates to what degree a particular kind of IP limits the free use of expressive or functional subject matter. Copyright stretches from poems to computer programs, for instance, whereas trade secret's comparatively narrow protections cover only commercially useful ideas.

The arrows on the map show the steps that various types of IP pass through as they develop. Each sort of IP begins at the center, as no more than an idea. Following the arrows shows how a mere idea can change, over time, into a recognized form of IP. In general, as the arrows move away from the center of the map, rights grow

- more developmentally mature,

- more powerful,

- harder to obtain, and

- more public and more in the federal realm.

Copyright, more than any other type of IP shown on the map, moves quickly and easily from a mere idea to purely federal privileges. Figure 2 shows two possible precursors to copyright: common-law protection of literary property and state statutory restrictions on unfixed expressive works. The former legal right expired on January 1, 1978, when the Copyright Act preempted it,[108] and appears here solely as a historical marker. The latter legal right has won general recognition in California legislation, which offers copyright-like privileges for unfixed works of authorship,[109] and narrower recognition in New York, which has enacted criminal sanctions on recording a public performance without permission and with the intention of profiting from doing so.[110] Neither common-law literary property nor state statutes restricting unfixed works offer much legal shelter. In most cases, therefore, ideas now speed directly to federal, statutory copyright without making any intermediate stops.

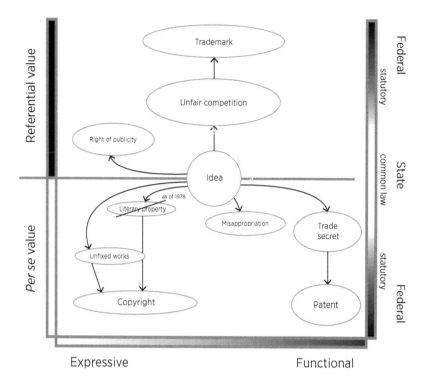

Figure 2. A Map of IP

Notably, figure 2 does not include what some courts and commentators have called "common-law copyright." The Supreme Court long ago established that US copyright restrictions originate not in the common law but, "if at all, under the acts of Congress."[111] Granted, the common law did protect expressive works from unauthorized first publication. But that created only "literary property," which is something quite distinct from, and distinctly weaker than, copyright's exclusive publication rights.[112] As noted copyright authorities Melville B. Nimmer and David Nimmer explain, the common law's protection of authors' rights over unpublished works was "referred to somewhat inaccurately as common law copyright."[113] Figure 2 eschews that misleading label.

The protean nature of the common law allows other interpretations of its scope, admittedly. New York courts have in recent years created— "recognized" would overstate the case, given that the courts did not claim to uphold any customary practice—a common-law right against the unauthorized duplication of publicly distributed sound recordings made before February 15, 1972, the date on which federal copyright first extended to such works.[114] The decisions of only one state's courts hardly suffice to define the common law, however, especially when all other states that have considered the question have reached a contrary conclusion.[115] It also remains a bit cloudy whether the common law's protection of literary property extends to unfixed works; several courts have denied that it does[116] while a few courts have hinted at a broader right.[117] With regard to these questions, as with regard to interpreting case law generally, it seems wisest to claim only the most widely respected legal principles as common-law rights.

5. COPYRIGHT VS. THE COMMON LAW

Because copyright stands in sharp contrast to the common law, we can learn about the former by studying the latter. This section offers a quick sketch of the common law, describing how custom, courts, and commentary have together generated an admirable body of rules for governing social behavior. As Richard A. Epstein has observed, the common law comprises just a few simple rules—simple, and yet together very powerful.[118] At its most basic, the common law protects three fundamental goods: our persons, our property, and our promises. This section describes the origins and effects of those protections, concluding that common-law rights might very well do as good a job of promoting progress in science and useful arts as does that statutory privilege, copyright.

A Bird's-Eye View of the Common Law

In the magisterial *Origins of the Common Law*, Arthur R. Hogue cautions, "The greater a man's knowledge of the law, the more hesitant he will be in answering the question: What is common law?"[119] He described his favorite subject well. The common law resists a hard, fast, and comprehensive definition. Like a vast and rugged mountain range, it offers many vistas.

Hogue saw the common law as a creature of medieval royal courts, and he defined it as "a body of general rules prescribing social conduct, enforced by the ordinary royal courts, and characterized by the development of its own principles in actual legal controversies, by the procedure of trial by jury, and by the doctrine of the supremacy of law."[120] Others see the common law in every judicial pronouncement of nonstatutory law. Richard A. Posner, for instance, defines it as "any body of law created primarily through judges by their decisions rather than by the framers of statutes or constitutions."[121] Seen from yet another angle—the one adopted here—the common law appears as a development of custom, courts, and commentary. *Black's Law Dictionary* offers the following as its first definition of the common law: "the body of those principles and rules of action, relating to the government and security of persons and property, which derive their authority solely from usages and customs of immemorial antiquity."[122] The common law resists easy summation, but it seems fair to say that it has been tried and tested over hundreds of years and thousands of cases and done a commendable job striking a fair balance between rank anarchy and suffocating control. It arises from an abiding regard for rights in persons, property, and promises.

According to that view, the common law originates in custom, wins recognition in courts, and develops in commentary. Custom naturally comes first.[123] It long ago gave rise to a set of social practices, such as avoiding bloodshed, honoring borders, and upholding oaths, that permitted people to live in peace and prosperity. Today, reference to custom continues to help common-law courts resolve disputes. A judge might for instance determine reasonable conduct in a tort case by looking to community standards,[124] award legal rights to someone who has long and openly used property technically entitled to another,[125] or interpret a contract's language by light of trade usage.[126] In these and other ways custom inspires (though hardly mandates) the common law.[127] Commentators, looking back over many court decisions and across many years, are able to follow the common law's development. Figure 3 illustrates.

Figure 3 traces the common law's origins from unarticulated customary practices, found in actions but not words, through the administration of justice, to purely verbal commentaries on the law. Up to a point, then,

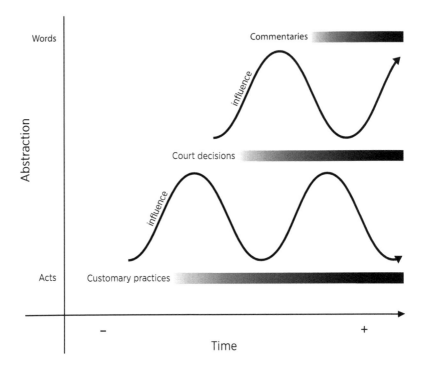

Words

Commentaries

influence

Abstraction

Court decisions

influence

Acts

Customary practices

−

+

Time

Figure 3. The Common Law's Development

the common law grows increasingly abstract over time; hence the initial upward cast of the arrows of influence laid out in figure 3. But the forces driving the common law's development also flow downward, toward more concrete results. Legal commentary sometimes persuades a judge, balanced on the cusp between two plausible claims, to choose one over another. Legal decisions sometimes affect customary practices, as when businesspeople adapt to local precedents concerning the solemnization of contracts through seals. The threads of custom, court, and commentary intertwine, weaving over time a tapestry of actions, words, and well-ordered social life. That may offer an idealized picture of the common law, granted, but what it lacks in detail it makes up for in scope.

At its most basic and elegant, the common law comprises just a few basic rules. Epstein boils the common law down to five fundamental principles: self-ownership, the right of first possession, voluntary exchange, protection against aggression, and a limited privilege based in necessity.[128] I here condense the first two of Epstein's five principles into respect for persons and property, and set aside the necessity defense as one of the common law's subtleties that, however important in lifeboat situations, has little bearing on copyright.

Thus refined, the common law embodies three fundamental principles: (1) aggress only in self-defense, (2) do not trespass on another's tangible property, and (3) honor voluntary commitments. Put even more succinctly, the common law commands that we respect persons, property, and promises. We find it convenient and useful to follow these fundamental principles. They seem natural to us. They should: they have evolved alongside us during the long journey from tribes, through kingdoms, to states. They will doubtless continue to guide our progress toward other forms of social organization.

Rather than simply inventing it out of whole cloth, courts have defined the common law by deciding how customary rules apply to particular disputes. In their collective wisdom, over hundreds of years, judges and commentators in Britain, the United States, and other common-law countries have refined the principles of tort, property, and contract law. They have bequeathed to us a detailed set of time-tested and mutually supporting rules, well chosen to safeguard our peace and prosperity.

Nobody planned that happy outcome. The common law instead evolved spontaneously, over many centuries and in countless cases, to protect our persons, property, and promises. Tort law, property law, and contract law do the heavy lifting. Beyond those three, at the core of the common law, bloom a variety of more specialized sets of rules, such as those pertaining to agency, restitution, and trusts.

Many commentators have observed that the common law tends to protect natural rights;[129] others add that it tends (or at least did tend) to promote economic efficiency.[130] My own review of the common law's deep structure reveals a related but distinctly different feature: the justification of legal relations varies by degrees and measures consent.[131]

The common law includes sophisticated mechanisms for distinguishing among various grades of consent, on a scale that ranges from express consent, through implied and hypothetical consent, and down into hypothetical, implied, and express unconsent. The common law tends to afford more justification to transactions nearest the top of that scale, enforcing expressly consensual transactions under the law of contracts, for instance, while condemning expressly unconsensual transactions as torts. To put this in the most fundamental terms, common-law rules tend to maximize the consensual disposition of property.

What property rights does the common law respect? Those honored in custom and long recognized by courts, such as the rights a person exercises over him- or herself, moveable goods, and land. In defining the rules for property rights, as with other common-law rules, judges have largely respected custom, though they have also stood ready to correct habitual injustices such as slavery.[132] Treatises and restatements of the law summarize, clarify, and systematize the common law's rules.[133] Those foundational sources say nothing about copyright, instead aiming only to capture the principles of property, tort, contract, and other areas of the common law. Copyright is not a form of property long recognized by custom, courts, and commentators; it instead arises as a constitutional power and a statutory privilege.

Looking beyond Copyright

Because it originates in our customs, the common law naturally fits our social needs. Its rules for respecting persons, property, and promises form a necessary framework for civil life. Perhaps the common law could provide a sufficient framework for supporting original expressions of authorship, too. That remains an open question, and one well worth asking in copyright's case. Can the common law beat the Copyright Act in terms of promoting the progress of science and useful arts?

The world enjoyed fixed expressive works—the works of Shakespeare, for instance—before copyright came along. The common law evidently suffices to encourage *some* authorship. How?

Authors can use property law and tort law to keep their draft works private. They might release authorized copies only on mutually agreed-to terms, enforceable under contract law. An author, or more likely an author's publisher, might publish copies only subject to built-in technical defenses, ones that the common law can help to nurture by keeping labs under lock and research confidential.[134] Even though the common law does not protect an author's expression per se, it protects the author's person and physical copies of the author's work. Even absent copyright, authors can profit from selling such things as live performances, originals, signed copies, and custom works. Authors can also benefit from the right, bestowed by the common law on each of us, to transfer what we own to whomever we please. The common law respects productive labor and honest begging alike, empowering authors to sell their services, or the physical artifacts they produce, or the public honors bestowed on patrons of the arts.

Other as yet undiscovered arrangements of common-law rights could do a great deal to stimulate the creation and distribution of works of authorship. Whether the common law could thereby match copyright in the race to "promote the general Welfare"[135] and "the Progress of Science and useful Arts" remains uncertain.[136] To help unravel that mystery, we should encourage authors and copyright holders to experiment with common-law alternatives to copyright. If copyright were thereby to become an unnecessary stimulus to authorship, it would be an improper one. The common law alone would then better serve the common good. That brings us to the question of the optimal policy for copyright, the topic of the next chapter.

CHAPTER 2

COPYRIGHT IN PUBLIC POLICY

opyright, Justice Oliver Wendell Holmes explained, "restrains the spontaneity of men where, but for it, there would be nothing of any kind to hinder their doing as they saw fit";[1] namely, copying others' original expressions. What public policy does copyright, that notable statutory exception to our common-law rights, pursue? Courts and commentators explain it as a response to market failure—as a cure for situations where property rights and voluntary transactions fail to serve the general welfare. This chapter elaborates, tracing copyright's path from a toll good, toward a public good, and—thanks to the Copyright Act[2]—back to a toll good. Next, the chapter reviews the standard economic model of copyright and amends it to better describe the effects of copyright infringement. That exercise leads to a suggestion about how public policy could in theory optimize copyright's contribution to social welfare—a suggestion that comes freighted with a crippling admission: lawmakers lack both the incentives and the information needed to implement an ideal copyright policy.

1. COPYRIGHT'S PUBLIC POLICY PATH

Works of authorship usually originate in private, kept safely under lock and key, confidentiality agreements, or other common-law protections. Once published, however, expressive works become what we might call *data ferae naturae*—wild and natural information. As such, expressive works roam and reproduce freely. We sometimes capture expressions in copies, caging them in atoms or bits. But once the public has enjoyed an expressive work, it tends to retain relatively cheap access to it. Or, rather, the public *would* freely enjoy published expressive works *if* copyright did not intervene.

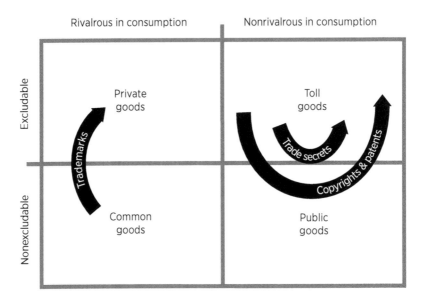

Figure 4. The Paths of IP

Note: For more details about the chart, including discussions of trademarks, trade secrets, and patents, see the full version, available at www.tomwbell.com/teaching/IP_Paths.pdf.

Copyright law limits public access to expressive works, herding works off the commons and into private hands. The Copyright Act aims to provide a sort of ranch to authors, giving them a place to nurture and sell their expressive works safe from the deprivations of grasping strangers. Authors enjoy those special privileges not as a natural right, but solely thanks to a public policy authorized by the US Constitution and implemented through the Copyright Act. Figure 4 illustrates the policy path that copyright, together with some of its legal next-of-kin, takes from its origins toward its ends.

Figure 4 offers a variation on economists' familiar fourfold classification of different types of goods. The table's rows indicate whether one who holds a given good finds it cost-effective to fend off nonholders. Excludable goods, such as apples or clubhouses, readily yield to fencing. Nonexcludable goods, such as the open seas or a shared language, prove uneconomical to defend from unauthorized access. The table's columns indicate whether a good tolerates only one-time use or, instead, offers a flowing stream of shared benefits. A good qualifies as rivalrous in consumption when to enjoy it you have to extinguish it. When you eat an apple, for instance, you end up with only a core; feed your sheep on the village green and you leave less clover for your neighbors. In contrast, all can enjoy a toll good (such as a cable TV transmission) or a public good (such as a broadcast TV signal) without exhausting it. Cross those two columns with those two rows and you end up with four types of goods.

Figure 4 uses that fourfold table to portray how copyright and some related legal rights wend their way through public policy. Expressive works (as well as trade secrets and patentable inventions) begin as toll goods, excludable but nonrivalrous in consumption. In other words, authors can at first keep others from consuming their expressions thanks merely to common-law tort, property, and contract rights. They can keep their works in private, under lock and key, and release them only upon solemn oaths of secrecy. Those with whom they share their work can enjoy it without decreasing the authors' enjoyment of the same; authors can sing their songs or study their paintings just as well if others enjoy their own copies. That marks all works of authorship as nonrivalrous in consumption. (The same holds true of trade secrets and patentable inventions.)

An author's expression retains its nonrivalry in consumption if the author publishes the work. The work then tends to lose its excludability, however. Unless the author can enforce a contract with everyone who encounters this published work or protect it with technological locks (devices used to limit access to services, such as Tivo or Netflix), the author has to rely on copyright to prevent others from accessing the work. Copyright steers published works back into toll goods' territory, empowering authors to assess fees and impose other limits on those who would use their works. (Patent law plays a similar role in preserving the excludability, and thus profitability, of publicly disclosed inventions. Trade-secret law, in contrast, helps to prevent certain types of commercially useful information from ever suffering public disclosure; the arrow in figure 4 tracing the fate of trade secrets thus shows them veering away from the pitfalls of nonexcludability.)

Why does copyright policy follow that particular path? Though we might ask out of mere curiosity, in copyright's case we might also ask because we demand a justification. The privileges created by the Copyright Act, because they restrict everyone but the author from freely enjoying a copyrighted work, defy natural and common-law rights. Without copyright, after all, we could freely copy expressive works. Why, then, does copyright dare to restrict our liberty?

Copyright negates the public good offered by expressive works in order to generate an even *greater* public good: the creation and distribution of new expressive works. So runs the most popular justification for copyright. Copyright takes away freedom and gives fees, licensing, and outright denial in return. We the People arguably profit from that policy bargain, given that copyright encourages the production and distribution of new works of authorship. The Founders evidently thought that copyright offered a good deal for the fledgling United States, because they established a Constitution that specifically empowers federal lawmakers to enact "necessary and proper" legislation to "promote the general Welfare" and "the Progress of Science and useful Arts." The result: the Copyright Act of 1790.

As chapter 1 explained, the Copyright Act gives the author of a fixed work certain exclusive rights to use that work in certain ways. The exclusive rights created by the act cover such things as the reproduction, public distribution, creation of derivative works, public performance, and public display of the work.[3] A copyright holder can treat those rights much as any piece of property, limiting access to them, selling them, or abandoning them to the public.[4] And, like tangible property rights, copyrights may prove valuable.

What makes copyright's exclusive rights valuable? They grant to a copyright holder the privilege of directing state action against unauthorized users of a restricted work. With that grant of state power, a copyright holder can enjoin and extract money from infringing defendants. People respond to incentives. The threats of getting dragged into court, suffering fines and orders, and landing in jail suffice to discourage a great deal of infringement. Many would-be infringers instead become willing consumers of copyright-restricted music, books, movies, games, pictures, maps, computer programs, and so forth. Some of copyright's revenues flow to authors, rewarding their work and encouraging more.

Perhaps we cannot say everybody is happy with copyright policy. Still, it seems like a plausible and good-faith attempt to protect us from a poverty of authorship. Copyright policy works imperfectly but it has hardly proven a disaster. It may, however, prove redundant. Handling expressive works solely with common-law tools might prove both more equitable and more efficient than relying on the Copyright Act. That remains a question of fact—one an economic model of copyright might help to answer. The next section shows the standard approach to that problem, preparing the way for the updated economic model that follows thereafter.

2. THE STANDARD ECONOMIC MODEL OF COPYRIGHT

Creating a work often costs an author a lot, whereas copying a work usually costs others very little.[5] Without copyright's help, authors might find it discouragingly difficult to recoup their expenses, and they might underproduce fixed expressive works and leave the public facing a market failure. To avoid that policy tragedy, the Copyright Act empowers authors to control certain reuses of their fixed expressive works. By selling those special statutory privileges, authors can offset their production costs. Copyright thus arguably does what the common law cannot: it ensures that the public enjoys an adequate supply of expressive works.[6]

The benefits of copyright policy come at a price, however. Absent copyright's restrictions, fixed expressive works would qualify as nonexcludable and nonrivalrous in consumption.[7] Copyright, in other words, bars the public from enjoying public goods.[8] Instead, the act vests copyright holders with the power to charge whatever the market will bear to escape liability for infringement. Though the monopoly rents that copyright holders thereby win allegedly provide a necessary stimulus to creativity, nonholders suffer the opportunity costs of losing cheap access to fixed expressive works.[9] Most commentators thus understand copyright policy to aim at striking a balance between giving authors sufficient incentives to create expressive works and providing the public with adequate access to the works thereby created.[10] Figure 5 illustrates this standard economic model of copyright policy.

As portrayed in figure 5, authors incur large costs upon creating a fixed work but very low marginal costs of production (MC) thereafter.

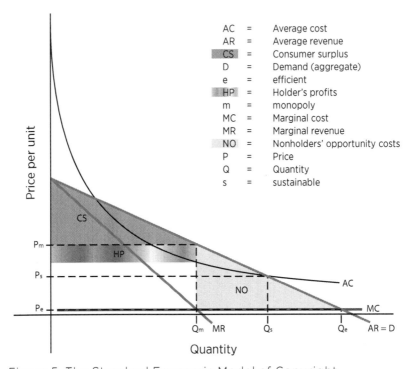

AC	=	Average cost
AR	=	Average revenue
CS	=	Consumer surplus
D	=	Demand (aggregate)
e	=	efficient
HP	=	Holder's profits
m	=	monopoly
MC	=	Marginal cost
MR	=	Marginal revenue
NO	=	Nonholders' opportunity costs
P	=	Price
Q	=	Quantity
s	=	sustainable

Figure 5. The Standard Economic Model of Copyright

Note: This portrayal of the standard model comes largely from Christopher S. Yoo, "Copyright and Product Differentiation," NYU Law Review 79 (2004): 227, fig. 1, which both sums up the traditional view among legal academics of the economics of copyrights and corrects it by setting the proper bounds for measuring profit. My chart differs from Yoo's, however, in showing average costs to exceed average revenue at low levels of production. That assumption, while not strictly necessary, doubtless describes most copyrighted works more accurately.

Authors' average costs of production (AC) thus drop with each additional copy they—or, more likely, the party to whom they sell their copyrighted work—produce. They face the usual sort of downward-sloping aggregate demand curve (D), which also marks the average revenue (AR) they can make by selling any given number of copies.

How many copies should they sell? Were public welfare alone the test, they would sell the quantity (Q_e) corresponding to the point where their marginal cost curve crosses the demand curve, earning the corresponding price (P_e). But that would discourage them (and later would-be authors) from creating fixed expressive works, as it would not allow them to recover their average costs. For them to break even in the authorship business, they would need to sell at least the quantity corresponding to the point where their average cost curve crosses the demand curve (Q_s), thereby earning a sustaining price (P_s).[11] Happily for them, though, the monopoly privilege afforded by copyright law allows them, at least in theory, to sell even fewer copies (Q_m), and at a higher price (P_m). Specifically, they will want to sell a quantity that corresponds to the point where their marginal revenue (MR) curve crosses their marginal cost curve. At higher quantities, their marginal costs would exceed their marginal revenues, giving them marginal losses.

If our hypothetical authors manage to sell at the monopoly quantity and price that maximizes their benefits, they will earn profits (HP) equal to the amount their revenue exceeds the amount necessary to recoup their average costs. In that event, consumers to whom they sell will enjoy a surplus (CS) representing the difference between what they pay and how much they value the authors' work. Non-owners unwilling to pay what the authors demand, however, will suffer opportunity costs (NO) equal to how much they would have paid for the uses barred by the authors' assertion of copyright.

We could doubtless say more about the standard economic model of copyright, adding complications,[12] quibbles,[13] and criticisms.[14] I will say more in chapter 10, where I explain why the United States stands a good chance of outgrowing copyright. For now, though, let us assume that figure 5 offers a useful economic model of copyright.

3. THE SPECTER OF COPYISM

In the standard economic view of copyrights, as in the economic view of other monopolies, average revenue equals demand. Those two measures trace one and the same line. Why? Because for most products and services, consumption closely matches supply at the market-clearing price. Sales reveal consumer demand and, in the case of copyright and other supposed monopolies, only one seller reaps revenue from those sales. Thus, for instance, a utility's average revenues faithfully track the aggregate consumer demand for electric power.

Even a so-called monopolist might face competition, however. An electrical utility might for instance suffer theft from unauthorized taps on power lines, competition from home-generated electricity, and exit to gas appliances. So, too, might the sole authorized seller of hard liquor fail to capture the entire market of drinkers, losing some to the resale of stolen goods and others to hand-brewed moonshine.

The caveats to "monopoly" prove especially applicable in the case of copyright, which permits some uses of privileged works—such as fair uses—that copyright holders do not authorize, and which fails to prevent many uses—such as infringing ones—that copyright law expressly forbids. We might fairly say that uses in the former category, because copyright holders have no statutory power to bar them, do not really cut into the market share for a copyrighted work. Copyright holders cannot lose what they never had, according to that view. The same cannot be said of infringing uses, however: by definition, they violate copyrights. A copyright holder thus never commands a true monopoly in the market for expressive works.

Instead of simply calling copyright a monopoly, we should talk about it in terms of market power.[15] Whether or not it hands out monopolies, after all, the Copyright Act *does* give a powerful subsidy to those it favors: the privilege of invoking state power to inhibit infringing uses of expressive works. The standard economic model of copyright usefully captures that effect, but somewhat exaggerates it. We can get a more accurate picture of copyright by splitting consumer demand from average revenue.

Thanks to pirated copies and other unauthorized uses, the consumption of an expressive work may greatly exceed the supply legally permitted under copyright law. This breaks the relationship between revealed demand and average revenue. Some consumers effectively treat copyrighted works as public goods, paying only the low marginal costs necessary to enjoy an unauthorized use. Free-riding consumers still pay, of course. But they pay not in cash but in the costs of arranging an unauthorized use—sneaking into a theater or walking to the library, for instance. None of those kinds of payments go to copyright holders, leaving them legally wronged, possibly aggrieved, and sometimes litigious. But copyright holders seldom find it worthwhile, or even possible, to fully defend their statutory privileges. Many infringing acts go undetected or for other reasons elude enforcement. Figure 6 illustrates that phenomenon,

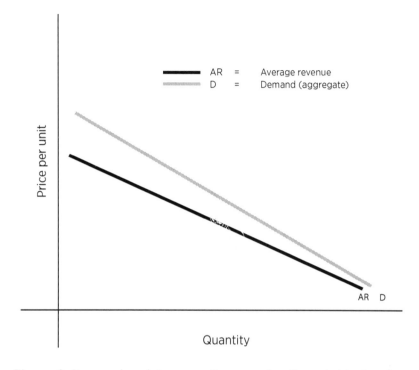

Figure 6. Demand and Average Revenue for Copyrighted Expressions

showing how aggregate consumer demand for a copyrighted work can diverge from the copyright holder's average revenue.

Copyright holders understandably object when, due to infringement, they earn less revenue than the law entitles them to. But why should the rest of us care? Recall that copyright aims to cure a looming market failure: we will suffer an undersupply of expressive works if authors cannot recoup their production costs. Copyright aims to cure that failure by giving authors the privilege of controlling, and thus profiting from, certain uses of their works. Infringement threatens to upset that statutory mechanism, depriving authors and their transferees of revenue that might otherwise stimulate the production and distribution of expressive works.

We might call that threat, after Marx and Engels, "the specter of copyism."[16] And, as the allusion to their manifesto suggests, we should all

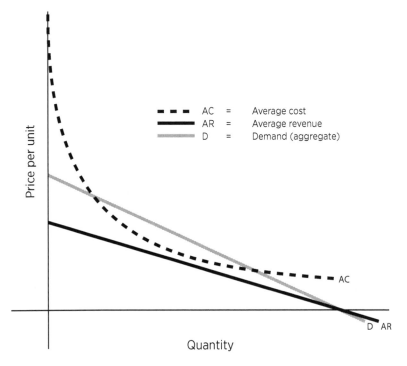

AC	=	Average cost
AR	=	Average revenue
D	=	Demand (aggregate)

Figure 7. When Unauthorized Uses Discourage Authorship

worry that poverty will follow if production does not pay. In the case of copyright policy, in other words, we should worry that infringement will decrease copyright holders' revenues below the level necessary to sustain authorship. As figure 7 illustrates, that threatens to deprive the public of new expressive works.

As figure 7 indicates, infringement threatens to drive a wedge between aggregate consumer demand for a work (D) and the average copyright revenue generated by the work (AR). Depending on the work's average cost curve (AC), infringement might thereby stymie the production of original expressive works. Copyright holders might not find it worthwhile to produce a work absent the prospect of recovering at least their average costs, even though consumers would willingly expend more than the work's average cost to have it. Thus might the specter of copyism curse us with market failure.

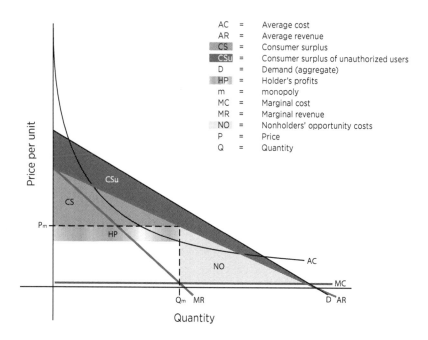

AC	=	Average cost
AR	=	Average revenue
CS	=	Consumer surplus
CSu	=	Consumer surplus of unauthorized users
D	=	Demand (aggregate)
HP	=	Holder's profits
m	=	monopoly
MC	=	Marginal cost
MR	=	Marginal revenue
NO	=	Nonholders' opportunity costs
P	=	Price
Q	=	Quantity

Figure 8. When Unauthorized Uses Increase Consumer Surplus

4. OPTIMIZING COPYRIGHT

While rightly shuddering at the specter of copyism, we should also recognize that the unauthorized use of copyrighted works can, if it does not go so far as to undercut authors' incentives, increase social wealth. Consider, for instance, an impoverished entrepreneur relying on pirated software to start a business. If this entrepreneur cannot afford to buy an authorized copy, and if the unauthorized use will not depress software production, the infringement will generate a welcome consumer surplus. The same would hold true of, say, someone who enjoys an infringing copy of a CD despite being unwilling to pay its retail price.[17] As figure 8 illustrates, these exceptions to the strict enforcement of copyright law could in theory benefit us all without discouraging the production and distribution of expressive works.

Figure 8 shows unauthorized and unpaying uses effectively competing with revenue-generating uses that respect copyright. Authorized users of the work pay the copyright holder price P_m to enjoy the work. That prices some law-abiding consumers out of the market—those non-owners who forgo the work rather than infringe it. They suffer the opportunity costs marked by area NO. These sorts of economic and legal constraints do not trouble certain users, however, whom I here style "unauthorized users" of copyrighted works.[18] Unauthorized users pay for access to an expressive work not by honoring copyright's demands, but rather by taking a path around the law.

Unauthorized users usually do not have notable fixed start-up costs; they do not need to invest in equipment or the like but instead pay only their marginal costs (MC) to access copyrighted works.[19] They typically do not pay in coin, but rather in terms of time, effort, and risk. That does not make a difference according to a purely economic view, which regards a cost as a cost, regardless of whether it arises due to lost time, labor, money, or anything else of value. It does matter, however, that to some consumers the gains of an unauthorized use may outweigh its costs, providing an opportunity for profit that unauthorized users seize. In figure 8, the surplus gains of all such unauthorized uses fill the area below the aggregate demand curve (D) and above the average revenue curve (AR), all the way down to where that demand curve crosses the low, low marginal cost of production curve (MC).

The large consumer surpluses in figure 8 look appealing, especially since they coexist with copyright holders' monopoly profits. Figure 8 surely offers too sanguine a view of the effects of copyright infringement, however. Without the limitations imposed by copyright law, some consumers who would otherwise willingly pay for *authorized* uses might instead opt to save their money by joining the unpaying masses of *un*authorized users. The resulting exodus, from respecting copyright to infringing it, would risk decreasing the revenues afforded by copyright, bringing about the policy tragedy portrayed in figure 7. Why? Because the market described in figure 8 would not generate enough revenues to support the monopoly price (P_m) for the monopoly quantity (Q_m). Under competitive pressure from unauthorized uses, the demand curve for the authorized uses of the work would sink. If any copyright holders remained in such an unremunerative market and the exodus continued unchecked, they would eventually find that they could sell their works only at their marginal costs. The specter of copyism stirs again.

How does copyright law dispel the looming threat of copyism? By imposing high marginal costs on infringing uses of privileged works. Absent the Copyright Act, and especially in digital works, an infringer would generally face the same low marginal production costs as a copyright holder.[20] Thanks to the Copyright Act, an infringer might instead have to pay actual or statutory damages, lost profits, costs, or attorney's fees.

How high should lawmakers set the marginal costs of infringement? We would not want them to under-deter infringement, lest the specter of copyism become all too real. Nor would we want lawmakers to over-deter impermissible uses, given that a modest level of infringement can deliver social gains. Theory suggests that lawmakers, taking into account that only some infringing uses get caught and litigated, should set the marginal costs of infringement just high enough to ensure that authorized users will have no incentive to opt for paying less than enough to sustain authorship.[21] In other words, lawmakers should set the marginal costs of unauthorized uses (MCu) equal to a price just sufficient to sustain authorship (P_s). Figure 9 illustrates.

It bears noting that this portrayal of copyright differs from the one offered by William M. Landes and Richard A. Posner, who instead offer an economic model of copyright in which the marginal costs of infringers slightly rise with the number of uses.[22] Their assumption certainly seems likely with respect to some infringers, given that larger copying operations tend to run greater risks of detection and prosecution. With regard to distributed mass infringement, however, individual copiers may find safety in numbers, thus incurring lower marginal costs as the number of unauthorized uses increases. Remaining agnostic about how those and other effects might in practice affect the marginal cost of unauthorized use, and favoring theoretical simplicity over actual error, figure 9 draws MCu as level.

The story does not end with figure 9, however. Even after the law artificially inflates the marginal costs of infringing copyrighted works, consumers will still migrate from authorized uses to unauthorized ones. The market-clearing price for a work will thus tend to settle very close to the marginal cost of infringing the work. Authorized and unauthorized uses of the work effectively compete, after all. The costs of infringement—set by the law—determine how much copyright holders stand to earn

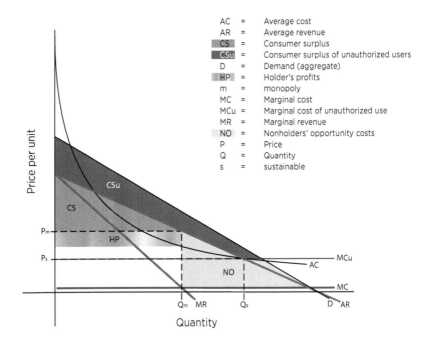

Figure 9. Copyright Increases Marginal Costs of Unauthorized Uses

by enforcing statutory privileges and, indeed, whether enforcing those privileges offers any net gain at all. Where, then, should lawmakers set the marginal costs of unauthorized uses of copyrighted works (MCu)?

Copyright policy should not aim to price all unauthorized uses out of the market. The unauthorized uses that it does allow will, granted, decrease copyright holders' profits. Copyright policy rightly aims at affording copyright holders only just enough revenue to cover their average costs, however. Any amount above that level unjustifiably runs up nonholders' opportunity costs, sacrificing the public good. To maximize the net social benefits of copyright, therefore, legislators should price the marginal costs of unauthorized uses at a level sufficient to allow copyright holders to recoup their average costs. This would tend to encourage consumers wavering at the margin between authorized and unauthorized uses to opt for authorized ones. Over time, in the main, and holding all else equal, we should expect copyright holders' revenues to drop to a level

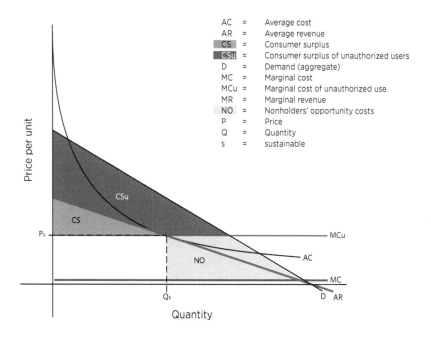

Figure 10. Effects of Setting Marginal Costs of Unauthorized Uses at an Authorship-Sustaining Price

just sufficient to allow them to recoup their average costs. Eventually, copyright holders would enjoy no monopoly rents at all; they would instead find that they could sell immunity from the exercise of their statutory privileges only at a price just sufficient to sustain an optimal level of authorship. Figure 10 illustrates.

Comparing figure 9 with figure 10, we see that competition from unauthorized uses of the copyrighted work in question has pushed the average revenue (AR) curve backward and down. In figure 10, where consumer demand (D) exceeds the marginal cost that copyright law imposes on unauthorized uses of the work (MCu), consumers rationally disregard copyright law. By instead opting to engage in unauthorized uses of the work, consumers enjoy large surpluses (CSu). Consumers who respect copyright law, but who value the work at greater than its market price, also enjoy surpluses (CS). Copyright holders caught in the world portrayed by figure 10 no longer extract monopoly profits; instead, they find that the market supports sales at a quantity (Q_s) and price (P_s) only just sufficient to recoup the average costs (AC) of producing the work. Even at that low price, copyright enforcement still imposes opportunity costs (NO) on consumers, who would have paid less for the work absent copyright. Copyright restrictions get in the way of consumer surplus. That arguably constitutes a necessary evil, however, given that a lower price would leave copyright holders unable to recoup their costs and, thus, unwilling to supply the market for expressive works.

So goes copyright in theory. In practice, as will be seen in chapters 10–12, lawmakers lack both the information and incentives to calibrate copyright policy so precisely or so well. Economic models can explain only how copyright law *should* work—not how it *does* work. And given how copyright policy does work—at best as a necessary evil—we would better serve the general welfare by encouraging the development of alternative mechanisms, based not in statutory law but in the common law, for promoting the production and distribution of original expressive works. After all, the economic analysis offered in this chapter considers only what level of copyright restriction we should aim at if we assume unhindered and unpaying infringement as the alternative. A fuller analysis would recognize that common-law mechanisms—property rights in tangible goods, contractual arrangements, gifts, and so forth—might also restrict unauthorized uses of expressive works and thus help fund their creation.

Given the fact that the prevailing defense of copyright casts it as a response to market failure, the common law by implication stands accused of failing to do enough to promote authorship. But perhaps that gives the common law too little credit. Perhaps we should instead worry that the common law might go too far, overprotecting intangible goods and so decreasing the public good. It certainly does not seem as if the Supreme Court thinks any such problem looms,[23] however, and the threat that common-law rights might restrict expressive works even more than copyright does can only, given the latter's current influence, appear slightly ludicrous.

What should lawmakers do? For now, in a world where copyright's influence predominates over the common law, good public policy should aim at setting the marginal cost of infringement equal to the authorship-sustaining price for winning access to restricted works. In the longer run, however, given that we cannot realistically expect copyright law to hit so small and moving a target, legislators should embrace a public policy that encourages authors to rely more on the common law and less on copyright.

CHAPTER 3

COPYRIGHT, PHILOSOPHICALLY

D ifferent people—reasonable and informed people—voice widely differing views about the proper philosophical approach to copyright. Perhaps we could pass over that debate without missing much; perhaps copyright *law* matters far more than copyright *philosophy* does. Philosophy finds traction in the law, however, giving abstract principles real effect. And even apart from its practicality, musing about the ultimate foundations of copyright provides a fresh perspective on old questions such as the origins of property, the existence of natural rights, and the justification for state action.

This chapter offers some philosophically flavored observations about copyright. That is not to say that no law appears at all, however; section 1 describes a general legal principle, respected from before the Constitution until today, that statutory enactments such as the Copyright Act give way to the common-law rights in all but the enactments' most undeniable commands. Even if it were a natural right, therefore, copyright would play second fiddle to the common law. As section 2 argues, however, those who originally proposed and ratified the US Constitution did not mean for it to treat copyrights as natural rights. On this point, history should instruct our philosophy. Section 3 wraps up the discussion with a review of property theory, surveying arguments for and against copyright. I conclude, as do others who appreciate Locke, that labor-desert theory does not suffice to justify copyright. Nor does Kantian theory.

John Locke and Immanuel Kant do not offer the only explanations of natural rights to property, however. Professor Randy E. Barnett of Georgetown University's School of Law offers as an alternative a natural legal positivist argument that, following Friedrich A. Hayek's lead, justifies property rights conditionally, tying them to the preferences for social peace and prosperity. I offer a related justification for natural rights, one that looks to the rights we can credibly assert without the benefit of state enforcement. Neither of these non-Lockean justifications of natural property rights appears to fit copyright very well, however. Philosophically speaking, copyright stands or falls on utilitarian grounds. It either maximizes social welfare or it does not. If the former, we can at least grant copyright grudging respect. If the latter, we would be better off without it.

1. THE QUESTION OF COPYRIGHT'S NATURALNESS

Who cares whether copyright qualifies as a natural right? Not many lawmakers, judges, or lawyers. They regard the question as settled. According to the conventional view, detailed in chapter 2, copyright represents nothing more than a tool of public policy. Courts and commentators do not rank its provisions with those of the Bill of Rights.[1] They see it as merely a possibly useful way to promote the general welfare and the progress of science and useful arts—not as a natural right.

That pragmatic dismissal of the question certainly saves time and effort. Even if copyright qualified as a natural right, after all, it would merely join a panoply of other natural rights. Nothing would authorize copyright to trump other natural rights, such as the rights to freedom of expression and the peaceable enjoyment of tangible property.

Even though I argue below that the original meaning of the Constitution did not treat copyrights as natural rights, I must admit that the point remains contestable. We simply cannot achieve certainty at so long a remove and about a topic not evidently all that important to those who first proposed and ratified the US Constitution. Even an originalist who regards copyright as a natural right should recall, however, that the Founders by no means set up a federal government to trample our common-law rights in tangible property, nor our rights at common law to enforce promises, nor to resist torts. An originalist Constitution treats common-law rights with the utmost respect, infringing only within sharp limits and only when necessary and proper to promote the public welfare.

As proof of that historical claim, consider that state copyright laws from the Founding Era did not include preemption clauses.[2] To the contrary, those statutes often took care to constrain copyright from unduly interfering with common-law rights. Connecticut's pre-constitutional copyright act provides, for instance, that "nothing in this act shall extend to affect, prejudice or confirm the rights which any person may have to the printing or publishing of any book, pamphlet, map or chart, at common law, in cases not mentioned in this act."[3] That provision, like similar ones in other state laws of the era, reflects a general principle: the Founders regarded statutes as legislative attempts to remedy salient defects of the common law and interpreted statutes against the backdrop of that general aim.[4] It thus seems very unlikely that the Founders would have understood copyright—whether a natural right, a fundamental civil liberty, or a statutory privilege—to automatically trump the common law.

Because it embraces that same canon of statutory interpretation that the Founders did, the Supreme Court would regard common-law rights with similar solicitude. The court has long held that "statutes which invade the common law . . . are to be read with a presumption favoring the retention of long-established and familiar principles, except when a statutory purpose to the contrary is evident."[5] Congress legislates against a background of common-law principles;[6] it "does not write upon a clean slate."[7] The Supreme Court has consequently held that common-law doctrines "ought not to be deemed to be repealed, unless the language of a statute be clear and explicit for this purpose."[8] The Copyright Act of course offers no exception to that general principle of interpretation.[9]

Elevating copyright to a natural right therefore would hardly render it inviolate. Courts and legislatures would still need a rule for settling conflicts between copyrights and other natural rights, such as those traditionally embodied in constitutional and common law.[10] We would have little reason to automatically favor copyrights–*qua*–natural rights over other natural rights, ample reason to instead favor the latter, and every reason to let the holders of expressive works choose which rights to exercise.

Admittedly, then, the question of copyright's naturalness has little bearing on much of this book's argument. Regardless of philosophers' disputes, the law would continue to require that copyright generally defer to common-law rights, and we would still want the sort of equitable and efficient public policies that respect for common-law rights can engender. Some readers might thus want to presume copyright's unnaturalness and turn directly to the next chapter. Others might prefer to stay, joining me in this chapter's investigation into whether copyright qualifies as a natural right.

2. COPYRIGHT'S UNNATURAL ORIGINS

We cannot be absolutely sure what the Founding generation thought about copyrights. They did not get much attention during public discussions about the newly proposed Constitution and, of course, interpretations of what the Founders said varies. It seems safe to say, however, that we have less reason to think that the Founders viewed copyright as a natural right than we do to think they regarded it as a statutory exception designed to promote the people's general welfare. Granted, some states under the Articles of Confederation had prefaced their copyright laws with invocations of natural rights. Set in context, however, those preambles sound more like excuses than justifications. At any rate, the rhetoric of those state copyright statutes makes the solely utilitarian language of the US Constitution copyright clause all the more conspicuous. The musings of the Framers likewise fail to recognize copyrights as natural rights. To the contrary, even copyright's most prominent defender among the Framers, James Madison, described it as "among the greatest nusances [sic] in Government."[11]

Original Meaning via State Copyright Acts

Twelve of the thirteen states governed by the Articles of Confederation passed copyright acts.[12] Of those twelve acts, seven had preambles that invoked natural rights.[13] The historical context of those statutes, however, gives their rhetoric an air more of apology than philosophy.

State legislators must have realized that they were contradicting the view, pervasive during the Founding Era, that such statutory monopolies favored special interests over common liberties.[14] The Maryland Declaration of Rights, for example, had decreed in 1776 "that monopolies are odious, contrary to the spirit of a free government, and the principles of commerce; and ought not to be suffered."[15] State legislators almost certainly realized, furthermore, that they had indeed enacted copyright statutes to appease a special interest—a small but influential lobby of authors and publishers led by Noah Webster, author of the famed speller, grammar book, and dictionary.[16] By invoking the rhetoric of natural rights, state legislators discouraged criticism that they had, after less than a decade of independence, disinterred statutory monopolies of the sort that earlier had helped spark the Revolution.

The states evidently invoked natural rights merely as rhetoric, however, given that none of their copyright statutes actually treated copyright as a natural right. A natural right would last indefinitely and cover all expressions; state copyrights lasted only a few years and covered just a few types of expressions. No state copyright statute covered paintings, prints, sheet music, or sculptures. The broadest of them covered only "literary" works.[17]

A natural right would protect all authors; state copyrights generally covered only US authors.[18] A natural right would disregard publication dates; most states denied copyright to any work printed before the statute took effect, regardless of its originality.[19] A few states even discriminated between different types of original expressive works, allowing maps and charts to qualify for copyrights regardless of when they were printed while denying copyrights to books and pamphlets printed before their statutes took effect.[20]

A natural right would arise, well, naturally. In contrast, no state allowed copyright as a matter of course. New Hampshire and Rhode Island demanded that authors identify themselves[21] and all the other state copyright acts imposed registration requirements of one sort or another.[22] North Carolina demanded that copyright holders forfeit a copy to the secretary of state[23] whereas Massachusetts demanded that two copies go to "the library of the University of Cambridge."[24] Several states went so far as to demand that copyright holders provide works at reasonable prices and in sufficient numbers.[25] No natural right would admit all the many sharp, artificial, and arbitrary limitations seen in the state copyright statutes. Despite their invocation of natural rights rhetoric, the states in fact treated copyright purely as a utilitarian tool for promoting arts and sciences in general, and special interests in particular.

At any rate, every iota of faith that one invests in the view that some state legislatures embraced a natural rights view of copyright ultimately ends up weighing against the view that the Constitution embodies the same philosophy. Those taking part in the Constitutional Convention almost certainly had state copyright practices in mind as they crafted the copyright clause.[26] Indeed, they quite possibly heard from the first copyright lobbyist, Noah Webster. Although the secretive nature of the Constitutional Convention obscures the extent of his influence,[27] circumstantial evidence strongly suggests that Webster, who had already done much to bring about various states' copyright acts, also successfully lobbied the Philadelphia delegates to add a copyright clause to the Constitution.

The absence of any reference to natural rights in the Constitution's copyright clause thus suggests that the Framers considered and rejected the natural rights defense of copyright. The same conclusion follows from the natural rights language that appeared in the report of the committee that the Continental Congress charged with considering "the most proper means of cherishing genius and useful arts through the United States by securing to the authors or publishers of new books their property in such works."[28] As mere legislative history, the claim of the committee's May 10, 1783, report that "nothing is more properly a man's own than the fruit of his study" carried even less legal weight than similar rhetoric appearing within the statutes passed by the states.[29] More to the point, the fact that James Madison and Hugh Williamson served as both members of the committee and delegates to the subsequent Constitutional Convention leaves very little room for doubt that those who drafted the Constitution must have considered and rejected justifying copyright on similar grounds.

Nor will it do to assert that the Constitution's terse language precluded any claim that copyrights protect natural rights. The clause's command that copyright "promote the Progress of Science and useful Arts"[30] shows the Framers completely willing and able to retain the utilitarian rhetoric of the state copyright statutes.[31] The *expressio unius* rule of interpretation, which holds that to list some items is to exclude others, strongly suggests that the Constitution does not support a natural rights justification of copyright, while the plain language in the clause itself invokes nothing beyond utilitarian goals. That the clause calls for legislation "securing" copyrights implies, if anything, that federal law should render more secure the rights formerly covered, in piecemeal fashion, under various state laws, thus comporting with Madison's defense of the clause: "The States cannot separately make effectual provision for" copyright.[32] As federal lawmakers later explained of the Constitution's copyright and patent clause, "There is nothing said about any desire or purpose to secure to the author or inventor his 'natural right to his property.'"[33]

Original Meaning via Madison on Copyright

Finding no record of substantive discussions about copyright in the Philadelphia Convention or in the state ratification debates, commentators intent on reconstructing how the Founders understood the Constitution's copyright and patent clause have largely relied on Madison's brief analysis of it in the Federalist Papers.[34] Here is Madison's full defense of the power granted to Congress in the copyright and patent clause:

> The utility of the power will scarcely be questioned. The copyright of authors has been solemnly adjudged, in Great Britain, to be a right of common law. The right to useful inventions seems with equal reason to belong to the inventors. The public good fully coincides in both cases with the claims of individuals. The States cannot separately make effectual provision for either of the cases, and most have anticipated the decision of this point, by laws passed at the instance of Congress.[35]

Like the grandiloquent preambles that some states added to their copyright acts, however, Madison's defense of copyright sounds more like rhetoric than logic.[36]

Intentionally or not, Madison misrepresented copyright's standing in common law. He presumably relied on the 1769 decision of the King's Bench in *Millar v. Taylor*, which read the Statute of Anne not to abrogate common-law protection of authors' works.[37] But the House of Lords overruled that case five years later, in *Donaldson v. Becket*[38]—thirteen years before Madison published Federalist No. 43. Madison's claim that copyright "has been solemnly adjudged, in Great Britain, to be a right of common law," therefore had as much truth as would a modern claim that, based on long-outdated cases, slavery has been solemnly adjudged constitutional.[39] Though neither represents an out-and-out falsehood, both statements unnecessarily risk causing confusion.

Notwithstanding Madison's reference to solemn adjudications at common law and to the "claims of individuals" to copyrights, moreover, he does not seem to have held a natural rights view of copyright. The telling evidence appears in what he said—or rather what he did *not* say—in his correspondence with Thomas Jefferson. Jefferson had written from Paris critiquing the proposed Constitution for failing to include a bill of rights, advocating in particular that it "abolish . . . Monopolies, in all cases." Jefferson explained that "saying there will be no monopolies lessens the incitements [*sic*] to ingenuity . . . but the benefit even of limited monopolies is too doubtful to be opposed to that of their general suppression."[40] Madison's remarkable reply merits lengthy quotation:

> With regard to Monopolies they are justly classed among the greatest nusances [*sic*] in Government. But is it clear that as encouragements to literary works and ingenious discoveries, they are not too valuable to be wholly renounced? Would it not suffice to reserve in all cases a right to the public to abolish the privilege at a price to be specified in the grant of it? Is there not also infinitely less danger of this abuse in our Governments than in most others? Monopolies are sacrifices of the many to the few. Where the power is in the few it is natural for them to sacrifice the many to their own partialities and corruptions. Where the power, as with us, is in the many not in the few, the danger can not be very great that the few will be thus favored. It is much more to be dreaded that the few will be unnecessarily sacrificed to the many.[41]

Madison said three things that bear note. First, contrary to his claim in Federalist No. 43 that the "utility of the power" granted to Congress in the copyright and patent clause "will scarcely be questioned," in private

Madison recognized Jefferson's concerns as potentially fatal for copyright. Second, note that Madison appears never to have followed up on his suggested remedy for the abuse of copyright's privileges—namely, abolishing the privilege after paying its holder a specified price. Third, Madison's assessment of the relative power that the many, who suffer monopolies, hold over the few, who enjoy them, ignores what public choice theory would predict and what experience has amply confirmed: the few who enjoy copyright have in practice more power to determine the scope of their privileges than do the many tasked to obey them.

Madison's reply to Jefferson's critique of the copyright and patent clause is most noteworthy, however, for what it does not say. Madison nowhere defends the clause as a measure necessary to protect the natural rights of authors and inventors (much less to protect their common-law rights). Madison's silence on that point would prove remarkable in any context.[42] Here, though, writing to one of the foremost advocates of natural rights, in reply to Jefferson's call for a bill of rights, and in defense of the copyright and patent clause, Madison's silence speaks tomes. Could any context cry out more loudly for an appeal to the supposed natural right to copyright? Madison instead treated copyright as nothing more than an admittedly dangerous tool for advancing industrial policy, and one of dubious efficacy at that.[43] Madison's defense of copyright uses "natural" only in describing political incentives—not rights.

Before closing this exploration of Madison's thought, it bears noting that a thoroughgoing originalist—one devoted to following the Founders in matters of both substance and process—might question the propriety of interpreting the Constitution's copyright clause by light of the original understanding of "copyright." The Founders generally agreed that extrinsic evidence of legislative intent ought not to shape statutory language; they demanded fidelity to the plain meaning of the text.[44] In this particular case, however, it appears that the Founders regarded copyright as an infringement, albeit perhaps a necessary one, on common-law rights to person and property. Because the Founders viewed statutes as attempts to remedy the defects of the common law, they thought it proper to construe ambiguous statutory language against the backdrop of that general purpose.[45] Questions about the original understanding of copyright thus neatly join with questions about how to interpret the Constitution's language on copyright. The Founders regarded copyright as an uncommon exception to common-law rights—a statutory privilege, in other words—and would have interpreted the Constitution to treat it exactly as such.

3. COPYRIGHT IN NATURAL RIGHTS THEORY

Perhaps natural rights do not exist. Many clever people say as much, arguing that humans enjoy rights thanks only to the state. According to that view, all rights equate to privileges—all issue from an institution that can credibly claim a monopoly on initiating coercion within a particular geographic area. Even in that view, as discussed earlier in this chapter, copyrights should defer to common-law rights. And, of course, copyrights logically could not in that view qualify as natural rights. Philosophizing about copyright would then reduce to a utilitarian cost-benefit analysis. There might still be good reason to support at least some form of copyright—as Richard A. Epstein appears to do, for instance[46]—but we would do so only tentatively, as a matter of prudence rather than of principle. I argue elsewhere that the realities of copyright law and policy, as well as the fundamentals of economics, should at least leave us doubting whether we need as much copyright as we now get, and should arguably have us seriously consider whether we need copyright at all. But those points speak more to philosophy than to practice.

What if natural rights do exist? In that event, there might be good reason to philosophize about copyrights not just as tools of public policy but as rights on par with those humans enjoy in their persons, property, and promises. This sections considers several justifications of natural rights: Locke's labor-desert theory, Barnett's naturalist legal positivism, and my preferred, somewhat existential one. The first offers the greatest hope for those who argue that copyright ranks as a natural right. Locke's theory suffers telling criticisms at the hands of Epstein and others, however. Friends of natural rights should not despair at that; they should instead embrace the possibility that property theory has advanced beyond Locke's early, imperfect effort. More modern explanations of natural rights, such as Barnett's natural legal positivism or a theory that, returning to the roots of Locke's approach, looks for rights humans can credibly assert without state enforcement, arguably do a better job of justifying property.

Those latter-day explanations of natural rights do not, however, appear to justify copyrights. Whereas we can justify property rights in tangibles (as well as in enforceable promises) on both deontological and consequentialist grounds, therefore, we can justify copyrights, if at all, only on the grounds that on net they promote the general welfare.

Locke's Labor-Desert Justification of Property

Some commentators have defended copyrights as natural rights under Locke's labor-desert theory of property. According to that view, copyright qualifies as a natural right for the same reason that tangible property does: because authors mix themselves, through their creative effort, in their expressions.[47] Ayn Rand, Herbert Spencer, and Lysander Spooner represent prominent libertarian proponents of that justification of copyright.[48] More recently, theorists from other schools of thought have pressed the same point.[49]

That initially plausible extension of Locke's theory looks problematic, however, upon closer scrutiny.[50] His labor-desert justification of property gives authors clear title to the particular tangible copy in which they fix their expression. If an author has already acquired property rights in paper and ink by dint of creating them or, more likely, consensual exchange, and then mixes those two forms of chattel property, tracing ink words on cellulose paper, then the author enjoys natural and common-law rights in the newly arranged physical property. But it remains a separate— and contestable—question whether that argument establishing rights in *atoms* also justifies giving an author property rights to a parcel in the imaginary realm of ideas.[51] Locke himself did not try to justify intangible property.[52] He appears, in fact, to have viewed copyright as merely a policy tool for promoting the public good.[53] Modern commentators who would venture so far beyond the boundaries of Locke's thought, into the abstractions of intellectual property, thus go further than Locke ever dared and further than they should in his name.

Query how well Locke's theory justifies any natural property rights, much less copyrights. A frank assessment shows that Locke's theory has certain debilities. In its original version, for instance, we do not own ourselves. Locke allows that "every man has a *Property* in his own

Person. . . . The Labour of his Body, and the *Work* of his Hands, we may say, are properly his."[54] Self-ownership only goes so far in Locke's account of property, however: "Men being all the Workmanship of one Omnipotent, and infinitely wise Maker; All the Servants of one Sovereign Master, sent into the World by his order and about his business, they are his Property," explains Locke.[55] We hold ourselves only in trust, in Locke's view, rather than in fee simple, and each of us labors under a duty to serve the will of the Sovereign Master, our Creator and Lord.[56] The modern secular mind bridles at the notion that no person owns him- or herself. Libertarians thus tend to interpret Locke, if at all, washed of his theological presumptions.

Even thus updated for modern sensibilities, Locke's theory of property has a long gantlet to run. Epstein, for one, fires off a series of criticisms. Locke "gives no account as to which resources should be regarded as owned in common, and if so, why,"[57] he complains. Locke's labor theory of value works at cross-purposes, moreover, to the principle of initial possession; "Locke in a sense has it all backwards," says Epstein.[58] That readers remain left with the hard question of what counts as property within Locke's system—that they cannot, for instance, agree on whether copyright qualifies as a natural right—counts as a mark against the theory. Epstein ultimately abandons deontology entirely, instead adopting "a form of closet consequentialism" in which the law embodies rules chosen "behind a veil of ignorance, so that . . . limitations on liberty are justified by the gains that they yield from the social ownership of property."[59] Epstein argues that "theories of natural rights in property cannot stand because the power of the state is needed to extend possessions beyond the situations of actual control,"[60] opts for a utilitarian analysis of copyright, and concludes "that a sensible system of copyright is not such a bad trade-off after all."[61]

Unlike Epstein, I find that natural property rights theory can helpfully explain a broad range of human behavior and offers a useful tool for assessing the justifiability of social institutions. Like him, however, I doubt that Locke's theory can justify copyright. To Epstein's trenchant critiques, I add one targeted at any supposed natural property right in expressive works: copyright contradicts Locke's own justification of property. Locke described legislation authorizing the Stationers'

Company monopoly on printing—the nearest thing to a Copyright Act in his day—as a "manifest . . . invasion of the trade, liberty, and property of the subject."[62] Today, by invoking government power a copyright holder can impose prior restraint, fines, imprisonment, and confiscation on those engaged in peaceful expression and the quiet enjoyment of tangible property.[63] Copyright law violates the very rights—the tangible property rights—that Locke set out to defend.[64] It gags voices, ties hands, and demolishes presses. But when they do not live under the command of a sovereign, Locke explained, humans enjoy "a *State of perfect Freedom* to order their Actions, and dispose of their Possessions, and Persons as they think fit, within the bounds of the Law of Nature, without asking leave, or depending upon the Will of any other Man."[65] By nature, in a "State of perfect Freedom," we can freely echo each other's expressions.

Of all the theories of natural rights reviewed here, Locke's probably has the greatest likelihood of influencing contemporary copyright policy. Kant and Hegel run distant second in most accounts of US copyright law, and only in theoretical accounts at that. Despite its relative prowess, though, Lockean property theory runs little risk of convincing lawmakers or courts to forsake the prevailing, instrumentalist view of copyright. The Lockean labor-desert theory has only one viable road to real influence—via original meaning jurisprudence.[66] Many judges find appeals to the original meaning of constitutional language, such as that embodied in the copyright clause,[67] quite persuasive.[68] As our careful review of the historical record has showed, however, the Founders probably did not regard copyright as a natural right.

Many intelligent, informed, and reasonable people argue that Locke's theory of property justifies regarding copyright as a natural right. We should disagree only after careful deliberation. The discussion here gives several good reasons, however, to conclude that Locke's theory of property cannot easily include both tangible property rights and intangible copyright rights. The latter conflict with the former, and, unlike them, do not exist in a state of nature. Property rights cannot qualify as natural in Locke's account unless they can arise in a pre-state society, a test that copyright manifestly fails. People enjoy copyright only in a state—not in a state of nature. Copyright's nonexclusivity means it must rely on state power for its enforcement; copyright's nonrivalry in consumption means that, to give its privileges any content, lawmakers must defy natural rights.

These observations only go to show that we should resist extending Locke's theory of property to copyrights. It remains a separate question whether we should reject Locke's theory of property entirely. Tradition deserves respect; it carries a great deal of time-tested wisdom and functions in ways mysterious to our merely human understanding. Still, even long-popular theories can fall into disfavor, outshone by newer and better ones. The next two sections thus consider some alternatives to Locke's justification of natural property rights, and how copyright fares under their standards.

Barnett's Positivist Account of Natural Rights

Randy E. Barnett justifies natural rights conditionally, basing them on our appreciation of certain social goods. He emphasizes that *"if we want a society in which persons can survive and pursue happiness, peace and prosperity*, then we should respect the liberal conception of justice—as defined by natural rights—and the rule of law."[69] Not everyone values freedom, harmony, and wealth, of course.[70] Most of us do, though, and together we easily number enough to enjoy the comforts and pleasures of human society.

We live together amicably because we recognize and respect certain natural rights. Which ones? Barnett names private property—including our property rights in our bodies—and freedom of contract.[71] Since the former protects both the right to peacefully enjoy property and the right to fend off trespassers, it corresponds to the common law's property and tort rules. Freedom of contract, which includes both the right *to* contract and the right to *not* contract, parallels the common-law rules for contracts. As Barnett describes them, then, our natural rights find voice in the rights to persons, property, and promises at the heart of the common law.

Barnett expressly includes "physical resources" in his description of property rights.[72] "Such property rights are 'natural' insofar as, given the nature of human begins and the world in which they live, they are essential for persons living in society with others to pursue happiness, peace, and prosperity."[73] Do copyright rights qualify as natural according to that same description? Probably not; they are not essential to our lives but rather merely useful, at best.

Barnett offers a positivist account of natural rights, an approach shared by Hayek. Social values evolve and develop to enable human flourishing, Hayek explains. "Groups which happen to have adopted rules conducive to a more effective order of actions will tend to prevail over other groups with a less effective order," he writes.[74] This hardly means that groups with especially efficient rules conquer and crush their less-developed neighbors: "It is more likely that the success of the group will attract members of others which then become incorporated in the first."[75]

This competition between social orders spontaneously generated natural rights long before states arose. "Long before man had developed language to the point where it enabled him to issue general commands, an individual would be accepted as a member of a group only so long as he conformed to its rules," Hayek theorizes.[76] David Hume expresses the same point with characteristic grace:

> But tho' it be possible for men to maintain a small uncul-
> tivated society without government, 'tis impossible they
> shou'd maintain a society of any kind without justice,
> and the observance of those three fundamental laws
> concerning the stability of possession, its translation by
> consent, and the performance of promises. These are,
> therefore, antecedent to government, and are suppos'd
> to impose an obligation before the duty of allegiance to
> civil magistrates has once been thought of.[77]

Our rights to persons, property, and promises qualify as "natural" because they have evolved to enable human social life. They long predate the state. Copyright, in contrast, arose only relatively recently, in complete reliance on a non-customary, exceptional, statutory privilege. Barnett's naturally positivist, conditional defense of natural rights cannot, it seems, justify copyright.

Natural Rights, Here and Now

Perhaps, though, we do copyright a disservice by defining natural rights only in terms of the long-evolved customs that help humans live together. Natural rights have survived the establishment of the state, after all. Even today, we respect others' rights in person, property, and promises simply because we think it proper to do so—not because we grudgingly cringe under the compulsion of state power. If we aspire to adopt a coolly positivist approach to natural rights, basing them on our observations of human society, it seems wholly appropriate to use up-to-date data.

According to that view, we can find natural rights by looking for claims we can credibly defend, in the here and now, absent state aid. What happened long ago matters only as evidence of general principles, not as a binding limit on the choices we of necessity make in the present. As archpositivist Felix S. Cohen puts it, "The state of nature is a stage of analysis rather than a stage of history. It exists today and has always existed, to a greater or lesser degree, in various realms of human affairs."[78] The rights to tangible property certainly qualify as natural on that basis. We live in many various and overlapping customary and voluntary social organizations that recognize and respect our persons, real and chattel property, and promises. Contrary to Epstein's supposition that "the power of the state is needed to extend possession beyond the situations of actual control,"[79] ample evidence demonstrates that humans can live together in relative peace and prosperity without the bounds of any institution that claims a monopoly on the initiation of coercion within a particular geographic area.[80] The state can help us to perfect the enjoyment of our natural rights, granted. But its services come at some cost to those rights. Whether we come out ahead under that arrangement remains, as Epstein would doubtless take the lead in asserting, a question of fact.

More particularly, whether or not copyrights—or an institution largely like them—could survive without state aid must also remain an open question. It seems safe to say that non-state copyrights do not exist. It remains unclear, moreover, how our natural rights could combine to create copyrights. We can combine our natural rights to persons, property, and promises in ways that encourage authorship, of course, such as by contracting for a personal performance or buying a material copy. Common-law institutions can thus go very far in promoting copyright's most general aim: guarding against a market failure in the supply of original expressions. Cobbling together tort, property, and contract rights can result only in legal mechanisms that achieve copyright's *ends*, however; the same process cannot recreate copyright's *means*. For that, copyright depends on state power.

Ideally, the state helps to define and protect natural rights. Even without its help, however, we can credibly assert rights to our persons, properties, and promises. Loners cannot defend their natural rights easily, of course, but (as many a zombie movie has endeavored to demonstrate and as history well documents) humans can band together to defend their natural rights without going so far as forming a state.[81] Social contracts need not create monopolies.

Copyrights, in contrast, exist only in states. Copyrights cannot survive in a state of nature because, by definition, they demand exclusive rights over nonexcludable works. Only a monopoly can give (or at least credibly promise to give) that. Suppose that in a state of nature you composed and performed an original song—a yodel, say. Even if you could get several large friends to help enforce your complaint, you would find it extraordinarily difficult to stop even just one singer from copying you in admiration. Imagine trying to defend your song against copying by an entire village, or a whole people, in a state of nature.

Locke's theory of natural property rights doubtless owes some of its popularity to the vivid tale he tells of a man gathering acorns in the wild. True to his example, we can also tell a tale that demonstrates how natural rights surround us even today, amid towering buildings and vastly complex social institutions. We generally treat each other with respect simply because we do not seriously consider any alternative; to recognize certain rights comes naturally to us. As chapter 4 will show, copyrights evidently do not evoke the same response among everyday folk, who instead violate the Copyright Act with uncaring and unaware impunity.

Imagine what would happen if the state were to suddenly disappear—not because of a natural disaster or intervening enemy, but just because all agreed it was not worth the trouble. We can easily imagine that people would continue to respect each other's basic rights in persons, property, and promises; social chaos might increase, but it would not necessarily overwhelm basic decency. Even in a condition of nature—*especially* in a condition of nature—a spontaneous order of customs, institutions, and on-the-ground practical reasoning supports property rights in tangible goods. It is very hard to imagine, however, that people would pay homage to the strictures of the Copyright Act if they did not face the prospect of terrible sanctions. They hardly do so even now, under the shadow of state coercion.

Does that thought experiment sound too speculative to instruct? Recall that states have not always existed, nor do they exist everywhere in the world today. They may or may not exist a thousand years from now. Even now, at this moment, those of us who think of ourselves as upstanding citizens live our day-to-day lives largely free from the direct influence of state power. With those reflections in mind, it should not prove too difficult to picture a state of nature ready at hand. Do copyrights live on in that world? Probably not; their fortunes rise or fall with state power.

Because they rely on the exercise of state power, copyrights cannot number among the natural rights that we bring to the table when we enter into a social contract. Nor can we take them with us, now, if we walk away from that supposed deal. Only rights that we can credibly assert without state help can give us any leverage when we bargain with Leviathan. Our natural rights explain our rights to personal freedom, chattel and real property, and reliable promises, but they do not go so far as to give us the power to justly silence another throat, pen, or press.

Authors exist in nature even though copyrights do not. Some authors create as naturally as the rest of us breathe. Others trade their expressions for value, sharing them with the aim of winning gifts and allies in return. Through many various mechanisms, existing and yet to be discovered, common-law rights can combine to encourage authorship. Indeed, chapters 11 and 12 will show how they might do better job at it than copyright does.

4. CONCLUSION

Philosophically speaking, we can best describe copyright in utilitarian terms. The instrumentalism that pervades cases, legislation, and commentary about US copyright law leaves scant room for a natural right to copyright.[82] The Supreme Court has, for instance, described copyright as "the creature of the Federal statute" and observed that "Congress did not sanction an existing right but created a new one."[83] Little suggests that the men who wrote and ratified the US Constitution considered copyrights to be natural rights, either. To the contrary, they evidently viewed copyright as a policy tool, one aimed at promoting the progress of science and useful arts. They begrudged copyright's interference with natural and common-law rights, like the government they formed, as a necessary evil. They calculated that neither civility nor copyright could survive in a state of nature, so they put both under a state.

Natural rights theory joins the Founding generation on that count. Copyrights do not fare well under Locke's labor-desert account of property. Nor do they answer to Barnett's positivist description of natural rights. Because we cannot credibly claim copyrights without the state's backing, they cannot survive in a state of nature. In sum, we should consider copyright an unnatural statutory privilege that violates our natural rights and can claim only as much justification as can the state itself.

CHAPTER 4

COPYRIGHT IN EVERYDAY LIFE

Most people pay relatively little attention to copyright. Perhaps they should, though, since most of them routinely and repeatedly violate the Copyright Act. Their ignorance of the law provides no defense, because the act imposes strict liability. Section 1 describes how infringement pervades our everyday lives and explains why only dire measures will get people to take copyright seriously. The fact that we violate the Copyright Act does not mean we have no regard for the welfare of authors, however. As section 2 explains, most people tend to frown on the fraudulent misattribution of authorship, while regarding the obligation to pay authors as akin to the obligation to pay taxes: a question more of prudence and civic virtue than of simple good or evil.

1. THE BATTLE OF JOHN AND JANE

Professor of law John Tehranian has carefully documented the likely instances of copyright infringement committed on an average day in the life of a hypothetical law professor, called (perhaps not so hypothetically) "John."[1] John does nothing evidently outrageous; he replies to some emails, hands out copies of an article in class, doodles during a boring meeting, sings "Happy Birthday" in a restaurant, and otherwise peacefully whiles away the hours. By the end of the day, though, John "has committed at least eighty-three acts of infringement and faces liability in the amount of $12.45 million (to say nothing of potential criminal charges)."[2] Tehranian's hypothetical infringer could stand for almost any of us. These days, almost anyone but a hermit runs an overwhelming risk of routinely and repeatedly violating the Copyright Act.

It was not always so, of course. Until comparatively recently, copyright subsisted in relatively few expressive works and most people lacked ready means to infringe. Now, though, every new fixed expression automatically wins copyright protection under US law and digital technologies make it cheap and easy to reproduce, publicly distribute, and otherwise infringe copyrighted works. In some contexts—especially online—casual copyright infringement has become the norm.

Does that trend mean that copyright will wither into irrelevance? Possibly. A great many people—federal lawmakers among them—will not likely embrace that outcome, however. To judge from recent trends, they will instead respond by increasing the penalties for copyright infringement.

If they took that logic to its dread extreme, lawmakers might consider imposing the death sentence for copyright pirates. To understand the appeal of making infringement a capital offense, try putting yourself in the shoes of Jane, a hypothetical Hollywood executive. For decades, copyright has served your industry well. You produced expressive works, consumers calmly lined up to pay, and everybody seemed pretty happy about the arrangement. Your long years in the business have seen American culture suffuse the planet. "What vases were to ancient Athens," you proudly claim, "music, films, and TV are to Hollywood."

Now, though, you see your cultural empire crumbling. Inspired by anticopyright rhetoric and taking advantage of lax enforcement, mobs have swept through the marketplace. They boldly break the locks protecting copyrighted works, greedily grab the goods, and disappear into the crowd. "We cannot make money under these conditions!" you exclaim. "Lawmakers need to act or we will abandon the market."

What would you have lawmakers do? "The same thing they do whenever mobs start breaking into stores," Jane replies. "The police need to fire a few shots over the infringers' heads. And if the looting continues, they should shoot some of the looters. That may sound severe, but we face a *breakdown of civil order*. Wouldn't police—or perhaps the National Guard—do the same if mobs threatened to take over Wall Street, Rodeo Drive, or Constitution Avenue? You can bet they would. Hollywood deserves the same protection. The time has come to get tough on infringement. The Copyright Act lacks the muscle to do the job. We need a Copy*riot* Act!"

Step outside Jane's fevered point of view and consider her complaint objectively. However extreme her rhetoric, she makes a valid point.

Suppose, as seems plausible, that copyright protects property and promotes the public good. Suppose further that, as John's tale showed, the odds of getting caught violating copyright have plummeted. Holding all else equal, then, if lawmakers want to preserve copyright's delicate balance between private and public interests, they should increase the disincentives to infringement. So runs the core of Jane's argument.

How hard a blow, according to that view, should the law inflict on infringers? Our disgruntled hypothetical executive, Jane, would have National Guard troops shoot film pirates. Lawmakers could increase the disincentives for copyright infringement without resorting to summary execution, however; they could impose the death penalty, for instance, with all its many procedural protections. Even mandatory life in prison would go further to discourage copyright infringement than present laws do. Exactly how much punishment copyright infringers should suffer of course remains subject to empirical study. Regardless, however, we ought to seriously consider Jane's argument: if technology allows almost all copyright infringers to escape punishment, the law should inflict extraordinarily harsh punishments on the few infringers that it does manage to catch.

Jane can also cite precedent for her view that extraordinary civil unrest calls for extraordinary law enforcement. As John's case showed, the Copyright Act evidently no longer suffices to discourage rampant infringement. We might thus say, to quote federal laws pertaining to insurrection, that a technological condition has arisen that "so hinders the execution of the laws" as to deprive copyright holders of "a right, privilege, immunity, or protection named in the Constitution and secured by law"—namely, their copyright rights.[3] The same laws provide that if state or local authorities "are unable, fail, or refuse to protect that right, privilege, or immunity, or to give that protection," the president "may employ the armed forces, including the National Guard in Federal service" to restore public order.[4] According to that view, a Copy*riot* Act does not seem so far-fetched.

In addition to keeping copyright policy in balance, those who would answer infringement with severe sanctions can argue that their approach offers efficiency gains. Cognitive psychologists tell us that humans routinely overestimate the likelihood of so-called "dread" risks—those that capture our imaginations with the prospect of spectacular crashes and terrible pain. Most travelers wrongly regard airplanes as more dangerous than automobiles, for instance, fearing a spectacular death more than a plain one. Lawmakers could economize on the costs of enforcing copyrights by inflicting especially dreadful penalties for infringement. It should take only a few high-profile prosecutions—giving some file-sharers the Guantanamo treatment, for instance—to discourage a great many other would-be infringers. Although that may seem cruel, "mercy to the guilty is cruelty to the innocent," as Adam Smith observes.[5]

So goes the case, here offered as a *reductio ad absurdum*, for radically increasing the penalties for copyright infringement. Despite the impassioned plea of our imaginary Hollywood executive, Jane, and the ruthless logic we might marshal in her support, I suspect that most who read this essay will reject Jane's call for a Copyriot Act. What explains this hesitation?

Perhaps simple self-interest drives us to deny copyright holders the fullest advantages the law can offer. Not being Hollywood executives, after all, few of us stand to lose our jobs and our fortunes to copyright infringement. We might instead relish the prospect of winning unrestricted access to formerly protected works. We might, in other words, want to join the mob of looters decried by our imaginary Hollywood executive, Jane.

I doubt that so crass a motive can fully explain our hesitation to view widespread copyright infringement as little better than looting, however. Despite their rhetoric equating infringers to thieves, and copyrights to cars, handbags, or televisions,[6] even copyright industry representatives have not (yet) called for anything so merciless as a Copyriot Act. Perhaps that will come; powerful lobbies have, after all, consistently sought and won broader and more powerful copyright privileges.

More likely, though, even Hollywood executives regard their mansions, Bentley sedans, and Sony HDTVs as more deserving of rigorous legal protection than they do the movies, television programs, and songs they sell. On that count, our everyday moral intuitions reflect the same view taught by economic reasoning, political philosophy, and sound public policy: copyright represents a statutory privilege designed to maximize social utility—not private property we can claim by natural or common-law right.

If lawmakers should not react to the advent of cheap, easy, and widespread infringement by treating it like an outbreak of looting, how should they react? On that question, one might write a book (or at least a chapter in one). Suffice it to say here that lawmakers should not seriously consider passing anything like the Copyriot Act. If saving copyrights requires a measure so extreme as that, they are not worth saving. Thankfully, as part III of this book explains, common-law rights look likely to pick up the slack where copyrights have failed. We can thus look forward to a world where property rights in tangibles, together with contracts and tort law, suffice to ensure that original authors receive ample recompense. If they can escape from copyright into the common law, Jane and John both might live happily ever after.

2. THE MORALITY OF UNAUTHORIZED COPYING

Even though many or most people fail to obey the strictures of the Copyright Act, they do not thereby demonstrate a total disregard for the welfare of the authors whose works they enjoy. Even those of us who have studied copyright's foundational principles and found scant support for the view that copyrights constitute natural rights need not, and should not, violate copyrights pell-mell. To say that copyright does not protect any natural rights is not to say that it has no ethical justification. As this section explains, our everyday morality of unauthorized copying may not mirror the Copyright Act, but it does stand for something.

As the first subsection explains, most people frown on unauthorized and misattributed copying, and rightly so. The second subsection explores the practical limits of most people's willingness to pay for expressive works, and counsels respect for copyright out of gratitude for authors' labors. The third subsection compares the Copyright Act to the tax code, and argues for regarding authors as akin to recipients of public welfare.

Fighting Expressive Fraud

A singer who claims authorship of a song written by another commits a sort of fraud on his or her listeners. Most of the time, that kind of fraud does not cause any serious harm and thus does not justify litigation. We typically do not rely to any substantial detriment on the accuracy of an expressive work's description; if we like a work we like it, regardless of its source.

Misdescriptions of authorship can trick us into buying the wrong expressions, granted. We don't need copyright to vindicate that sort of wrong, however; the common law and various state and federal statutes already suffice. Consumers of misleadingly labeled goods or services can plead fraud under tort law.[7] In some cases, they might also plead breach[8] or promissory estoppel[9] under contract law. The licensee of a materially misdescribed work would enjoy a strong contract law defense, one voiding any agreement alleged by the licensor-publisher.[10] An author who sees his or her work sold under another's name would, as a wronged competitor, have standing to sue for unfair competition under state or federal law.[11] The publisher of such an author might likewise enjoy legal and equitable remedies for passing off.[12] The Federal Trade Commission and its many state counterparts can protect consumers and competitors of falsely labeled expressive works, while various federal and state executive officers can fight such wrongs with the criminal sanctions levied against the many guises of fraud.

Even without copyright, the law does not like it when artists claim false credit. A wide range of powerful legal tools give society ample ways to discourage materially harmful misdescriptions of expressive works. We don't need copyright to satisfy our moral intuitions on that front, and most people's condemnations of unauthorized copying don't go much beyond harmful lying. Does honest copying, even when done for profit and without an author's permission, typically rouse moral indignation? Not evidently. People across many cultures buy unauthorized works without compunction. At one time, in fact, US copyright policy deliberately *encouraged* the practice with regard to foreign authors.[13] Nonetheless, many authors ardently object even to fully attributed, unauthorized copies of their work, complaining that such uses amount to theft. How far does morality suggest we should go in remedying such pleas?

Copying without Paying

If you made an unauthorized copy of a CD and gave it as a gift to a friend, would you feel guilty of committing a moral wrong? Many people would not, judging from their unrepentant acts. Nonetheless, even such friendly copying constitutes actionable (if very small-scale) copyright infringement. Most casual copiers probably know as much, too. They evidently think that you can infringe a copyright, and admit to breaking the law, without also admitting to the commission of some terrible wrong. By analogy, a good driver on an empty road can speed with a clear conscience. Breaking the law in such a case harms nobody, even if it does thumb its nose at authority.

To use a still more apt example, many citizens drive dangerously close to the tax code's edges. Most of us obey the tax code, no doubt, and for good reason: to misjudge could lead to loss of liberty and property. Voluntary payment of excess taxes remains very rare, however; most people evidently pay under compulsion rather than joy. Many people evidently regard their obligation to obey the Copyright Act in a similar light.

Both the tax code and the Copyright Act rely on positive legislation; both create regulatory regimes; both redistribute private assets (money in the one case, common-law rights in the other). We grudgingly accept that the tax code and the Copyright Act create special beneficiaries of state power, the former by way of tax credits, the latter by way of exclusive privileges.[14] Both the tax code and the Copyright Act have ardent fans, of course, who celebrate the efficiency and equity of helping those whom the market might otherwise callously ignore. But the attractions of compulsory charity hardly establish a natural right to welfare. Neither does our natural regard for authorship establish a natural right to copyright.

Those caveats to the moral status of copyright do not justify infringement, however. Speaking only for myself, I try to respect copyrights. Admittedly, I probably misjudge at times. Copyright law contains many subtleties, even to a dedicated student, and its application often relies on contestable facts. We often don't know what constitutes infringement unless and until a judge tells us. Regardless, copyright does not excuse innocent mistakes. I shudder when I recall that, like you and everyone else subject to the Copyright Act, I am held strictly liable for my infringements. I console myself with the thought that copyright law does not burden me terribly and offers an apt way to express my heartfelt appreciation of skilled authors.

Copyright's beneficiaries have no more natural right to my obedience than, say, Medicare's beneficiaries have a natural right to my tax payments. Authors, like the poor, may merit our concern and material aid, but only as a matter of private morality. Government programs turn such charitable obligations into legal mandates and all too often operate with dismaying inefficiency and unfairness. For the same reasons the United States reformed federal welfare, easing its recipients into the rigors of the working world, it should also reform copyright, weaning authors from their special privileges and encouraging them to live under the same common-law rules that bind us all.

The Copyright Tax Code

Like most people, you probably try to not egregiously violate copyright law. Why? We recognize copying limits, like speed limits and tax codes, as legislation designed to maximize social utility, created by statute for presumptively good reasons and thus, unless manifestly inefficient or inequitable, enjoying some claim to our obedience. We follow such laws out of patriotism, unreflective habit, grudging acceptance, or fear—but not because they protect fundamental human rights.

So, to judge from actions, go the moral intuitions of most folks. We regard violations of persons, property, and promises as serious matters, dire deviations from acceptable social behavior. We regard casual copyright infringement, in contrast, as little worse than driving 80 mph in a 65 mph zone, or exaggerating the value of a charitable donation on a tax form.

Authors, admittedly, sometimes express with profound outrage that unauthorized copying, even when it gives credit where due, equates to theft.[15] Their understandable pique does not, however, suffice to establish a claim of right. The nonrivalrousness of expressive works means that copying does not hinder the use or enjoyment of any single copy. A painter fully owns his canvas even if another photographs it without his permission. What authors care about in such instances is not the use and enjoyment of their works, but rather their lost copyright revenues.

Copyright can provide authors with revenue, a benefit that infringement threatens to reduce. Authors understandably feel disappointment and anger when their works suffer unauthorized use, but that hardly shows that copyright infringement violates a natural right. It only shows that authors, like almost everyone else, prefer more money to less. There can be no copyright infringement absent copyright. Only by circular reasoning can the complaint that infringement reduces authors' revenues justify copyright; it presumes the very end we ask it to explain. Far from an inviolate right, a copyright holder has only a conditional privilege.

CHAPTER 5

THE LANGUAGE OF COPYRIGHT, AN INTELLECTUAL ~~PROPERTY~~ PRIVILEGE

What should we call the legal powers granted by US law to the author of a fixed expressive work? Typically, we call them "copyrights." We classify copyrights as a species of intellectual property, abbreviating it as "IP." We say that people *own* copyrights—first a work's author or authors, then, often, a transferee. Eventually, the copyright expires and the public comes into its possession. We thus speak of copyright in tones redolent of property.[1] This chapter describes an alternative way to talk about copyright, one consistent with the observation that copyright more closely resembles a privilege—a special statutory benefit—than it does the sort of right, general in nature and grounded in common law, that deserves the title "property."

Though copyright doubtless has some property-like attributes, it can claim none of them without qualification. "Privilege" arguably fits copyright better and for that reason alone merits wider use. Though this is an alternative way of talking about copyright, it hardly represents a radical shift; calling copyright a "privilege" follows legal and popular usage, past and present.[2] Nor would broadening the way we talk about copyright prove especially burdensome. Both "intellectual property" and "intellectual privilege" devolve into "IP," conveniently enough. We can just as readily speak of "copyright *holders*" as "copyright *owners*," and emphasize that copyright does not *protect* expressive works so much as it *restricts* their unauthorized use. These are not mere matters of rhetorical fashion. Speaking about copyright in terms of privilege will encourage salutary policy results, protecting property's good name and counterbalancing the public choice pressures that have come to strongly shape copyright policy.

1. WHY TO CALL COPYRIGHT A "PRIVILEGE"

Courts and commentators have often described copyright as a legal privilege,[3] a usage consistent with the view that copyright represents a statutory exception to our common-law rights. More generally, copyrights represent (along with patents) a species of intellectual privilege authorized in the US Constitution[4] and effectuated through legislation.[5]

The Copyright Act entitles a copyright holder to enlist agents of the state in *prima facie* violations of nonholders' common-law rights.[6] Absent copyright, we would remain free to employ our persons and property in echo of others.[7] Copyright sharply limits those natural and common-law rights.[8] Perhaps it does so for good reason and for the common good.[9] What looks like theft to us might look like the seizure of infringing copies to a judge;[10] and an apparent threat of false imprisonment might come at court order.[11]

Nonetheless, rightly or wrongly, copyright represents an exception to the general rule that we can freely speak the truth. It thus won't do to call copyright simply a "property right." We should at least append the qualifying phrase "and an *anti-property* right," because copyright's power comes at the expense of our rights in our pens, presses, and throats. Should we also call copyright an *anti-person* right? It endures only at cost to our liberties, after all. At any rate, copyright does not qualify for the title "property"; it instead ranks as a privilege, all-powerful in its scope but sorely dependent on state power for its effect.

Copyright as a Statutory Exception to the Common Law

Copyright fits squarely within the first definition of "privilege" provided in *Black's Law Dictionary*: "A particular and peculiar benefit or advantage enjoyed by a person, company, or class, beyond the common advantages of other citizens. An exceptional or extraordinary power."[12] The Copyright Act gives copyright holders power to bring civil actions against infringing nonholders, winning equitable and legal remedies.[13]

Common-law rights, presumptively violated when a copyright plaintiff invokes state power, provide no redress to the infringer. *Black's Law Dictionary*'s definition of "privilege" speaks to this phenomenon, too: a privilege is "that which exempts one from a liability which he would otherwise be required to . . . sustain in common with all other persons."[14] An ordinary, average citizen enjoys no just power to break down your door, cut your communications, rifle through your accounts, seize your assets, or, if you show contempt, throw you in jail. You would ordinarily have every right to defend yourself against anyone who committed, threatened to commit, or wrongly encouraged public officials to commit such wrongs. And yet, the Copyright Act excuses those and other apparent torts.

Does this definition of "privilege" conform with the exacting requirements of Yale Law School's legendary professor Wesley Hohfeld?[15] He used the word interchangeably,[16] and confusingly,[17] with "liberty."[18] It would sorely mislead, however, to call copyrights "copy liberties." In fact, that term would better describe the rights that each of us enjoys—or, absent the Copyright Act, would enjoy—to freely use others' expressions.[19]

Nonetheless, the definition tendered here does help to clarify that copyright holders claim special immunities from the obligations that each of us has, in a state of nature and under the common law, to respect others' rights to peaceably enjoy their persons and properties.[20] Hohfeld explains that "a privilege is the opposite of a duty, and the correlative of a 'no-right.'"[21] Applying his theory to copyrights, we might say that a copyright privilege is the opposite of a duty to respect others' natural and common-law rights, and the correlative of the absence of rights for defendants guilty of infringement.

That offers a more fully and fairly positivist description of copyright, and one more true to Hohfeld's project, than descriptions blandly observing that all rights limit each other.[22] To the contrary, our common-law and natural rights carry more normative weight, and thus presumptively more legal weight, than the special rights created by the Copyright Act.[23] A thoroughgoing positivist committed to clarity would therefore do best to call copyright not simply property, nor (with all due respect to Hohfeld) a liberty, but rather a type of privilege.

Copyright as Not a Fundamental Civil Right

Privileges come in different flavors. The *copy* privilege represents a statutory exception to common-law rights and obligations that grants special powers and immunities to copyright holders. It thus stands in sharp contrast to another type of privilege: a fundamental civil right enacted to defend citizens' natural and common-law rights.

Professor Adam Mossoff of George Mason University School of Law has convincingly argued that in the United States, in the Founding and Antebellum eras, commentators justified certain positive enactments on grounds that they were crucial for the protection of natural rights and liberties.[24] They counted among such fundamental civil rights the judicial enforcement of contracts, trial by jury, and the writ of habeas corpus.[25] Though he suggests we should extend the definition of "fundamental civil right" to patents, Mossoff cites no source from the eighteenth or early nineteenth centuries that applies that label to patents. Perhaps that simply reflects the peculiar phrasings of the day rather than anything of deeper meaning. Nonetheless, as Mossoff admits, many commentators past and present have described patents as monopoly privileges—a telling usage.[26]

As Mossoff ably explains, privileges *qua* fundamental civil rights reinforce and protect natural rights.[27] The right to judicial enforcement of contracts renders personal vows more secure, for instance, while jury trials and the habeas corpus writ protect citizens from an overweening government. Such privileges, far from contradicting natural rights or liberties, safeguard them.[28]

The same cannot be said of patents or copyrights. Those sorts of privileges violate the rights we naturally enjoy in our persons, estates, and chattels.[29] Perhaps they do so for good reason and for the common good. So, too, do our natural rights suffer the indignities of regulation, taxation, and conscription. But that is only to say that patents and copyrights burden us for good reason—it is not to say that they represent fundamental civil rights. To the contrary, those privileges represent statutory exceptions to our common-law and natural rights.

2. WHY TO NOT CALL COPYRIGHT "PROPERTY"

Discussions of copyright have long included language casting it as property.[30] Some such talk has come in the form of rhetoric obviously aligned with its speaker's interests. When asking lawmakers to mandate broadcast flag technology to prevent consumer copying of television programs, for instance, Jack Valenti, president of the Motion Picture Association of America, said, "We just want to protect private property from being pillaged."[31] Similarly, Hilary Rosen, president of the Recording Industry Association of America, said of the unauthorized distribution of sound recordings, "It is simply not fair to take someone else's music and put it online for free distribution. No one wants their property taken from them and distributed without their permission."[32] But even evidently disinterested parties have thoughtfully argued that copyrights, no less than real estate or chattels, fully qualify as property.[33] That claim, even if it has not convinced many courts or commentators, merits consideration.

According to the view now prevalent among legal scholars and judges, property comprises a bundle of rights.[34] Foremost among those rights, legal authorities rank the right to exclude non-owners. Other property rights include use, alienation, acquisition, preservation, and compensation for takings. According to an alternative view, property sits at the center of a web of relationships with and around the owned object. Let us test each of those, the *properties of property*, against copyright's features. We will find, as have most courts and commentators, that "intellectual property" fits copyright only awkwardly, at best.

Right to Exclude

Legal authorities regard the right to exclude non-owners as property's signature attribute.[35] In contrast to owners of tangible property, however, copyright holders depend on the Copyright Act to allow them to exclude.[36] Even under the act, moreover, copyright holders enjoy only relatively weak exclusion rights. True, the Copyright Act defines certain rights as "exclusive." It does so only subject to a very wide range of exceptions, however.[37] The act does not exclude anyone from a broad (if vaguely defined) range of personal uses of a copyrighted work, such as singing a pop song in the shower, for instance,[38] and in many cases, such as a scathing review that quotes its target liberally, even allows use of a work over the objections of its holder.[39]

Copyright law thus offers even weaker exclusionary rights than does patent law, the other constitutionally authorized form of IP.[40] If the nominal owner of a plot of land had no power to exclude the public from putting it to *personal* use, nor to exclude competitors from putting the land to *profitable* use, would we confidently claim that the owner enjoyed exclusive rights to it? To speak frankly, we would do better to admit that the owner has at best only a limited privilege to that land. So, too, should we speak of those who hold copyrights.

Use

Some scholars cast the right to use—to employ, to occupy, or to profit from[41]—property as one of its fundamental attributes.[42] Emphasizing use rights does nothing to recast copyright as a natural property right, however, because absent the Copyright Act's extraordinary restrictions, the author of a fixed expressive work would have no more right to use it than anyone else.[43] Even taking the statute as given, moreover, does little to establish a copyright holder's right to use (as opposed to exclude others from using) a given work. Strictly speaking, the Copyright Act does not so much empower certain parties to use a certain work as it restricts *other* parties from doing likewise. Even a more narrow characterization of copyright's use right—as the right to use a work profitably—does not make it look much like property, given that the many loopholes in a copyright holder's exclusive rights effectively limit many potentially profitable uses of a work. As much as those who hold copyrights in sound recordings would like to charge radio stations for playing their musical works, for instance, the Copyright Act denies them the right to do so.[44]

Alienation

Commentators understand the power of alienation—the power to transfer title to another party—as a fundamental feature of property. Thanks to the Copyright Act, copyright holders doubtless enjoy very broad alienation powers.[45] Indeed, that constitutes one of copyright's most salient virtues, one that encourages the efficient allocation of assets. Notably, however, copyright holders depend on the Copyright Act to ensure their alienation rights; without the act they would have no greater power to alienate a published work than anyone else because all would enjoy equal access to it. Even under the act, moreover, copyright holders do not enjoy such broad alienation powers as the owners of tangible property do.

Several sections of the Copyright Act allow authors to terminate—in other words, revoke without paying recompense—copyright rights that they have freely and willingly granted to others.[46] Those termination rights appear somewhat exceptional when compared to the law's typical respect for voluntary transfers of rights.[47] The Copyright Act refuses to respect any agreement contrary to a termination right, saying that such a right "may be effected notwithstanding any agreement to the contrary, including an agreement to make a will or to make any future grant."[48] Nor does the act requires terminators to compensate losing grantees. More precisely, sections 203, 304(c), and 304(d) do not speak about any requirement to make compensation, pro or con. No authority has found such a requirement, however, and those provisions evidently assume that terminating holders *owe* nothing because, as the act defines copyrights, they *take* nothing. As those termination provisions demonstrate, copyright holders do not enjoy the full range of alienation rights generally afforded to owners of tangible property.[49] Copyright holders may even find that the act bars them from donating a work to the public domain.[50] Property owners do not usually face such sharp and unyielding restrictions on alienation.

Acquisition

As Richard A. Epstein observes, the natural rights arguments typically applied to justify tangible property do not fit copyright.[51] Copyrights can be acquired, of course. In contrast to tangible property, however, the acquisition of a copyright requires legislative backing. Even Locke recognized as much.[52] Absent the Copyright Act, authorship would garner title only to tangible copies of expressive works—perhaps protected by trade secrets, contracts, or automated rights-management schemes, but not protected against infringement. To acquire protection against infringement, the heart of copyright's power, authors require a special statutory right to invoke state power in violation of others' natural and common-law rights. Authors require, in other words, a privilege.

Preservation

Nobody stands to lose real estate or chattel goods after some specified term. To the contrary, we assume that those tangible properties
may remain privately owned indefinitely, through the years and across
the generations. Not so with regard to such intellectual privileges as
copyrights and patents. They persist only for specified statutory terms,
thereafter to lapse into the public domain, unowned and unownable.[53]
Tangible property endures, whereas copyright's intellectual privileges
evaporate.

Copyright holders have objected to that second-class treatment,
arguing that they deserve the same potentially unlimited term of
preservation afforded to property holders. Mark Twain, for instance,
complained about copyright's limited term. "You might just as well,
after you had discovered a coal-mine and worked it twenty-eight years,
have the Government step in and take it away," he objected.[54] How long
did Twain think copyright should last? "Perpetuity."[55] That such pleas
have not been fulfilled—and under the US Constitution cannot be
fulfilled[56]—indicates yet again how copyrights differ materially from
property rights.

Compensation for Takings

The right to receive just compensation for governmental takings[57] has
long represented a hallmark of property.[58] Does copyright afford such a
right? The exact question remains as yet unlitigated and, thus, still subject
to dispute.[59] By holding that no such right attaches to patents, however,
the recent case of *Zoltek Corp. v. United States*[60] strongly suggests that the
same outcome would obtain for copyrights.[61]

The Supreme Court denied *certiorari* to *Zoltek*, thereby letting the
case stand.[62] The court has elsewhere noted, moreover, that "property
interests . . . are not created by the Constitution. Rather, they are created and their dimensions are defined by existing rules or understandings that stem from an independent source such as state law."[63] Given
that copyrights exist only because the Constitution expressly authorizes
them,[64] the court's definition of "property" as something "not created by
the Constitution" hardly fits copyright.

Property as a Web of Relations

In contrast to the bundle of sticks model discussed above, some commentators argue that we should view property as a web of relationships.[65] Tony Arnold explains that web as "a set of interconnections among persons, groups, and entities each with some stake in an identifiable (but either tangible or intangible) object, which is at the center of the web."[66] He emphasizes, however, that the object at the center of such a web—the property—"must be relatively identifiable and definite."[67] That requirement alone should raise doubts whether copyright, which suffers notoriously vague boundaries,[68] qualifies as property under the "web of relationships" metaphor. Consider, too, that holders and consumers often have radically different views of what does—or, more generally, *should*—qualify as copyright infringement.[69] Can a web so weak and one-sided support the burden of proving that copyright constitutes property?[70]

3. DEFENDING PROPERTY[SM]

Especially among academics, much of the skepticism expressed about copyright-*qua*-property appears to reflect skepticism about property rights in general. Thus, for instance, Professor Peter Drahos inveighs not only against intellectual property, but also against the notion that *any* form of property can qualify as a fundamental value[71] or natural right.[72] Anyone with that point of view will doubtless find it easy—comforting, even—to regard copyright as a type of privilege rather than of property.

Friends of property should also regard copyright skeptically, however. As discussed above, the powers wielded by copyright holders come only at the expense of the property rights the rest of us hold in our persons, estates, and chattels, as discussed in chapter 3. That irreconcilable conflict should alone cause anyone who cares about property rights to cast a suspicious eye on copyright.[73] Copyright's corrosive effect on property goes deeper than mere inconsistency, however. In the guise of "intellectual property," copyright assumes a title to which it has scant claim. In so doing, copyright harms the very idea of property, eroding its distinctiveness, its popularity, and ultimately its strength.

Were this a case for unfair competition law, we would regard "property" as a service mark made distinctive by dint of long use.[74] Even if we did not go so far as to mark it with the superscript "SM," as businesses do to protect their service marks (and as jokingly suggested in this section's title), we would jealously safeguard the word as reliable proof that such traditional rights as exclusion, use, alienation, and so forth apply. Like a shoddy knockoff, however, copyright embodies those characteristics only imperfectly. To call it "intellectual property" thus risks confusing consumers of the law—citizens, attorneys, academics, judges, and lawmakers—about the nature of copyright. Worse yet, it confuses them about the nature of property. According to that view of the problem, the "property" mark suffers not merely *dilution* from copyright's infringing use, but *tarnishment*, too.[75]

As a relative latecomer to the law, copyright has scant claim to property's good name. To protect property, we must protect "property." And to protect "property" we should revisit "*intellectual* property."

4. RHETORICALLY REBALANCING COPYRIGHT

A delicate balancing of the many interests affected by copyright may well exceed lawmaker's powers, to say nothing of their motives. Still, we can aspire to at least roughly balance the public choice pressures that affect copyright. Casting copyrights as intellectual privileges would help in that effort; casting them as copy*privileges*, not owned but *held*, would help still more.

We can employ such clarifying terminology without intending any slight to the copyright-as-property model. Copyrights admittedly exhibit some property-like features, which property-talk does a fair job of portraying. But to call copyright "property" risks vesting copyright holders with more powers than they deserve.[76] To call it "privilege" offers a rhetorical counterbalance, reminding copyright holders of what they owe to the public and recalling lawmakers to their duties.[77]

5. CONCLUSION

Why care about finding the right name for copyright? Because words work legal magic, transmuting intentions into actions. Words influence what the public thinks, what lawyers argue, and what courts decide.

Calling copyright "intellectual property" invites misunderstanding. Calling it "intellectual privilege" describes copyright more modestly and accurately, helping to inform and improve public policy.

Perhaps no single label can fully capture the unique and protean nature of copyright. In that case, just as comparing flat maps based on different projections can help us to better understand the spherical Earth, so too could we benefit from comparing different views of copyright. At the very least, the language of privilege offers an alternative perspective on copyright, one that usefully contrasts with the perspective offered by property theory and that reveals an important and neglected aspect of copyright.

CHAPTER 6

COPYRIGHT POLITICS: INDELICATELY IMBALANCED

ourts and commentators often claim that copyright policy strikes a delicate balance between public and private interests.[1] This chapter, in contrast, portrays copyright as a lumbering, sprawling, messy compromise between various lobbies, few of which have the public interest in mind. According to this view, copyright policy wobbles precariously on the verge of tipping over and falling into statutory failure. Rather than "delicately balanced," we might more accurately describe copyright policy as "indelicately imbalanced."[2]

Perfect policy equipoise will always elude us. We don't have the information necessary to put copyright's various factors into exact balance. How can we quantify the importance of Picasso's *Guernica*, for instance, or of Dr. Seuss's *Yertle the Turtle*? In most cases, the numbers simply do not exist. What numbers we can discern, moreover, appear to us only in a haze of uncertainty.

We can, however, keep an eye open for evident policy disasters, taking care to steer clear of obvious hazards. We should moreover guard against letting copyright maximalists seize the tiller, lest they overemphasize their particular interests to the detriment of other interests, both public and private. The Constitution gives us a lodestar, calling lawmakers to "promote the general Welfare"[3] and "the Progress of Science and useful Arts,"[4] a navigational challenge that will sometimes call for trimming copyright's sails.

1. COPYRIGHT'S IMBALANCE

Since they passed the first copyright act in 1790, federal lawmakers have steadily increased copyright's duration, scope, power, and complexity.

The Copyright Act's few narrow, judicially created limitations have done very little to counteract that trend. Those facts alone do not suffice to show that copyright policy favors copyright holders' private interests over others' private and public ones. One might argue, after all, that lawmakers have by continually expanding the copyright privilege merely kept it delicately balanced. One might even argue that despite their efforts lawmakers neglect to adequately protect expressive works, cheating not only copyright holders but ultimately the general welfare and progress in science and useful arts. This section aims only to document how lawmakers have steadily expanded the legal privileges afforded by copyright. It remains for section 2 to explain that trend as the result not of a delicate balancing act but rather an indelicate one.

Duration of Copyright

The term of copyright has steadily expanded under US law. The 1790 Copyright Act set the maximum term at fourteen years plus a renewal term (subject to certain conditions) of fourteen years.[5] The 1831 Copyright Act doubled the initial term and retained the conditional renewal term, allowing a total of up to forty-two years of coverage.[6] Lawmakers doubled the renewal term in 1909, letting copyrights run for up to fifty-six years.[7] The 1976 Copyright Act changed the measure of the default copyright term to life of the author plus fifty years.[8] Recent amendments to the Copyright Act expanded the term yet again, letting it run for the life of the author plus seventy years.[9] Figure 11 illustrates the growth of the general US copyright term over time, including the effects of various statutory extensions.[10]

Note the overhanging ledges in figure 11. Those show how often lawmakers have reached backward in time, extending the copyright term even for works that had already been created. The Supreme Court has held that legislative trick constitutional,[11] notwithstanding copyright policy's implied aim of stimulating new authorship—not simply rewarding extant authors.[12]

Scope of Copyright

The subject matter covered by copyright has steadily expanded, too. The plain language of the Constitution authorizes legislation limiting access

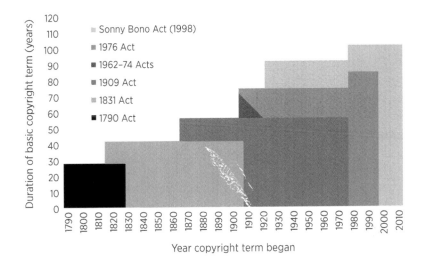

Figure 11. Trend of Copyright Duration in US Law

Notes: In calculating copyright terms based on the life of the author, the table conservatively assumes that authors create their works at age thirty-five and live for seventy years.

Sources: Copyright Act of 1790, 1 Stat. 124 (1790), reprinted in Copyright Office, Library of Congress, Bulletin No. 3 (Revised), *Copyright Enactments: Laws Passed in the United States since 1783 Relating to Copyright* (1973), 22; An Act to Amend the Several Acts Respecting Copyrights, 4 Stat. 436 (February 3, 1831), reprinted in Copyright Office, *Copyright Enactments*, 27; Copyright Act of 1909, 17 U.S.C. § 23 (1909) (repealed 1978); 17 U.S.C. § 302(a) (2012); Sonny Bono Copyright Term Extension Act, Pub. L. No. 105–298, 112 Stat. 2827 (1998), codified at 17 U.S.C. § 302(a)–(b). Professor John Rothchild helped me to correct a draft version of this chart, which first appeared in Tom W. Bell, "Escape from Copyright: Market Success vs. Statutory Failure in the Protection of Expressive Works," *University of Cincinnati Law Review* 69 (2001): 741–805.

only to "writings."[13] Lawmakers began almost immediately to read that grant broadly, extending the 1790 Copyright Act to cover not only books but also maps and charts.[14] Subsequent legislation increased the scope of copyright's restrictions, bit by bit, to include prints;[15] musical compositions;[16] performance rights in dramatic compositions;[17] photographs and negatives thereof;[18] paintings, drawings, chromos, statutes, and models or designs intended to be perfected as works of the fine arts;[19] motion pictures;[20] for-profit public performances of nondramatic literary works;[21] sound recordings;[22] computer programs;[23] and architectural works.[24] My research has revealed only one instance in which a statute arguably reduced the subject matter covered by copyright: this was with regard to publications of the federal government.[25] The Copyright Act

has expanded even beyond the bounds of copyright, covering artists' moral rights,[26] new designs of vessel hulls,[27] and technological systems that themselves protect copyrights.[28]

Power of Copyright

The exclusive rights granted by copyright law have expanded, as well. The 1790 Copyright Act restricted merely the reproduction and distribution of covered works.[29] The present statute gives copyright holders exclusive rights to the reproduction, distribution, preparation of derivative works, public performance, and public display of covered works.[30] Remedies for infringement have also grown from the mere destruction of infringing works and payment of statutory damages[31]—today the act vests copyright holders with a broad panoply of powers. Current remedies include the impounding of infringing articles and devices used in infringement;[32] statutory damages or actual damages and profits;[33] costs and attorneys' fees;[34] bars on the importation of infringing articles;[35] the power to subpoena digital service providers to disclose the identity of an alleged infringer;[36] and criminal sanctions including fines and imprisonment.[37]

Complexity of Copyright

The Copyright Act itself has exploded in size and complexity over the years. The Copyright Act of 1790 had just seven sections and no subsections. It ran 1,224 words.[38] The current version of the Copyright Act comprises eleven chapters, 122 sections, and a superabundance of subsections, sub-subsections, and so on. It lumbers along at about 70,400 words.[39]

Limits on Copyright

The Copyright Act has come to include a number of limitations on the exclusive rights that it establishes. Most of these limitations, such as those that excuse secondary transmission of television stations for private home viewing,[40] reproduction and distribution of works adapted for disabled persons,[41] and automated or innocent infringement by Internet service providers,[42] undoubtedly mean far more to special interests than to the rest of us.[43] The act does include some copyright limitations that apply more generally. Most of these apply only in circumstances so narrowly defined as to aggrieve few copyright holders, however.[44] The fair use[45] and first-sale[46] doctrines carry some punch, granted, but they came from the courts rather than Congress.[47] Copyright policy combines all the elements of a public choice tragedy: concentrated benefits, diffuse costs, and state power.

2. COPYRIGHT'S INDELICACY

Public choice theory—the observation that political actors respond to incentives, such as campaign donations or the prospect of future employment as lobbyists, no less than private ones do—readily explains copyright's steady growth.[48] Those who create or market expressive works know who they are, what they want, and how greatly they want it. Unsurprisingly, the procopyright faction approaches Congress as a well-defined, highly motivated, and apparently effective lobby.[49] In contrast, those who might benefit from a less expansive Copyright Act typically have disparate, inchoate, slight, or nonmonetized wishes. Advocates for common-law rights and the public domain thus find themselves outgunned when it comes to influencing the legislative process.

The problem runs deeper than the act's all-too-obvious public choice affliction. Even lengthy, open, and sincere civil discourse would of necessity fail to set copyright law into delicate balance.[50] Authorities cannot measure even the economic factors that would have to go into such a calculation, much less the myriad fluctuating and intangible ones.[51] Even if they could *measure* all the relevant economic, legal, technological, and cultural factors, politicians could not *balance* them.

Copyright law reaches so deeply into our lives that it has become not simply a matter of industrial policy, or even of information policy, but of *social* policy. Copyright law limits what we sing in church, what we post on our blogs, and what we read to our children. Federal lawmakers cannot possibly quantify the value of such things, so how could they delicately balance them?

Does that make the prospect of delicately balancing copyright policy sound unlikely? It gets worse. Public choice theory teaches that even if lawmakers could get and compare all the data necessary for delicately balancing the public and private interests affected by copyright and patent law, it wouldn't matter.[52] Lawmakers would not use the data—or, more precisely, it would have little impact on the laws they make. Instead, lobbying by special interests would invariably ensure that copyright policy favors select private parties against all others. That is not to say that politicians are always corrupt or that democracy must fail; rather, it simply means that politicians respond to the same incentives as the rest of us and that, consequently, democracies tend toward predictably biased outcomes.

As an illustration of the public choice pressures that drive copyright policy, consider the fate of the copyright in *Steamboat Willie*, a 1928 cartoon that the Walt Disney Company cites as establishing its copyright claim in Mickey Mouse.[53] Scholars have made a surprisingly strong case that, because the requisite formalities of the 1909 Copyright Act were not satisfied, *Steamboat Willie* has fallen into the public domain.[54] The Walt Disney Company has responded to such claims by threatening to bring suit for "slander of title," demonstrating how seriously it takes its copyright in *Steamboat Willie*.[55] Let us take Disney's alleged copyright seriously, too, then, to better understand its public choice effects.

Figure 12 illustrates how the duration of the copyright that the company claims in *Steamboat Willie*—marked by the black line—has twice approached expiration—a limit marked by the bottom of the chart. In both instances, federal lawmakers amended the Copyright Act to extend copyright's duration, both for subsequent copyrighted works and for works such as *Steamboat Willie* that predated the amendments. The line marking the copyright term in *Steamboat Willie* jogs upward both on the effective date of the 1976 Act (January 1, 1978)[56] and again on the effective date of the Sonny Bono Copyright Term Extension Act (October 27, 1998).[57] (*Steamboat Willie* did not receive the maximum possible copyright duration under either extension due to complications arising from the work's status as a work in its second term under the 1909 Copyright Act.)[58] No one can, of course, say with certainty whether or to what degree lobbying by the Walt Disney Company drove those copyright term extensions, which fortuitously or not saved the (supposed) copyright in *Steamboat Willie* from falling into the public

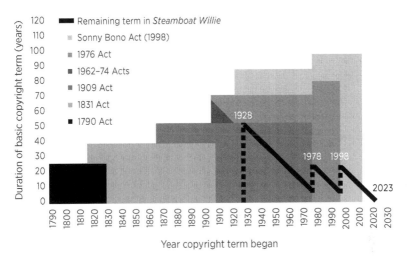

Figure 12. Copyright Duration and the Mickey Mouse Curve

domain.[59] It does not take a great deal of skepticism, however, to predict that federal lawmakers will extend copyrights again before 2023, at which time *Steamboat Willie* will once more risk sailing beyond the limits of copyright's duration.

Given the rough-and-tumble of real-world lawmaking, does the rhetoric of "delicate balancing" merit any place in copyright jurisprudence? The Copyright Act does reflect compromises struck among the various parties that lobby Congress and the administration for changes to federal law. A truce among special interests does not and cannot put all the interests affected by copyright law into a "delicate balance," however. Not even poetry can license that metaphor, which aggravates copyright's public choice affliction by endowing the legislative process with more legitimacy than it deserves. To claim that copyright policy strikes a delicate balance does worse than simply mislead; it aids and abets a statutory tragedy.

3. HOW TO ASSESS COPYRIGHT POLICY

To delicately balance the many interests affected by copyright policy exceeds politicians' capabilities, to say nothing of their motives. Still, though, we might aspire to *roughly* balance the public choice pressures that affect copyright. I suggest some fixes in part II of this book. Casting copyrights as intellectual privileges, as I suggested earlier, would help too.

Granted, even roughly balancing copyright policy might prove beyond us. In that event, we could at least avoid obvious disasters. We cannot tell whether copyright law at present offers would-be composers the optimal set of incentives for maximizing social wealth, for instance, but we can tell whether the public suffers an utter dearth of new musical works.[60]

Even though no one can tell whether copyright and patent law have achieved that mythical "delicate balance" of public and private interests, we *can* tell when lawmakers have plainly put matters out of whack. Sentencing copyright infringers to death would, for instance, clearly go beyond the pale. Perhaps some current laws go too far, too. The point is not to settle such questions but simply to observe that imprecise knowledge should not preclude rough justice.

That copyright policy can never delicately balance all the private and public interests it touches means that it always, to a lesser or greater extent, fails. We must therefore keep close watch over copyright, constantly guarding against a policy disaster. Even at its best copyright remains a necessary evil. If copyright's costs obviously outweigh its benefits, we should reform it. The speed of reform should of course depend in part on the settled expectations to buy peace from the retiring regime. But salient policy failures call for serious policy reforms.

At the very least, we should challenge the absurd argument that copyrights have become so important to the national economy that they must reach further still.[61] To the contrary, the fact that a rich and powerful lobby supports copyright demonstrates that no market failure in the production of expressive works looms on the horizon. Far from trumpeting the prodigious revenues, jobs, and exports that their clients generate, those who lobby for increasing copyright's power should have to prove that the public suffers terribly from a gross deficiency of fixed expressive works.

Perhaps copyright has expanded not just to the limits of its justification, but beyond. Perhaps authors would do just as well without it. The public appears to suffer no material deficiency in original perfumes, recipes, clothing designs, furniture, car bodies, or uninhabited architectural structures,[62] even though US law affords no effective protection to them *qua* original expressions (nor *qua* novel inventions covered by patent law).[63] Perhaps the same would hold true of subject matter now covered by copyrights, were their privileges revoked.

4. CONCLUSION

We cannot count on lawmakers to resolve the question of whether copyright strikes a delicate balance. We cannot count on them even to have much resolve in asking the question. The problem of encouraging the creation and distribution of original expressions and novel inventions mirrors other difficult problems of social coordination; in no such case can we expect a central political authority to have the information and incentives necessary to identify and implement an efficient and equitable public policy. Here, as in general, we should—insofar as possible—rely on the decentralized enforcement of common-law rights and remedies.[64] Although the common law cannot replicate copyrights and patents, those unnatural and purely statutory creations, it might nonetheless supplant them.

Given copyright's inevitable and indelicate imbalance, we should favor policies that reduce its influence over information policy so as to protect as many innocents as possible from copyright's misdirected wrath. If the public choice pressures feeding copyright's growth threaten to turn it into a monster, we should consider going entirely without it.

PART II

FIXING COPYRIGHT

Copyright does not work as well as it could or should. The next three chapters offer some fixes. Chapter 7 describes how the "fared" (aka "commercial") use of copyrighted works can limit the fair use of them and offers some principles for balancing the two. Chapter 8 argues for codifying copyright misuse, an obscure but potentially powerful doctrine that could both protect fair use and encourage the development of common-law alternatives to copyright. Chapter 9 offers policy guidelines and statutory language for deregulating expressive works, safeguarding the health of the public domain.

CHAPTER 7

FAIR USE VS. FARED USE

"Information wants to be free," claim those who decry the overpowering grasp of copyright law.[1] But they cannot mean what they say. *Information* wants nothing at all. The epigram speaks not to what information wants, but rather to what people want: they want information for free.[2]

So restated, the catch-phrase still rings true. Who would not prefer to get information—that vital good—at no cost? But information never comes for free. We can only try our best to fully account for its costs, minimize them, and allocate them fairly. If we must have copyright, then, we should insofar as possible subject it to market processes. This observation does not justify copyright itself; that remains subject to dispute. But if we are going to make copyrights, we should make sure they make sense.

Copyright users necessarily bear costs when they search for, interpret, and collect information. This holds true even when the fair use defense allows consumers to avoid paying *cash* for the right to use a fixed expressive work. Copyright holders likewise bear costs when they create, copy, and distribute works. Unsurprisingly, they seek remuneration of those costs and, if possible, profit.

Just as copyright itself represents a response to market failure, as demonstrated in part I, so does fair use. And just as common-law rights and technological developments look increasingly likely to overcome the market failure that alone justifies copyright—a claim that I will explore in detail in chapters 9–11—so too do they look increasingly likely to trim the effective scope of the fair use doctrine. Courts tell us that the doctrine should give up ground where opportunities to purchase or license copyrighted works advance.[3] If you can buy the right to use an expressive work at a market-clearing price, after all, you have little excuse to use it without paying. Fair use avails you nothing in such a case; you should license the work or go without. You should, in other words, rely on *fared* use rather than *fair* use.

Although you might at first bridle at having to pay a fare for what you would otherwise simply take, you should in fact welcome the change. Fair use is not free use, after all. Whether in cash, time, or trouble, you always pay when you consume copyrighted work. Thanks to technological advances—digitalization, computers, and the Internet—paying a fare for access to an expressive work often costs less, all told, than using the work without permission. Most consumers appear to welcome the advent of convenient markets for copyrighted works, at any rate; thus has Apple's iTunes service flourished.

This chapter explains why fair use will and should give way as fared use expands. Fair use will and should remain potent, however, when a copyright holder entirely refuses to license access.[4] The market does not simply fail in such a case; it fails to even exist, giving good reason to excuse the unauthorized use of the suppressed work. Fair use thus plays a vital role in protecting critical reviews, parodies, and investigative reporting.

What if copyright holders employ common-law tools, such as licenses or automated rights management, to bar even the fair use of a work? In that case, we might well judge that copyright policy has failed, on net, to promote the general welfare, the progress of science, and useful arts. To remedy that wrong, however, we should not attack common-law rights. If copyright and the common law combine to give copyright holders too much power, we should trim back the former. After all, as a special exception to the common law, the Copyright Act remains at best a necessary evil.

This chapter argues, in sum, that

- the scope of fair use will shrink as fared use grows, though fair use will continue to safeguard works against suppression;

- copyright holders may use common-law devices, such as licenses or technological protections, to limit fair uses; and

- if in combination copyright and the common law restrict too much expression, we should direct our reforms at the former rather than the latter.

1. FAIR USE

Fair use limits copyright's power. A party that engages in the fair use of a copyrighted work enjoys a legal defense against claims that the use infringes copyright. Section 107 of the Copyright Act codifies the doctrine.[5] Despite that codification, fair use remains a notoriously uncertain defense. We often can only guess whether a given use qualifies as "fair" under section 107; it almost always depends on contestable facts. Be that as it may, most legal authorities regard fair use as a crucial part of copyright policy.[6] Fair use counterbalances the overenforcement of copyright, promoting the general welfare and progress in the sciences and useful arts by classifying certain expressive acts as noninfringing. The First Amendment requires at least that much.

Fair use has the salutary effect of freeing the flow of information. That boon does not come at no cost, however. Because it decreases copyright's potential power, fair use perhaps dampens the ardor of some would-be authors. In a world without fair use, after all, copyright holders would enjoy the privilege of enjoining or licensing almost any use within the scope of section 106's panoply of exclusive rights, including the rights to reproduce, prepare derivative versions of, publicly distribute reproductions of, publicly perform, or publicly display expressive works. If it weren't for fair use, singing a parody of Carly Rae Jepsen's "Call Me Maybe" in the high school cafeteria could land students in jail.

Who wants to live in that world? Even the beneficiaries of copyright would probably find it irksomely constraining, given that artists and authors inevitably draw on older works to create new ones. Fair use protects us from the statutory failure that would follow if copyright were to expand into every corner of our culture, regulating even the most inconsequential and private uses of others' expressions. Whatever the costs of the uncertainty fair use casts on the scope of copyright, however, it probably ends up promoting the general welfare. All of us—even copyright holders—can celebrate that.

Fair Use Is Not Free Use

We may have less cause to celebrate fair use in coming years, however. The development of more efficient market mechanisms for regulating access to copyrighted works makes it look likely that practical impact of the fair use defense will shrink. Trends suggest that extant law and technological advances will combine to make it easier and easier for copyright holders to demand and receive licensing fees. Consider, for example, how iTunes has changed music listening (and copying) practices. Consumers have no sound reason to object to paying market-clearing rates for permission to use copyrighted works, however. Granted, consumers might at first feel aggrieved to find that they must pay for uses that formerly they enjoyed free of charge—but we should not confuse fair use with free use. In fact, fair use is never free.[7] Fared use simply makes the costs of accessing copyrighted works more obvious.

Because a copyright does not give its holder the right to require licensing fees for uses falling within the scope of section 107,[8] parties availing themselves of *fair* use typically regard it as *free* use. But fair use seems free only because copyright holders do not demand money for it. In one way or another, consumers have to pay when they use a copyrighted work. Even if fair use excuses them from paying the copyright holder, they incur costs when they photocopy and distribute newspaper stories for spontaneous classroom use, for instance, or when they search for quotations and type them into their papers. It makes no difference that we pay licensing fees in *money* whereas we pay fair use's transaction costs in *lost opportunities*. Economically speaking, a cost is a cost. As Richard A. Posner explains, "one of the most tenacious fallacies about economics" is the notion "that it is about money. On the contrary, it is about resource use, money being merely a claim on resources."[9]

Paying licensing fees might easily prove cheaper, all told, than paying fair use's costs. Not too long ago, you might have invoked fair use to make cassette copies of your albums, allowing you to listen to your favorite music on the go. These days, you would probably instead pay iTunes to let you load copies of your favorite songs onto your iPod. We can thank the prospect of licensing fees for driving the technical innovation that made such new and better ways of accessing expressive works possible. Before you did not pay to carry your favorite music with you; now you do. Has that made you worse off? Surely not. Consumer demand demonstrates that Apple's *fared* use offers a better deal than analog's *fair* use. We should not assume that fared use imposes a net cost on consumers; indeed, the contrary seems far more likely.

Fixing Market Failure

Sometimes transaction costs make contracting to sell or license access to a copyrighted work prohibitively expensive. Copyright holders might decline to license a use simply because the trouble of so doing exceeds the prospective revenue, for instance, or would-be users might calculate that obtaining permission to use a work poses too much of a hassle. Fair use corrects those sorts of market failures by permitting such uses free of charge.[10] As professor of law Wendy J. Gordon describes it, "Courts and Congress have employed fair use to permit uncompensated transfers that are socially desirable but not capable of effectuation through the market."[11]

Understanding fair use as a response to market failure does much to explain the vagaries of its development in the case law. Consider the decision in *American Geophysical Union v. Texaco, Inc.*: the court reasoned that "a particular unauthorized use should be considered 'more fair' when there is no ready market or means to pay for the use, while such an unauthorized use should be considered 'less fair' when there is a ready market or means to pay for the use."[12] In other words, the scope of the fair use defense rises and falls with the transaction costs of buying access to copyrighted works.

Maintaining Copyright's *Quid Pro Quo*

As courts and commentators often have noted, the Constitution demands a public benefit as justification for the limited statutory privileges created by the Copyright Act.[13] In contrast to the view that the fair use doctrine represents a second-best response to pervasive market failure, therefore, some commentators regard it as an integral part of this constitutional *quid pro quo*.[14] According to this view, fair use provides a public benefit—unbilled access to copyrighted works in certain contexts—to balance copyright's private privileges. The spread of fared use at first appears to threaten this supposed bargain, because it seems to impose new limits on the public's access to copyrighted works without offering any public benefit in return. More careful consideration of the issue shows, however, that fared use appears likely to benefit copyright holders and copyright users alike.

By reducing transaction costs throughout the market for copyrighted expressions, fared use benefits the public both directly and indirectly. Having emanated from an intentionally vague statute[15] and developed in various, occasionally contradictory cases, the fair use doctrine necessarily blurs the boundary between valid and invalid copyright claims. Thus did Judge Learned Hand describe the fair use doctrine as "the most troublesome in the whole law of copyright."[16] Though the resultant uncertainty obviously harms producers and sellers of copyrighted works, it also harms consumers. Academics, artists, commentators, and others desirous of reusing copyrighted works without authorization must borrow at their peril, consult experts on fair use, or, sadly, altogether forgo reusing the works. The clarifying power of fared use directly benefits those who would reuse copyrighted works—and through them their public audiences—by creating harbors safe from the threat of copyright litigation.

Moreover, fared use benefits the public indirectly by increasing the transactional efficiency of the market for expressive works. Like other markets, the market for expressive works does not constitute a zero-sum game; the users of copyrighted works don't lose just because copyright holders gain. As Nobel laureate Ronald Coase observed of markets in general,

> It is obviously desirable that rights should be assigned to those who can use them most productively and with incentives that lead them to do so. It is also desirable that, to discover (and maintain) such a distribution of rights, the costs of their transference should be low, through clarity in the law and by making the legal requirements for such transfers less onerous.[17]

Fared use, by its systemic improvement of copyright's transactional efficiency, helps the United States discover and maintain a distribution of rights to expressive works that will increase net social wealth.[18] Fared use thus stands to benefit both producers and consumers.

Because fared use will increase the value of copyrighted works, moreover, it will encourage improvements in their quantity, quality, and availability.[19] Consumers will benefit. Although this cornucopia of expressive works may at first come only for a fee, some of it will eventually (in theory) fall into the public domain. Copyright holders might very well offer limited free access to their wares in an attempt to draw more extensive (and expensive) uses. Inspired by the prospects of licensing, entrepreneurs will undoubtedly create other services, at present utterly and inevitably unforeseen, to attract and satisfy consumers of information.

Because fared use creates well-defined and easily obtained rights to expressive works, it puts the power of the market in the service of consumer demand.[20] Fared use therefore will probably provide better public access to copyrighted works than fair use does or could. At any rate, no one can plausibly claim that fared use would necessarily serve the public interest any less well than copyright's current *quid pro quo*. Perhaps we would do even better with fewer copyright restrictions overall. So long as we have copyright, though, we might as well clarify its boundaries as well as we can and loose market processes on the problem of connecting consumers with the works they want.

Fair Use Continues to Bar Copyright Censorship

Despite the inroads made by fared use, fair use will continue to trump censorship-by-copyright. The court in *American Geophysical* allowed licensing to limit the fair use defense only "when the means for paying for such a use is made easier." The court thus conditioned its decision on the observation that "a particular unauthorized use should be considered 'more fair' when there is no ready market or means to pay for the use."[21] In this, it followed the Supreme Court's reasoning in *Campbell v. Acuff-Rose Music, Inc.*:

> The market for potential derivative uses includes only those that creators of original works would in general develop or license others to develop. Yet the unlikelihood that creators of imaginative works will license critical reviews or lampoons of their own productions removes such uses from the very notion of a potential licensing market.[22]

Although a thin-skinned copyright holder might like to stop wags who evade technical and contractual restrictions so they can reuse "liberated" works in objectionable ways, therefore, the fair use defense would shield such defendants from copyright infringement claims. Here, at least, fair use holds its ground.

Can you count on the fair use defense to excuse not only your objectionable reuse of a copyrighted work but also your refusal to pay for that use? Probably so. Reuses that qualify for the fair use defense do not, under section 107 of the Copyright Act, constitute infringement.[23] The act would thus not obligate you to pay. Requiring payment in such circumstances arguably make more sense, for the same reasons that support the spread of licensing generally.[24] Furthermore, excusing nonpayment might encourage the overproduction of reuses that aim, for purely economic reasons, to offend copyright holders.[25] True, parody and other criticism "can provide social benefit, by shedding light on an earlier work, and, in the process, creating a new one."[26] But too much of a good thing is no good at all.

Such theoretical considerations have yet to change copyright law. Unless and until they do, it looks as if information providers will have to suffer objectionable uses without remuneration, license them grudgingly, or try to prevent them by other means—including, most notably, by invoking their common-law rights.

2. FARED USE

Copyright holders generally try to exercise their statutory rights to recoup the costs of creating, copying, and distributing expressive works. Like most of us, they aim to win profits, too. The common law aids that effort by offering a trusted body of time-tested and reasonably efficient default rules. Thus, for instance, authors might license the use of their copyrights, relying on contract law to guide each deal. They would have a tort claim if they suffered fraud in the process. And they might use common-law property rights—in labs, workshops, and packaging—to put the copyrighted work under lock and key.

Most copyright holders rest content if they can combine their statutory privileges and common-law rights to simply earn money. Few have any interest in demanding more from their customers, such as wielding their copyrights to demand that licensees abandon their fair use rights. In most instances, trying to censor uses of a work that are offensive to the copyright holder is not cost-effective because it fails to provide the licensor with any greater monetary benefit than unconstrained licensing would provide. Only a copyright holder with some overriding nonmonetary objective, such as a powerful aversion to public criticism, would find anticriticism contracts worthwhile.[27] Licensors who want injunctive relief against offensive uses would not only have to forgo licensing fees for such uses and bear enforcement costs; they would also have to offer consumers something extra to make such censorious contracts attractive in the first place. That added inducement to suffer censorship would probably come in the form of lower licensing fees—another price that overly sensitive copyright holders would have to pay.

Notwithstanding those caveats, let us assume that some copyright holders, at least some of the time, will want to combine their statutory rights with their common-law rights in an effort to prevent the fair use of their works. Would such an effort succeed? It probably would, under current law. But should it?

If copyright and the common law combine to give copyright holders too much power, only the former bears the blame. Copyright, recall, represents a statutory exception to common-law rights. If copyright goes too far, it does so by transgressing our common-law rights to our voices, pens, and presses. It thus makes no sense to condemn the common law for copyright's excesses. Rather, we should recognize the cause of the problem, and cure it by trimming back copyright rights out of respect for common-law ones. Chapter 8 discusses how to do so.

3. CONCLUSION

Under current legal doctrine, the fair use defense shrinks as licensing opportunities grow. In this way, markets can overcome copyright's limitations. We should welcome that sort of development as both efficient and equitable. But fair use's power will endure nonetheless. It will continue to protect such things as reviews that critically quote copyrighted works, disclosures of otherwise confidential information, and parodies.

When fair use nullifies copyright holders' statutory rights, they might resort to common-law means of protecting their works. Perhaps the combination of copyright and common-law rights will prove oppressive. In that event, though, we should respond by limiting the former and respecting the latter.

CHAPTER 8
CODIFYING MISUSE

Copyright holders claim special statutory privileges. They also claim common-law rights, as when they form and enforce contracts, defend property rights in tangible goods, and win remedies for suffering torts. By combining their copyright rights with their common-law rights, copyright holders can expand their control over fixed expressive works. When this combination of statutory and common-law powers goes too far, such as when a copyright holder uses licensing to create a tying arrangement illegal under antitrust law or to forbid an otherwise fair use of a work, an accusation of copyright misuse may follow. How should copyright law react in such a case?

Here as elsewhere, the same general principle applies: because copyright represents a special exception to the common law's general background rules, copyright should give way when the common law alone suffices to promote the general welfare and the progress of science and useful arts. Chapter 7 used that principle to analyze copyright's fair use doctrine. This chapter uses it to analyze copyright's misuse doctrine.

How does copyright misuse work in practice? Consider an example. ThinSkin Inc. offers downloads of its copyrighted software, Bugfest, subject to payment of $20 and agreement to a click-through license. Among other terms, the license bars public criticism of Bugfest. Bill Snarky buys a copy of Bugfest, clicks "I agree," and thereafter blogs about the software's many flaws. Snarky's critique includes screenshots of Bugfest in action—too many, let us suppose, to excuse as fair use. ThinSkin sues Snarky, citing unauthorized reproduction of expressions covered by Bugfest's copyright[1] and violation of the software's license. Snarky answers by raising a copyright misuse defense. Under current doctrine, Snarky would probably win relief from ThinSkin's claim that his screenshot violated its copyright. The misuse defense would probably not protect Snarky from

ThinSkin's claim that he breached their agreement by publicly criticizing the software, however. To judge from the precedents, misuse limits only copyright privileges—not common-law rights.

The misuse defense to copyright infringement exists, at present, only in scattered judicial pronouncements[2] and in a somewhat uncertain form.[3] The US Supreme Court has only hinted at the doctrine,[4] and federal lawmakers have yet to codify it.[5] Nonetheless, lower courts appear increasingly willing[6] to recognize misuse as a defense to copyright infringement.[7] Misuse has now reached a stage of development similar to the stage that the fair use defense reached before its statutory enactment.[8] Just as precedents from patent law inspired courts to recognize the defense of copyright misuse,[9] the Patent Act's codification of misuse[10] should serve as a model for lawmakers, inspiring them to add a definition of copyright misuse defense to the Copyright Act.

To rationalize the doctrine, this chapter proposes a codification of copyright's misuse defense. Specifically, it suggests putting all that now appears in section 107 of the Copyright Act (which at present defines the fair use defense) into a subsection designated section 107(a), and adding the following paragraph to the act as section 107(b):

> It constitutes copyright misuse to contractually limit any use of a copyrighted work if that use would qualify as noninfringing under § 107(a). No party misusing a work has rights to it under § 106 or § 106A during that misuse. A court may, however, remedy breach of any contract the limitations of which constitute copyright misuse under this section.

The second sentence of the proposed section 107(b) summarizes the case law that has recognized and defined copyright misuse. It does so by denying copyright holders any of the rights set forth in sections 106 or 106A—the Copyright Act's two main provisions defining rights—during the pendency of any copyright misuse. As for the first and last sentences of proposed section 107(b), they advance a policy only implicit in the case law: when copyright and contract rights combine to give a copyright holder too much legal power, courts should decline to enforce only the holder's copyright rights. That deference to the common law conforms to copyright's foundational principles and would protect copyright from the public choice pressures that, as described above, threaten to expand it beyond its proper scope.

1. COPYRIGHT MISUSE IN THE COURTS

Copyright misuse currently exists solely as a judicial doctrine. Understanding how lawmakers should codify copyright misuse calls for first understanding how courts have shaped it. Many other commentators have tackled that worthy project in great detail.[11] Therefore, what I offer here is only a summary account of the extant case law.

The copyright misuse defense grew out of the patent misuse defense, where the doctrine originated to bar patent holders from wielding their statutory rights to put illegal restraints on trade.[12] Although some authorities have affirmed that using a copyright in violation of antitrust law likewise constitutes misuse,[13] most courts that have applied the doctrine have done so in response to other, less plainly actionable wrongs.[14] As the Fourth Circuit Court of Appeals put it, when it first recognized the doctrine of copyright misuse, "The question is not whether the copyright is being used in a manner violative of antitrust law . . . but whether the copyright is being used in a manner violative of the public policy embodied in the grant of a copyright."[15]

As that broad reference to public policy suggests, the exact scope of misuse remains a bit uncertain. The doctrine evidently applies when a copyright holder attempts to restrict by license competitive behavior otherwise permissible under copyright law.[16] Courts have also found misuse where copyright holders have attempted to use their statutory rights to inhibit what the fair use defense plainly allows[17] or what the Copyright Act otherwise leaves unprotected.[18] Based on the logic of such cases, and suggestive dicta from other cases, commentators surmise that the defense extends to attempts to contractually restrict users' fair use rights.[19]

At any time during which a copyright holder engages in misuse of a work, the holder cannot enforce copyright rights in it. The copyright holder can regain those rights, but only by ending the practices that constitute misuse.[20] Even then, judging from patent law precedent,[21] courts will not remedy alleged infringements that occurred during the period of misuse.[22] Because no copyright rights existed during that period, no copyright *wrongs*—i.e., infringements—could have occurred. (The sole exception to that view appears in one trial court's dictum summarily claiming that copyright misuse tolls not rights but only remedies. Under that idiosyncratic view, criticized below, copyright holders might, after ending their misuses, recover even for infringements that occurred during the period of misuse.[23])

According to the majority view, copyright misuse functions only as a defense. It does not create standing to sue for and obtain judicial relief.[24] Even in what was evidently the sole case where a court has recognized copyright misuse as an affirmative claim for relief, rather than merely as a defense for copyright infringement, the plaintiff sought only judicial declaration of its rights (rather than monetary or injunctive relief) and complained of practices that also violated antitrust law.[25]

A party need not suffer directly from misuse before wielding it as a defense for copyright infringement. Instead, it suffices to prove that a copyright holder engages in misuse of the allegedly infringed work *somewhere* and that the misuse affects *someone*.[26] Thus, for instance, a defendant might enjoy the defense because the plaintiff's licensing agreements with third parties unduly restrict the third parties' rights.[27]

Courts have not decisively resolved whether a party with unclean hands can benefit from copyright misuse.[28] In *Lasercomb America, Inc. v. Reynolds* the court, which largely pioneered the modern approach to copyright misuse, allowed the defendants the benefit of the doctrine, even though it affirmed that they had committed fraud.[29] The court in *Atari Games Corp. v. Nintendo, Inc.*, in contrast, found that the defendants' unclean hands barred them from invoking misuse.[30] Arguing that the *Atari* court had misread the relevant precedents, the court in *Alcatel USA, Inc. v. DGI Technologies, Inc.* held that the trial court had wrongly denied the defendant the misuse defense, even though the defendant had "very dirty mitts."[31] In sum, although it seems safest to say that copyright misuse can shield even a party with unclean hands, the issue remains unsettled and, in most jurisdictions, unaddressed.

Copyright misuse provides a defense against only copyright infringement claims; it offers no defense for breach of a contract or another common-law cause of action.[32] Courts have thus let misuse bar the enforcement of copyright rights while leaving contract and other rights unaffected.[33] Still other courts have suspended plaintiffs' copyright rights in light of misuse without mentioning—and thus evidently without disallowing—plaintiffs' common-law rights.[34] Though little celebrated by courts or commentators, this obscure quirk of copyright misuse has remarkable effects, and inspired the deregulatory approach embraced by my proposed addition to the Copyright Act.

2. A SENTENCE-BY-SENTENCE EXPLANATION OF PROPOSED SECTION 107(B)

Section 107(b) would codify copyright's misuse doctrine. Hitherto, courts have justified the doctrine by drawing comparisons to patent law, which has long had a codified misuse defense,[35] and by invoking general principles of equity.[36] Section 107(b) follows the Patent Act in codifying the copyright misuse defense, clarifying its scope, and defining its effect. Thus the statutory section proposed in this chapter, even if it never becomes law, serves to describe current doctrine and define the proper role of misuse in copyright policy.

Section 107(b) operates stepwise, through three sentences. The first sentence specifies when copyright misuse might occur. The second sentence describes the legal effect of the defense. The third sentence limits the scope of the doctrine. Taken as a whole, section 107(b) aims to ensure that, instead of combining copyright and contract law to limit fair use, copyright holders choose either the rights afforded under the Copyright Act or those afforded by contract law.

Sentence 1:
> It constitutes copyright misuse to contractually limit any use of a copyrighted work if that use would qualify as non-infringing under § 107(a).

This sentence aims to ensure that copyright and contract law do not combine to vest copyright holders with too much legal clout. Effectively, it forces a copyright holder to choose between respecting fair use and relying on contracts. By specifying that contractual limits on fair use qualify as copyright misuse, section 107(b) rationalizes the case law, capturing not just the holding of one particular court, but rather the logic and spirit of manifold judicial and academic opinions.

Notably, the first sentence of section 107(b) specifies only one particular way in which copyright misuse might arise. Query whether that would foreclose a court from justifying the defense on other grounds. If section 107(b) were law, for instance, could a defendant facing copyright infringement charges still argue that the plaintiff's antitrust violations constituted misuse? The absence of any exclusionary language and respect for established doctrines should convince courts to not read section 107(b) to bar recognition of other forms of copyright misuse. Misuse has traditionally been a child of the courts and section 107(b) would not ask them to abandon it.

The first sentence of section 107(b) aims only to clarify a particular, and particularly uncertain, form of copyright misuse. It does not foreclose the invocation of other, more clearly established grounds for finding copyright misuse. Nor does it foreclose courts from exercising their equitable discretion to remedy egregious, but novel, forms of copyright misuse. In this way, section 107(b) adopts an open texture akin to that of section 107(a).[37]

Sentence 2:

> No party misusing a work has rights to it under § 106 or § 106A during that misuse.

This sentence codifies the practice, consistently followed in copyright misuse cases, of suspending copyright rights in a work during the work's misuse. As a matter of simple logic, remedies cannot be justified if rights are not violated. Even copyright holders who end their misuses should not retroactively win copyright remedies for any alleged infringements that occurred during the period of misuse. In this regard, as in so many others, copyright misuse doctrine follows the path laid by patent misuse doctrine.[38]

The only judicial exception to this view is found in a dictum of the *In re Napster* court. The court opined that when and if the plaintiffs had ended their misuse, they might win copyright remedies retroactively—even for infringements that occurred during the period of misuse.[39] Since it did not rule out awarding interest on any monetary relief thereby delayed, the *In re Napster* court's approach to copyright misuse threatens to gut the doctrine. Such a lenient approach to misuse would give copyright holders little reason to fear the misuse defense.[40] The second sentence of section 107(b), because it suspends copyright *rights* rather than only *remedies*, rejects that suspect aside from *In re Napster*.

Sentence 2 also embodies the majority view that misuse merely tolls copyright rights; it does not permanently destroy them. As discussed above, courts and commentators have opined that a copyright holder facing a valid misuse defense may, by no longer misusing the subject work, regain copyright rights in it. This approach conforms to the theory, implicit in the case law, that the doctrine of misuse aims not to punish overreaching copyright holders but merely to deny them overweening legal powers.

Section 107(b) seeks to guard constitutionally protected freedoms of expression from the state power afforded to copyright holders.[41] The fair use defense has traditionally helped to ensure that the Copyright Act does not contradict the First Amendment.[42] Licenses that prohibit commentary about copyrighted works threaten to overwhelm that bulwark of liberty, however. Section 107(b) fortifies fair use, safeguarding that legal defense—and thus our freedoms of expression—from an unseemly combination of copyright and contract rights.

Sentence 2 goes beyond, but not against, the case law by clarifying that the copyright misuse defense bars not only the ordinary sorts of exclusive rights set forth in section 106 of the Copyright Act and covering such acts as reproduction, creation of derivative works, and public performances and displays, but also the so-called "moral rights" set forth in section 106A, which give fine visual artists privileges to claim their works as their own and in certain cases to prevent alterations to them.[43] Why extend section 107(b) to the latter? Not because anyone who enjoys the relatively limited rights afforded by section 106A poses a particularly great risk of misusing them. Rather, it is because no compelling reason suggests that such parties, when and if they misuse their copyright rights,[44] should escape the scope of the defense.[45]

Sentence 3:

> A court may, however, remedy breach of any contract the limitations of which constitute copyright misuse under this section.

The third sentence of section 107(b) codifies what courts have already held: copyright misuse serves as a defense against copyright claims only—not against claims arising under the common law in general or contract law in particular. Note that this provision says only that courts "may" remedy breaches of contracts that control access to expressive works. It does not guarantee the success of those claims, which must stand or fall under the law of contracts applicable to the dispute.[46]

The respect here shown for contract rights reflects a fundamental aspect of copyright policy. By forcing copyright holders who misuse their works to choose between their statutory rights and their common-law ones, section 107(b) would encourage the development of new ways of protecting expressive works. To the extent that such alternatives would cure the market failure that justifies copyright, they would render copyright superfluous. Thus, copyright *misuse* might promote the worthy policy of eventually ending copyright *use*.

3. SECTION 107(B) IN PRACTICE

Could the codification of copyright misuse proposed here survive the legislative process and pass into law? Possibly. As noted earlier, the doctrine of copyright misuse stands at a point in its development akin to that achieved by the fair use doctrine just before its codification.[47] This merely suggests copyright misuse may be ripe for codification, however; it hardly compels that result. To assess the prospects for section 107(b), we need to take account of the various factions that might lobby for or against it.

Though hardly a politically powerful faction, the various parties who generally favor opening wider access to copyrighted works—consumers, educators, librarians, students, and others—would almost certainly find much to like in section 107(b). The proposed statute would, after all, clarify and universalize what courts have already said: copyright holders must not leverage their rights under the act to commit wrongs against the public. In particular, section 107(b) would, by classifying contractual limitations on fair use rights as copyright misuse, clearly safeguard a vital mechanism for ensuring that copyright law does not infringe on our freedoms of expression.

A much more powerful lobby, including representatives of the entertainment and software industries, generally disfavors weakening copyright. Even those parties, however, might find much to like in section 107(b). First, the proposed codification of misuse would clarify a troublingly vague area of law, making the rights created by the Copyright Act more reliable and, thus, more valuable. Second, copyright holders wary of section 107(b) could easily safeguard their statutory rights by adding to their licenses appropriate saving clauses, avoiding the misuse defense by clarifying that the licenses do not limit any rights established by section 107(a).[48] Third, section 107(b) would reassure copyright holders that, even if they offend its definition of misuse, they might still enforce their rights under contract law.

How would section 107(b) work in practice? Return to the example offered earlier in the chapter, wherein software licensor ThinSkin Inc. leverages its copyright to force Snarky to waive his right to criticize its product. Section 107(b) plainly gives Snarky a misuse defense against ThinSkin's copyright infringement claim.[49] ThinSkin retains the right to sue Snarky for breach of contract, though.

What would suing only in contract get ThinSkin? While denied the generous monetary and near-automatic injunctive relief afforded by the Copyright Act,[50] ThinSkin would enjoy a good chance of winning contract damages—perhaps even liquidated damages, if the agreement has specified them in advance—and would have a fair chance of winning a court order enjoining Snarky from violating his promises.[51] Section 107(b) would not force copyright holders like ThinSkin to forgo all legal remedies—just those arising out of copyright law.

In the long run, section 107(b) would encourage copyright holders like ThinSkin to develop new ways of protecting expressive works. In some cases, after all, section 107(b) would flatly rule out reliance on copyright rights. It would, however, reassure copyright holders that they might still invoke contract law to good effect. Like a mother bird nudging her fledglings to the nest's edge, section 107(b) would embolden copyright holders to escape the confines of the Copyright Act, promoting both their own interests, and, more crucially, the development of common-law mechanisms for rewarding the production of original expressive works.

4. CONCLUSION

This chapter has described and defended a codification of copyright's misuse doctrine. The section it proposes adding to the Copyright Act largely follows the case law in defining the scope and effect of the misuse defense. By specifying that certain contractual restrictions constitute misuse of copyright protections, section 107(b) would also pursue a policy of ensuring that fair use continues to protect Americans' freedoms of expression. Thus codified, the misuse defense would promote the public good by making copyright less vague, less threatening, and ultimately less important.

CHAPTER 9
DEREGULATING
EXPRESSIVE WORKS

Copyright law regulates expression. Through it, copyright holders win the privilege of invoking state power to control how and what Americans communicate. The Copyright Act limits our freedom to reproduce, rework, publicly distribute, publicly perform, and publicly display certain works of authorship.[1] In many cases, even when the act does not utterly prohibit the unauthorized use of a restricted work, the Copyright Office sets the price for using it.[2] The rules regulating our access to original expressive works flow from the top down, out of Washington, DC, to the hinterlands, in excruciatingly detailed and nonnegotiable terms.

The common law operates on a very different basis. In general, it grows from the bottom up, through the decisions of manifold state courts, largely free from the influence of federal lawmakers, statutes, or administrative agencies. Relative to those authorities, the common law embodies a few elegant and robust principles, leaving details to particular cases, customary practices, and mutual consent. The common law thus offers a deregulatory alternative to copyright.

Why should we embrace the common law over copyright? Simple logic suggests the appeal of acquiring the benefits of copyright policy (access to authors' works) without incurring its costs (lost opportunities to use those works). The Constitution goes further; it demands that Congress abandon copyright if it discovers better policy options. If copyright is not necessary and proper to promote the general welfare and progress in science and useful arts, after all, it loses its sole justification. With regard to protecting expressive works as with regard to public policy in general, the common law offers a basic and presumptively sufficient set of rules for promoting the public good. Only if the framework of rights to tangible property, enforceable promises, and personal security that makes up the common law fails, grossly and avoidably, should we resort to legislative or administrative alternatives.

The common law evidently suffices to stimulate many original expressions. In chapter 1 we considered how perfumes, recipes, clothing designs, furniture, car bodies, and uninhabited architectural structures exhibit great innovation despite falling outside the scope of copyright law, patent law, or any like mechanism of statutory privilege. Perhaps the common law could do still more if pressed into service more broadly. Perhaps its fundamental principles of contract, property, and tort law could stimulate original expressive works even better than copyright can. Only by trying can we know.

We should thus promote policy experiments testing whether the common law alone would suffice to produce a socially optimal amount of expression. Those experiments will never happen, though, unless copyright holders have good reason to abandon their statutory privileges. At present, they have little reason to do so. True, abandonment would allow copyright holders to escape the risk of paying the attorneys' fees of defendants who succeed in fending off particularly outrageous infringement claims[3] (a risk that the common law does not pose), but that offers only a small incentive to forgo copyright's many advantages. It would help matters if the Copyright Act expressly guaranteed that federal preemption would prevent former copyright holders from trying protect their works through common-law mechanisms, such as by contracts limiting the unauthorized reuse of an author's works. Such a guarantee would greatly increase the incentives to abandon copyright and rely on the common law.

Should the United States favor the common law or a federal statute when it comes to controlling the creation, dissemination, and use of expressions? Commentators and courts largely agree on how to answer this question in the context of the First Amendment, allowing property- and contract-based restrictions on speech while forbidding statutory ones. No such consensus exists in the context of copyright, however. Indeed, scarcely anyone even asks the question in those terms. Extant Supreme Court jurisprudence treats copyright like a content-neutral, time, place, or manner restriction, like a ban on the use of loudspeakers in a public park, and thus subjects it to only intermediate scrutiny. In fact, however, copyright more closely resembles a content-based restriction on liberties protected by the First Amendment. Instead of punishing sacrilegious or anti-patriotic speech, however, copyright punishes unoriginal speech. As such, copyright should attract not intermediate scrutiny but the strongest review that courts can muster: strict scrutiny.

This take on the First Amendment status of copyright remains idiosyncratic, admittedly. The fault, however, lies not with the logic of the argument but with the precedents. To the question, "Should we favor the common law or a federal statute when it comes to controlling the creation, dissemination, and use of expressions?" we thus should answer, "Put the common law above copyright."

1. FROM CENTRAL COMMAND TO DECENTRALIZED DISCOVERY

We should encourage and respect common-law solutions to copyright's problems. Nobody—not lawmakers, not judges, and certainly not academics—can reliably dictate the single best means of regulating access to expressive works. The necessary information must come from those who actually participate in the market for expressive goods and services, and it will appear in the mosaic of their diverse experiments. Only by patiently studying their evolved preferences, in the fine and in the aggregate, will we discover the best way to promote the general welfare and progress in science and useful arts.

As copyright holders and consumers of copyrighted works tinker with copyright's default rules, they will test a wide variety of methods for managing expressive works. Assessing this exploratory and entrepreneurial process requires careful observations of actual results. The examples set by creative perfumes, recipes, clothing designs, furniture, car bodies, and uninhabited architectural structures—all of which flourish despite their uncopyrightability—strongly suggest that the common law can promote authorship. A robust market in once-copyrighted works would prove more probative. Perhaps because we lack clear ways of designating such works, no one appears to have run that experiment yet. The next chapter discusses a way to remedy that deficiency.

Would protecting fixed expressive works with only the common law protect the general welfare, too? It seems likely to do so at least as well as copyright does. The common law's decentralized and adaptable structure gives it ready access to tacit and local knowledge, driving gains in efficiency. Even if federal lawmakers wanted to, they could not tap that inchoate, fluctuating, and widely distributed information.

The common law offers equity advantages over copyright, too. Insofar as copyright law represents a balanced bargain between the various private and public interests it affects—a popular fiction, as shown in chapter 6—it epitomizes the type of take-it-or-leave-it offer that foes of adhesion contracts so dislike. Indeed, the same legal scholar who coined the phrase "adhesion contracts," Professor Friedrich Kessler, criticizes them on the grounds that they *too greatly* resemble legislation.[4] Neither authors nor their audiences have much real say in how lawmakers distribute rights to expressive works.[5] If you don't care for click-wrap licenses limiting access to fixed expressive works, you should especially disdain the one-sided and nonnegotiable terms of federal legislation.

When and if copyright holders and consumers of copyrighted works flee from the federal statute to the common law, we can pretty safely assume they have found it mutually beneficial to do so. Granted, sometimes licensing practices and terms go too far. Contract law already has in place ample safeguards against such abuses, however. And, granted, consumers might sometimes find technical locks and chains bothersome. But if we don't like the way a merchant packages his wares, we remain free to shop elsewhere, offer a lower price, or ask for something different. Such common-law arrangements thus deserve a presumption of enforceability.

2. ABANDONING COPYRIGHT

In chapter 7, we saw how copyright and the common law can combine to threaten the general welfare by overregulating expressive works, as when a copyright holder wields statutory privileges to force licensees to forfeit their fair use rights, and why lawmakers should respond by fixing copyright, not by limiting the common law. In chapter 8 we discussed how copyright's misuse doctrine implicitly follows that policy, and how codifying the doctrine might clarify and improve it. Copyright abandonment offers a similar but more lasting exit from copyright to the common law. Whereas misuse opens a thoroughfare between copyright and the common law, in other words, abandonment offers only a one-way street.

Courts[6] and commentators[7] agree that a copyright holder can abandon the Copyright Act's privileges.[8] Because such an abandonment of copyright happens only rarely—and sees defining litigation even less frequently—some interesting questions remain unresolved. Can a copyright holder abandon only some of the act's privileges and, to divide things still more finely, abandon them for only a certain period of time?[9] Do the Copyright Act's termination provisions, which effectively allow authors to renege on their promises in certain instances,[10] limit the effectiveness of an abandonment?[11] Such questions take us deep into the details of the Copyright Act. Happily, though, how they are answered affects only the means by which copyright holders voluntarily abandon their copyrights and cast their works into the public domain—not whether they can abandon them at all.[12] Abandonment remains an option regardless.

Would courts respect common-law restrictions on abandoned works? Whoever asserts such restrictions would have to frame the causes of action so as to avoid preemption under section 301 of the Copyright Act, the statutory provision through which federal lawmakers have defined the effective limit of claims brought under state law. States plainly cannot pass their own copyright acts; the Constitution gives the federal government supremacy in that area. State common-law claims over formerly copyrighted works do not, however, face a similarly dire threat of federal preemption under section 301.[13] Nor does the doctrine of copyright misuse appear likely to inhibit such claims, given that the doctrine aims to limit the power of statutory and common-law rights acting in concert. Indeed, as discussed in chapter 8, courts have invoked the copyright misuse defense to strike down statutory rights even as they let coincident common-law ones remain standing. To make a long story short: abandoned works would probably remain fully susceptible to common law–based restrictions, such as usage licenses or technological access controls.

Section 301 of the Copyright Act reflects a larger principle, one premised in the US Constitution's supremacy clause. "This Constitution, and the Laws of the United States which shall be made in Pursuance thereof . . . shall be the supreme Law of the Land," it provides.[14] In theory, the supremacy clause gives a basis for preempting state law restrictions on expressive works independent from, and more powerful than, that given in section 301. Even if state common-law claims over expressive works escape section 301 preemption, therefore, we should also question whether those kinds of claims would escape the kind of preemption implied by the supremacy clause. In practice, however, courts would probably never get to the question. Content to rely on section 301,[15] courts resist invoking implied conflicts preemption under the supremacy clause to determine the scope of preemption of common-law claims to fixed works of authorship.[16]

Suppose, though, that a court tested supremacy clause preemption against a common-law claim to an expressive work. What should the court rule? Rather than finding such claims preempted, it should return to fundamental constitutional principles, recognize that copyright represents an extraordinary exception to the common law's default rules, and favor the latter over the former. Given the uncertainties surrounding abandonment, a relatively untested legal tool, courts might benefit from a reminder along those lines. The next section offers legislation to do just that.

3. SAFEGUARDING COMMON-LAW RIGHTS

To deregulate expressive works, we must let them escape from under the Copyright Act into the common law's domain. Though the doctrine of copyright misuse is a promising way to promote that policy, it suspends the act's privileges only temporarily. Copyright abandonment, in contrast, works permanently, ensuring that a work placed into the public domain will remain there. There is even less case law to illustrate the effect of abandonment than of misuse, however. It is not yet clear whether and to what extent common-law rights survive copyright abandonment. This section thus proposes adding to section 301 of the Copyright Act[17] a provision called section 301(g), ensuring that common-law rights will always remain an option for protecting works of authorship:

> Nothing in this title annuls or limits any common-law
> restriction on the use of a fixed work of authorship if
> that work has been dedicated to the public domain.

Proposed section 301(g) guarantees the right to exit from copyright to the common law by assuring that anyone who abandons the former can take refuge in the latter. Notably, it merely *offers* that escape route; section 301(g) does not *force* copyright holders to give up their statutory privileges. Nor does anything else in the Copyright Act or the Constitution appear likely to do so. As will be described more fully below, however, the prospect of having to pay opposing parties' attorneys' fees might convince some copyright holders to abandon their statutory rights and rely on the common-law rights protected by section 301(g).

Does proposed section 301(g) have any chance of becoming law? Federal lawmakers have already made explicit their willingness, in the context of the first sale doctrine, to force copyright holders to decide between contract law and copyright law.[18] Section 301(g) would merely make that sort of choice more generally available.

Do lawmakers have authority to pass section 301(g) into law? The Constitution hardly mandates that they maximize copyright power; to the contrary, it limits them to necessary and proper means of promoting the general welfare and the progress of science and useful arts. Nor would the recent Supreme Court decision in *Dastar Corp. v. Twentieth Century Fox Film Corp.*[19] bar section 301(g). The court there expressly limited the scope of only federal statutory unfair competition law with regard to works in the public domain.[20] The court did not speak to the proper scope of common-law protections of such works.

Why would anyone want section 301(g) to become law? The copyright lobby would probably welcome it for offering a legal option not yet clearly understood. Consumers of copyrighted works would lose nothing by the clarification; rather, they would benefit from the discovery of better alternatives to copyright. Some politicians might disfavor the proposed provision as too likely to decrease their rent-seeking opportunities by removing some expressive works from the scope of the Copyright Act. That crass rationale should hardly sway the rest of us, though. Policymakers should interfere with private arrangements only on proof of imminent peril to the public interest, and provide the freedom to exit from the special regulatory privileges of copyright into the good, old, regular common law.

4. COPYRIGHT ABANDONMENT FOR FUN AND PROFIT

Why would copyright holders choose to abandon their statutory rights and rely solely on their common-law ones? A few authors, who create for the fun of it, might do so for nonmonetary reasons (see chapter 10 for further discussion). Thanks to the combined effect of copyright misuse and section 505 of the Copyright Act, however, even copyright holders focused on maximizing their profits might find abandonment attractive.

Under section 505, courts may in their discretion award attorney's fees to the prevailing party in copyright litigation. The Supreme Court has interpreted that provision to benefit copyright plaintiffs and defendants alike.[21] The court suggested that, among other factors, courts should base an award of attorney's fees under section 505 on "frivolousness, motivation, objective unreasonableness (both in the factual and in the legal components of the case) and the need in particular circumstances to advance considerations of compensation and deterrence."[22] Those factors could easily describe a typical case of copyright misuse. Not surprisingly, then, courts have found that defendants who suffered copyright misuse[23]—or even something less than misuse[24]—deserve an award of attorney's fees under section 505.[25]

The common law, like US law generally, takes a very different approach to attorney's fees. Under the so-called "American Rule," each party in civil litigation—even the winner—must pay for its own legal representation.[26] Section 505 of the Copyright Act represents a rare and notable exception to that rule.

Here, then, the common law treats authors better than copyright law does. The Copyright Act offers many benefits to copyright holders, of course, such as strict liability and statutory damages. Overzealous copyright holders might find that the doctrine of misuse denies those benefits, however, and that section 505 imposes the costs of paying for an opposing party's attorney. For some copyright holders, those combined effects might suffice to render abandonment a financially attractive option. That would hold especially true if copyright holders could count on their common-law rights to survive abandonment and if entrepreneurs continue to develop private alternatives to statutory restrictions on the use of expressive works.

5. CONCLUSION

To the extent that copyright holders and consumers of copyrighted works opt to manage expressive works solely by contract and other common-law devices, they will deregulate expressive works. Their various private arrangements will then supplant the allocation of rights that the Copyright Act defines as mere defaults. We should encourage that sort of experimentation, as it offers both a more efficient and more equitable option than the Copyright Act's centrally planned statutory privileges. Proposed section 301(g) would help that effort by clarifying what case law and sound theory already suggest: those who abandon their copyright rights preserve their common-law ones. Thus reassured, and eager to escape liability for paying opposing parties' attorneys' fees, copyright holders might find abandonment an attractive option.

PART III
BEYOND
COPYRIGHT

What would a world without copyright look like? The next two chapters describe a possible near future in which copyright is not so much abolished as ignored—rendered obsolete by surging technologies, refined business models, and a burgeoning humanity. Chapter 10 explains how the ardency of mere amateurs will increasingly suffice to stimulate the production and dissemination of original expressive works. Technology has made it easy for a garage band to perform for the world. Chapter 11 revisits the standard model of copyright and tests the effects of market growth, showing why efficiency demands that copyright restrictions shrink as market size increases. Together, these chapters suggest that we can look forward to a world that has outgrown the need for copyright and entered the fullest flower of its originality and expressiveness.

CHAPTER 10
UNCOPYRIGHT AND OPEN COPYRIGHT

For better or (more likely) for worse, copyright now automatically encumbers every new fixed work of authorship.[1] Copyright kicks in as soon as anyone writes an essay, doodles a sketch, or bangs out an email. The copyright's holder need not register the work[2] or put notices on copies of it[3] to win statutory privileges to restrict unauthorized uses.[4]

If you want to play it safe, you should thus assume that some sort of copyright claim binds every fixed work.[5] Even very old works often come with modern copyright strings attached. Consider, for instance, John Stuart Mill's classic work *On Liberty*. Though the book was originally issued in 1859 and has long since fallen into the public domain, my library's copy includes a notice reading, "Copyright 1978 by Hackett Publishing Company, Inc." Presumably, that copyright covers only the editor's introduction and selected bibliography. Yet Hackett's overbroad notice may discourage some people—especially those who know little about copyright law—from reproducing even the public domain parts of *On Liberty*.[6]

In that and other ways, copyright policy currently fails to admit to its limitations. Cautiously presuming that copyright covers every fixed work, and duped by inflated copyright notices, we fail to fully enjoy our rights to the public domain. We should aspire to a more open copyright system, one that encourages both the creation of new works and the liberation of existing ones. For that, we need a way to signal, clearly and reliably, when a work has escaped the bounds of copyright. We need an *uncopyright* notice.

1. THE UNCOPYRIGHT NOTICE

The Copyright Act provides that copyright holders can brand their works with "Copyright," or "Copr.," in lieu of the copyright symbol, ©.[7] An *uncopyright* notice would naturally read "Uncopyright" or "Uncopr." The uncopyright symbol? A Ø, per the international iconography of things forbidden. In cases where such graphics prove too troublesome, the cents character in parentheses—(¢)—would do nicely. (That some uncopyrighted works might come with common-law or technological protections that require payment before accessing the works makes the use of a monetary symbol all the more—critics would no doubt say "all too"—appropriate.) Table 1 illustrates the parallels.

Table 1. Copyright and Uncopyright Notices

Copyright	Uncopyright
Copr.	Uncopr.
©	Ø
(c)	(¢)

Where will uncopyrighted works come from? Some will come from clearly unprotected parts of the public domain. The worthy Project Gutenberg, for instance, offers favorite old texts on the web, unencumbered with copyright restrictions, in an easily accessible format.[8] New works, too, might carry Ø marks, put there by authors eager to help build the public domain.[9]

2. "BLOCKHEADED" AUTHORS?

Granted, not every author will want to forgo copyright's privileges. Perhaps only very few will. Every little bit helps, though, and over time even a trickle of uncopyrighted works might fill an ocean of information. But why would anybody author a work for the public domain? In short, because the willingness to subsidize the production and distribution of such works outweighs the costs.

Samuel Johnson claimed, "No man but a blockhead ever wrote, except for money."[10] He would doubtless have said the same about the other media—music, painting, motion pictures, computer software, and so forth—that copyright now covers. Regardless of how they express themselves, savvy authors demand remuneration for their creative labors. Copyright helps to ensure that they get it.

And yet "blockheaded" authors exist.[11] Some percentage of authors will, at least at some times, share their expressive works for very little or no pay. We can even imagine an author, eager for attention or burning with artistic passion, willing to pay others to experience his or her masterpieces. We might not always understand what motivates such authors (though we should call them "blockheads" only with affection; they are seldom fools). We need only observe that, as Johnson himself evidently recognized, nonmonetary incentives sometimes suffice to inspire authorship.

Blockheaded authors, like any authors, face fixed and marginal costs. Blockheaded authors do not rely on copyright law to recoup those expenses, however. Instead, they subsidize the costs of creating and distributing their works, paying for them out of pocket and then, typically, releasing them to the public. Blockheaded authors effectively pay to satisfy their own demand for their own works—in other words, they solipsistically supply a market comprising a single consumer. Rather than tracking the average revenue generated by blockheaded authors' works, therefore, we should track the average subsidy for blockheadedness. Figure 13 does so with the curve marked "AS," for "aggregate subsidy," showing how that subsidy might relate to a blockheaded author's production and distribution costs.

As in the picture of copyism's specter offered in chapter 2, figure 13 portrays a sort of tragedy. It shows what happens when the costs of creating and distributing a fixed work exceed the subsidy that its blockheaded author would have paid: the work goes unproduced. Thus, for instance, many a wannabe rock star has lacked sufficient funds to cut a single. The tragedy portrayed in figure 13 goes beyond mere artistic frustration, however. Assuming that a blockheaded author's creations would have found some willing audience, no matter how small, that author's silence represents a lost opportunity to increase human happiness.

More and more often, nonmonetary incentives suffice to stimulate authorship. Thanks to the same technological magic blamed for summoning the specter of copyism, authors find it increasingly cheap—in terms of money, time, and effort—to produce and distribute expressive works.

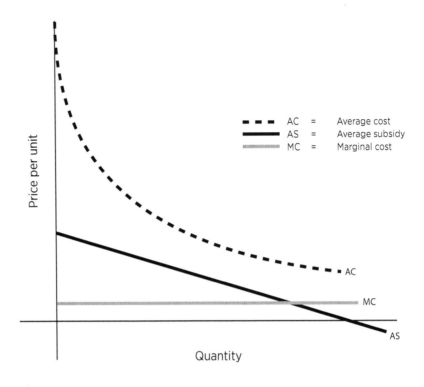

AC	=	Average cost
AS	=	Average subsidy
MC	=	Marginal cost

Figure 13. When Average Costs Exceed Average Subsidies, Discouraging Blockheaded Authorship

Whereas it once took many thousands of dollars to record and nationally distribute a new song, for instance, it now takes only a computer, an Internet connection, and some basic music production software—all easily available for under $2,000.[12] These days, almost anybody with a dream and a guitar can get a clean shot at the world's ear. Figure 14 illustrates that effect, charting how technological progress has lowered the average and marginal costs of supplying the market with original expressive works.

Figure 14 also illustrates how reductions in the cost of producing and distributing original expressive works encourage blockheaded authors to create. A blockheaded author with an average subsidy curve (AS) that passes above the author's average cost curve (AC) will find it worthwhile to pay the subsidy price (P_b) to produce a particular quantity

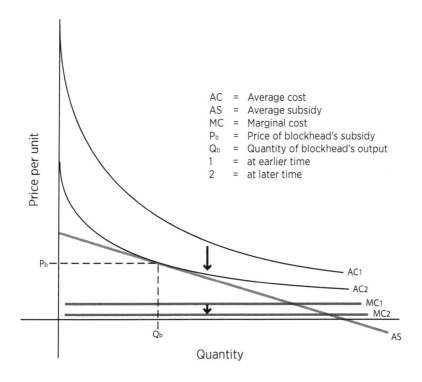

Figure 14. Effect of Technological Advances on the Supply of Blockheads' Original Expressive Works

of the work (Q_b). Overall welfare increases because the blockheaded author relishes self-expression and nonauthors gain access to an original expressive work. Figure 14 does not include a demand curve illustrating how much those nonauthors would pay—be it in currency, time, or effort—to access the blockhead's work. You could draw that sort of curve almost anywhere on the graph, however. So long as it *somewhere* exceeds their very low marginal costs of accessing the work, consumers will enjoy a surplus.

So understood, and holding all else equal, the willingness of blockheaded authors to subsidize the production and distribution of expressive works will tend to render copyright's legal restrictions inefficiently overprotective. In a relatively primitive society, such as that of the United

States in the late 1700s, policymakers might find that nonmonetary incentives do not stimulate an adequate supply of expressive works. Copyright, by helping to ensure that authors get paid for their expressions, can help to remedy that market failure. So, at least, the Founders evidently thought.[13] As technology advances, however, and the cost of supplying original expressive works drops, the number of authors for whom the lucre of copyright proves a necessary stimulus also drops.[14] Thanks to decreases in the cost of creating original expressive works, authorship need not entail crushing debts. Thanks to the very low marginal costs of reproducing and distributing such works, moreover, a relatively few blockheaded authors can entertain a very large market.

Those technological and economic trends tend, over time, to cure the same market failure targeted by copyright policy. They ensure that nonmonetary incentives will suffice to stimulate an increasing amount of authorship, and that blockheaded authors will thus supply more and more of the market's demand for expressive works. At some limit, for some works, copyright law will prove superfluous, and its burdens will exceed its benefits. Volunteer programmers might, for instance, supply computer operating system software free of charge.[15] As a general principle, then, as methods for producing and distributing expressive works grow increasingly efficient, they tend to tip copyright policy into inefficiency, making it more restrictive than necessary or proper for promoting the general welfare.

3. COMPOSING FOR LOVE, NOT MONEY

Want an example of how a copyright blockhead reasons? I'll provide one of a romantic nature. Though it is the most widely sung song in the world, "Happy Birthday to You" comes freighted with copyright's limitations.[16] The law does not bar anyone from singing the song in private, of course, nor for an audience consisting only of family and friends.[17] But copyright law does evidently discourage public celebrations, casting the pall of liability on unauthorized sing-alongs.[18]

Regarding "Happy Birthday to You" as a tired old bully of a song, I composed an alternative for my love: "We Celebrate Your Birthday." After I sang it for her, accompanied by our kids, I cast the song into the public

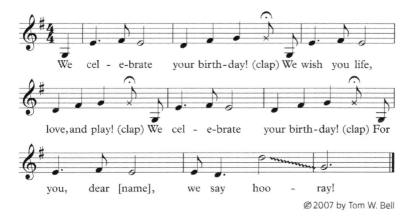

Figure 15. We Celebrate Your Birthday

Note: See http://www.tomwbell.com/music/Celebrate_Your_Birthday.aif for a sound recording of me and my kids performing "We Celebrate Your Birthday."

domain, hoping that others might sing it for their own beloveds. I here offer it for your own birthday party—see figure 15.

Though I will not defend "We Celebrate Your Birthday" as great art, I did think it through fairly carefully. The old standard, "Happy Birthday to You," boasts several catchy features, after all: a bouncy, easy melody; simple and appropriate lyrics; and room for any name. I leave it to you to judge how well my effort met those same criteria. Please feel at complete liberty to sing "We Celebrate Your Birthday" for family, friends, or even complete strangers. *My* birthday girl would *love* that.

4. FREE WILLIE?

As mentioned in chapter 6, scholars have made surprisingly strong arguments that *Steamboat Willie*, a cartoon the Walt Disney Company cites as establishing its copyright rights in Mickey Mouse, has fallen into the public domain. As a thought experiment, let us assume the truth of these scholars' claim. What would happen if nobody held a copyright in *Steamboat Willie*? Certainly, each of us would by default enjoy complete freedom to copy, distribute, display, or perform the cartoon, because the expiration of the work's copyright would also end the exclusive rights of the Walt Disney Company and its assigns to exercise those statutory privileges. So, too, would we escape copyright's limitations on making derivative versions of *Steamboat Willie*—versions that might show Mickey standing at a lectern rather than at a pilot's wheel, for instance, or have him expounding copyright law.

The Walt Disney Company would retain its copyrights in later, plumper versions of Mickey Mouse, of course. Contemporary artists wanting to reinterpret the character while avoiding the company's veto would have to draw inspiration primarily from the earlier, skinnier version. Given that the characters would share a common ancestor, however, even mice derived solely from *Steamboat Willie* might strongly resemble the modern-day Mickey Mouse.

Would the Walt Disney Company object to these unauthorized reuses of *Steamboat Willie*? It might, indeed. Some such uses might substitute for sales of the company's wares, after all, or cast its most prominent spokesmouse in an unsavory light. But copyright law would, per the assumption behind our thought experiment, offer the company no solace. The Walt Disney Company could not plausibly claim that patent or trade-secret law gives it the power to limit free use of *Steamboat Willie*, either. Nor could it invoke the right of publicity, which—though sometimes shockingly effective in limiting speech about celebrities[19]—has thus far not stretched to cover cartoon characters.

Trademark and unfair competition law would probably offer the Walt Disney Company its most potent weapon against any movement to emancipate *Steamboat Willie*. Generally speaking, that area of law allows the holder of a name, symbol, or other mark to prevent latecomers from using in commerce marks likely to confuse consumers about the source or affiliation of a particular good or service. Thus, for instance, Nike can bar anyone else from putting its famous "swoosh" on non-Nike clothes. The Walt Disney Company uses Mickey Mouse as a mark designating its goods and services. If a consumer did not know (*ex hypothesis*) that the image and voice of Mickey Mouse, qua the character Willie, had fallen into the public domain, and that consumer saw a cartoon of a substantially similar Mickey Mouse in a new context, the consumer might naturally, yet wrongly, assume that the newer Mickey

Mouse had issued from the same source as so many other cartoons featuring the character. According to that argument, consumer ignorance would give the company cause to censor derivative versions of the copyright-free Mickey Mouse.

Perhaps the addition of a disclaimer, such as the notice "Not a Walt Disney Company production!" in a cartoon's margin, would suffice to dispel consumer confusion. That would forestall only a "passing off" claim, however—one where a mark's holder accuses another party of selling bogus wares under that mark. The same disclaimer would set the defendant up for a "*reverse* passing off" claim—one where Disney would charge that the cartoonist wrongly sold Disney's product (intellectual creations about Mickey Mouse) under another's name. Disney could thereby damn those who use *Steamboat Willie* both if they *do* use disclaimers and if they do *not*. Happily for anyone who wants to free Willie, however, the Supreme Court has cut through that Gordian knot of liability.

The Supreme Court held in *Dastar Corp. v. Twentieth Century Fox Film Corp.* that, once a work has fallen into the public domain, its former copyright holder cannot use federal unfair competition law to demand credit from those who reuse the work.[20] Still more broadly, the court flatly excluded copyrighted works from the scope of section 43(a)(1)(A) of the Lanham Act, the federal law barring passing off, whether direct or reverse.[21] The court explained the policy reasons for limiting unfair competition law thus:

> Assuming for the sake of argument that [defendant] Dastar's representation of itself as the "Producer" of its videos amounted to a representation that it originated the creative work conveyed by the videos, allowing a cause of action under § 43(a) for that representation would create a species of mutant copyright law that limits the public's "federal right to 'copy and to use'" expired copyrights.[22]

Given that it voiced broad concerns, lower courts have read *Dastar* to have broad effect. They have extended it to bar state law claims of unfair competition, a result the US Constitution's supremacy clause, which establishes the preeminence of federal over state law, would apparently mandate.[23] Lower courts have also extended *Dastar* to bar unfair competition claims arising out of the use of uncopyrighted and uncopyrightable works.[24] Plainly, the case has done a great deal to ensure that copyright's privileges go no further than copyright itself.

The exact scope of *Dastar*'s preemptive effect remains as yet uncertain. Even if it suffered the uncopyrighting of *Steamboat Willie*, for instance, the Walt Disney Company might still bring suit under section 43(a)(1)(B) of the Lanham Act against anyone using liberated versions of Mickey Mouse to deceptively market non-Disney wares, such as by falsely advertising a new *Spaceship Willie* as a Disney original.[25] *Dastar* left open the question of whether courts should remedy such claims.[26] Lower courts have, however, read *Dastar* to bar section 43(a)(1)(B) claims alleging no more than false marketing about whether permission was granted for use of an uncopyrighted work.[27] Under that reasoning, the Walt Disney Company probably could not even stop the hypothetical authors of *Spaceship Willie* from selling it as "Mickey Mouse in the finest tradition of Walt Disney," or, conversely, "A wholly original take on Mickey Mouse." In that event, Mickey Mouse would escape its corporate master, win the freedom of the public domain, and join the likes of Santa Claus and Uncle Sam in the pantheon of towering cultural icons.

5. TOWARD AN OPEN COPYRIGHT SYSTEM

US copyright law too much resembles a roach motel: expressive works check in, but they don't check out. Even that gives present policies too much credit, however. Expressive works don't come looking for the Copyright Act's shelter; they get it by default. Most authors freely choose to enjoy copyright's privileges. Many probably wish it offered even better security against unauthorized copying. But even a haven can become a trap if it offers no freedom to exit. Recognizing uncopyright as an alternative to copyright, Ø as a counterpart to ©, would help make copyright policy more balanced, fair, and open.

Uncopyrighted does not necessarily mean unprotected. The common law or technological protections might limit the use of certain uncopyrighted works, as when trade-secret law safeguards a customer list or when watermarks hinder reuse of an image. Even in such cases, however, users would benefit from knowing that copyright does not lurk in the background.[28] More importantly, creative individuals who come across works unprotected by copyright, the common law, or technological tools—works found in the commons—would want very much to know that the works are free of copyright restrictions. The rest of us would want them to know it, too, so that they might fearlessly pick up the works and put them to good use. Attaching an uncopyright notice to such works would encourage others to recycle them.

The United States can best promote the progress of science and useful arts by developing new and better alternatives to copyright. By opening a clearly marked exit into the public domain, an open copyright system would stimulate the development of common-law and technological tools for protecting expressive works. Those devices, insofar as they reward the creation, reproduction, and distribution of fixed expressive works, would help to ease the statutory failure that now afflicts copyright policy. Ultimately, we may even find that nonstatutory protections for expressive works suffice to render copyright superfluous. In that event, *un*copyright might open the way to *no* copyright.

CHAPTER 11
OUTGROWING COPYRIGHT

D oes copyright offer the best means of stimulating the production of expressive works? Perhaps it does, at the moment. If so,
however, in the future copyright will probably restrict access to
expressive works too tightly. As the market for copyrighted works grows,
copyright holders will find it increasingly easy to engage in price discrimination, allowing them to find the customers most willing to pay a premium
for the particular expressions they most want. The profits afforded by copyrights, and the inducements to authorship, will thereby grow. This chapter
explains that effect and discusses how copyright policy should respond.[1]

To begin, let's take a moment to review the economic justification of
copyright. It costs a great deal to produce the first copy of many expressive works, including such notably valuable ones as movies, books, and
software. Copyright law helps to reassure would-be authors that they
will recover these fixed, up-front costs.[2] Alternative mechanisms—such
as tips, patronage, automated rights management, and contracts—risk
providing too little protection against unauthorized copying, leading to
market failure.

As the market in expressive works grows, however, it threatens to make
copyright law too powerful. As people join that market, whether by enter-
ing the world or by escaping isolation, they offer authors new sources
of revenue. Given the low marginal costs of reproducing and distributing expressive works, these larger audiences will tend to reward authors
with larger profits. At some point, those profits will give authors stronger
incentives than they really need.

Population increases also introduce new authors to the market,
granted, eager to compete with the extant ones.[3] So long as these new-
comers copy only the genre or general style of incumbent authors, no one

can justly complain. Copyright law forbids would-be competitors from offering the public substantially similar versions of copyright-restricted works, however.[4] In effect, copyright holders enjoy a competition-free zone around their works, allowing them and them alone to satisfy consumer demand for their particular expressions.

In sum, as copyright holders win access to larger audiences, they find it increasingly profitable to price discriminate by focusing on the consumers most willing to pay for a particular work of authorship. Yet the per-unit costs of creating and distributing expressive works will probably hold steady (or even, thanks to technological innovation and economies of scale, decline). Given a big enough market, almost any artist can find enough ardent fans to pay the bills. True, that larger market will include more competing authors, but copyright limits the degree to which new authors can compete with old ones.

As markets grow, therefore, copyright threatens to become too strong a medicine for the ills it was prescribed to treat. When copyright reaches that point, its social costs will outweigh its benefits. We can get there sooner or later, but the destination remains the same. Wise public policy should take that effect into account by making copyright smaller as markets grow larger.

1. AN ECONOMIC ANALYSIS OF THE EFFECT OF MARKET GROWTH ON COPYRIGHT

Markets can grow for many reasons—population increases, relaxed trade barriers, rising demand—but it all boils down to more transactions. Holding all else equal, that results in more demand for authors' services. Not all else is equal, though; with those new consumers come new authors who compete with the old ones. What overall effect does the resulting increase in both the supply and the demand of expressive works have on copyright policy?[5]

As the market for copyright grows, the profits from copyright rise. So do the burdens that copyright imposes on the public, however, because copyright holders gain at the expense of restricting others' common-law rights. Market growth thus causes copyright's costs to the public to eventually exceed its benefits. The following pages explain. Subsection 1 documents the assumptions behind this account of the relationship between market growth and copyright policy. Subsection 2 runs those assumptions through the standard economic model of copyright.

The Model's Assumptions

For the sake of simplicity, and because it seems plausible, let's assume that the ratio of authors to consumers holds roughly constant despite fluctuations in the size of the market for expressive works. If only 0.1 percent of adults compose music, for instance, we might assume that any given group of 1,000 babies will include one future composer and 1,000 potential consumers (since composers listen to music, too). Likewise, any market newly opened to trade in expressive works will expose domestic composers to one new competitor for each 1,000 potential consumers.

For present purposes, we need not specify the exact ratio of authors to consumers—a number that would prove slippery, at best. We can also concede that the real world may sometimes offer variations on the theme explored here. Winning access to Chinese markets, for instance, has thus far given Hollywood a huge new audience but few new rivals.[6] Nonetheless, it does not seem wildly implausible to assume that, in the long run and in the main, the ratio of authors to consumers holds roughly steady despite variations in the size of the market for expressive works.

It takes time for markets to grow. With the passage of time consumers win access to an increasingly large stock of old expressive works. Every new author thus has to compete not only against contemporaries, but also against authors who have already left their mark on the world. That increase in the number of competing works might to some degree decrease the rewards of new authorship, true, but copyright does not aim simply at making authorship profitable. Instead, it aims to ensure that consumers have ample access to expressive works, and it treats rewarding authors as merely a means to that end.[7] Growth in the stock of *old* expressive works, because it stands to lower the price of *all* expressive works, arguably helps to ensure that copyright policy can achieve that ultimate goal more easily.[8] The present model does not invoke that as yet another reason market growth tends to render copyrights overly restrictive, however, instead opting for a simpler analysis.

This analysis assumes that the costs experienced by authors and copyright holders do not change significantly as the market for expressive works grows. Some evidence suggests that, in fact, technological advances have made it increasingly easy for authors to create marketable works.[9] Other evidence suggests that technological advances have made it more expensive to enforce copyrights.[10] Those countervailing effects undoubtedly balance each other out to some degree, but at any rate they do not play a role in this model.

Consumers typically purchase only one copy of an expressive work. Exceptions exist, of course, but because the owner of a copy of an expressive work can consume it many times over, one copy generally satisfies any given consumer's demand.[11] An economist might thus describe copies of expressive works as goods nonrivalrous in consumption over time and intra-consumer. Within a household, in other words, copies of expressive works function like club goods if one member of the household excludes others from consuming the work,[12] or like public goods if not.[13] Each consumer of such a good will pay up to his or her reservation price (i.e., the highest amount he or she is willing to pay) for one copy and, finding that copy a sufficient supply of the work, generally will pay nothing for additional copies.[14] So, at least, this model assumes.

Modeling the Effect of Growth in the Copyright Market

As the market for expressive works grows, assuming that the proportion of authors to consumers does not change, copyright holders tend to earn larger profits. Why? Recall our assumptions that would-be authors represent a constant percentage of any given population and that population growth does not materially affect the cost of producing and distributing expressive works. Although new authors enter the growing market, the average number of consumers per author remains unchanged. The larger population gives each author—or, more generally, each party to whom authors transfer their copyrights—more consumers to choose from. The consistently low marginal cost of distributing expressive works makes it increasingly easy, moreover, for copyright holders to find those consumers who most want the particular works that each holder puts on the market. Copyright holders can focus on their best customers, providing great satisfaction while earning commensurate revenues.

In other words, population growth and consistently low costs of distributing works combine to make it easier for copyright holders to find the fans who will pay the most for any given work—to "price discriminate," in the jargon of economists. This allows copyright holders to earn higher revenues. Since marginal costs remain low and flat, that extra revenue equals extra profit, some of which finds its way into authors' pockets.[15] Authors make more money in that scenario. If copyright's incentives are not updated accordingly, they will eventually prove more restrictive than necessary to stimulate the optimal level of authorship. As markets grow, therefore, the need for copyright decreases.

Around the time that lawmakers passed the 1790 Copyright Act, for instance, authors in the United States had to cope with a comparatively tiny market for expressive works. An author who specialized in, say, novels about sailors would have found few readers burning to read these works and would have earned correspondingly paltry revenues. Today, in contrast, the United States has so large a market in copyrighted works that even authors who focus on very narrow themes can find thousands upon thousands of fans. And while a correspondingly large number of competing authors has also arisen since 1790, not all of them will be able to give exacting customers exactly what they want. At some point, for some fans, only one author's work will do, and competitors will find that they cannot fulfill the same demand without infringing on the original. In today's large markets, therefore, even authors specializing in very narrow topics can thrive.

Markets in copyrighted works can expand until they fill the universe. Once competition from other works has compressed them down to their hard core, in contrast, copyright's exclusive privileges admit no further competition. Together, these two effects ensure that as markets for copyrighted works grow, holding all else constant, the revenues generated per copyrighted work will grow too. Production costs per work don't look likely to rise, so profits per work probably will. Once copyright's privileges have exceeded their optimum level, as the profits they afford continue to grow along with markets, the Copyright Act will exceed its theoretically ideal level of restriction and tip into statutory failure.

2. WILL NEW ENTRANTS REDUCE MONOPOLY PROFITS?

As discussed earlier in this chapter, the analysis here assumes that the ratio of authors to consumers holds roughly constant as the size of the market for expressive works grows. The standard economic model of copyright does not seem to demand anything different; it does not evidently consider the possibility that the monopoly profits afforded by copyright will attract new authors who, eager to share those spoils, will dissipate them. Hence the criticism of the standard model offered by the University of Pennsylvania Law School's professor Christopher S. Yoo: it shows only a short-run equilibrium, whereas in the long run the prospect of monopoly gains would invite new authors to enter the market and "divide the available surplus into increasingly smaller fragments until no profits remain."[16]

I grant that Professor Yoo's criticism holds true for many applications of the standard model. In many markets, at least, any given copyrighted work faces considerable competitive pressure from substitute works. In the sort of very large market modeled above, however, I doubt that Yoo's analysis applies with much force. Why? Because copyright holders in such a market will tend to sell their works to a few high-demand fans, since a very large market can provide enough such fans to make great specialization remunerative. And, crucially, dividing the market into such narrow, specialized slices can protect a copyright holder from competition. At some limit, copyright law's ban on substantially similar copies will kick in, creating a very real barrier to competition.[17] Thus, for instance, might the author of folksy tunes about mountain flowers find enough fans, in a universe of billions upon billions of consumers, to make composition profitable—secure in the thought that would-be competitors would have to infringe her copyrights to win over her fans. The structure of competition in very large markets for expressive works thus appears to fall outside the range of Yoo's critique.[18]

3. DO THE FACTS FIT THE THEORY?

Markets in expressive works have grown extensive in recent decades, thanks both to population growth and lowering trade barriers. Have the economics of copyright changed as the above analysis would have predicted? Hard evidence on that count, pro or con, proves elusive. Analysts have observed, however, that as the market for expressive works has grown, it has grown increasingly fractured. Whereas US consumers once shared only three television channels and a few general-interest magazines and newspapers, for instance, they can now choose from hundreds of specialized cable channels and thousands of periodicals tailored to very narrow interests.[19] Notably, very specialized channels and periodicals often cost very much. Analysts have also noted that the Internet has, by making expressive works cheap and easy to access for more and more consumers, made even works located far out on the "long tail"[20] of popularity potential money-makers. Those developments conform to what the model offered here would have predicted.

Nonetheless, it appears that many authors have begun pursuing nearly the opposite strategy. Rather than enforcing their copyrights vociferously and targeting only their biggest fans, such authors instead rely on the combination of cheap distribution (typically via the Internet) and relatively low revenues per copy (often on a voluntary basis) to recoup their creative costs.[21] Does that contradict what the model of the economics of copyright in very large markets would predict? Not necessarily. Authors in a very large market for expressive works might find it worthwhile to forgo monopoly returns, instead marketing their works widely and cheaply. That strategy might at least allow them to recoup their fixed costs. With luck, it might even allow a small profit.

The fact that some authors in a very large market decline to focus on a few high-paying fans thus does not contradict the model offered here. To the contrary, it supports the model's policy conclusions. To the extent that a very large market in expressive works can stimulate authorship *even among those who do not rely on their copyrights*, it indicates that copyright policy may have begun slipping into obsolescence.

4. RAMIFICATIONS FOR COPYRIGHT POLICY

This chapter's analysis indicates that as markets for expressive works grow, copyright holders' monopoly profits increase relative both to the consumer surplus generated by copyright and to the opportunity costs—the cheaper forgone opportunities—of those whom copyright restricts. How should copyright policy respond? Given the near-universal view (discussed in chapter 2) that copyright policy aims to strike a balance between giving authors sufficient incentives to create expressive works and providing the public with adequate access to the works thereby created, this analysis suggests that copyright policy should respond to growth in the market for expressive works by one of the following tactics:

- weakening the privileges afforded to copyright holders,
- augmenting public access to copyrighted works, or
- some combination of both remedies.

Notably, however, it might turn out that copyright policy has long provided authors with too few incentives to create expressive works or the public with too many opportunities to encroach on copyright holders' prerogatives. In that event, growth in the market for expressive works might finally put copyright policy back into proper trim. What the analysis offered here suggests about what policymakers *should* do to copyright, in other words, depends on what they *have* done to it.

It certainly seems safe to say that the United States presently suffers no gross poverty of authorship. Even among households that the US Census Bureau officially defines as "poor," 97 percent have color televisions, 78 percent have a VCR or DVD player, and 62 percent have cable or satellite TV reception.[22] These appliances presumably get put to good use, leaving even the worst-off Americans very wealthy in expressive works. But I leave to others the question of whether copyright policy did, does, or will walk the fine line between private and public interests.[23] For present purposes it suffices to say that those who call for strengthening copyrights should bear the burden of proof. Markets for expressive works have expanded in recent years, and look very likely to continue doing so. Should lawmakers respond by likewise expanding the copyright privilege? Only for indisputable reasons.

5. THE BENEFITS OF CONSUMER SPECIALIZATION

As Adam Smith observed more than 200 years ago, producers can increase their profits by specialization.[24] Smith famously illustrated this point by describing the manufacture of nails,[25] but the same principle holds true for those who produce expressive works.

Granted, the gains that Smith described arose from the lower production costs afforded by economies of scale.[26] Market growth, in contrast, blesses copyright holders not only with similar savings[27] but also, and more significantly for present purposes, with the benefits of serving idiosyncratic consumer demands. As regards this latter factor, we might say that Smith's observation about producers applies just as well to consumers: Growth in the market for expressive works allows some to maximize the gains of trade by specializing in what they *consume*.[28] Copyright law, because it allows a copyright holder to bar competition from substantially similar works, allows copyright holders to reap that consumer surplus.

Authors, and copyright holders after them, thus stand to *gain* the most by focusing on what their customers *want* the most. In relatively small markets, overspecialization might not allow authors to recoup their fixed costs. As markets for expressive works grow, however, and as the costs of creating and distributing expressive works hold steady, specialization begins to make more financial sense. In very large markets, economic theory suggests that copyright holders could reap monopoly profits by marketing to the consumers most willing to pay for the work of authorship marketed. Market growth makes that sort of price discrimination cheap, easy, and lucrative.

Authors and copyright holders might well celebrate that result. It is not so evident that the public should applaud it too. Unless lawmakers have grossly underestimated the power of the privilege needed to stimulate an adequate production of expressive works, market growth stands to knock copyright policy out of whack. In that event, the social costs of copyright would outweigh its benefits.

Perhaps a lightly populated, large, semiagricultural nation, hampered by slow and costly communication, required copyright law to encourage an adequate production of expressive works. It seems that those who wrote and ratified the US Constitution thought so.[29] But however well that justification for copyright once worked, it works decreasingly well as markets for copyrighted works grow. If, as seems likely, that growth continues, we will end up living in a world where copyright has become utterly superfluous—one where technology, common-law rights, and simple generosity stimulate authorship more efficiently than copyright does. Indeed, we may already live in that world.

THE PACKET-SWITCHED SOCIETY

A s courts and commentators traditionally describe copyright, it arises through the collective deliberation of central authorities who, after a delicate balancing of competing interests and in the name of the general welfare, create statutory rights to expressive works. According to that model, lawmakers let copyright holders borrow the state's power to violate natural and common-law rights, empowering copyright holders to control others' pens, presses, and voices. That approach strongly recalls the policy model applied to earthbound, closed, circuit-switched networks, in which a central authority controls all communications.

Those who build circuit-switched networks invoke the state's power of eminent domain to justify violating common-law rights, laying wires that cut across private property. Regulators supervise the monopoly that results, imposing common carrier obligations, cross-subsidizing universal service, and controlling rates. So, too, goes the circuit-switched model of copyright: the Copyright Act empowers copyright holders to violate the common law, granting them statutory privileges that cut across customary rights, while lawmakers carefully calibrate the ebb and flow of expressions to maximize the general welfare.

This book has taken a fundamentally different approach to public policy, an approach inspired by packet-switched networks like the market, person-to-person communications, and the Internet. In such a network, message-bearing packets flow from point to point over any of many different paths, routed not according to the dictates of a central authority but rather by generally accepted protocols. So long as a packet follows a few simple rules, it can take any route it likes. Packet switching has many virtues:

it often proves more flexible, robust, and scalable than circuit switching, for instance. It supports layer upon layer of complexity, too, encouraging a wealth of unplanned order. Most importantly for present purposes, packet-switched networks offer us an apt model for understanding that vast web of consent-rich relations we call the liberal society.[1]

Each of us in a free society pursues a variety of goals, some shared and some unique. We each follow a unique route through a shared network of voluntary connections. No central authority directs how we pursue our goals. Nor could it, given the complexity of the system and the distribution of information. Our packet-switched society instead relies on a few simple rules—based in natural rights and implemented through the common law—to define a protocol universally just and locally fair.[2] Our society spontaneously generates peace and prosperity, the fruit of conscious action but not of conscious design.[3]

As wire-bound parts of the Internet demonstrate, a packet-switched network sometimes runs on a circuit-switched infrastructure. Similarly, liberal societies typically rely on some measure of state intervention to help patch the gaps where private mechanisms fail. But in neither situation should we confuse an old fix for a necessary feature. Thanks to open-access[4] and packet-switched radio communications,[5] for instance, the Internet can—and probably should—escape from circuit-switched bottlenecks, which prove all too susceptible to disruption and censorship.[6]

The common law now stands ready to finally cure the market failure that alone can justify copyright's statutory privileges. When thus rendered superfluous, the Copyright Act transforms from a necessary evil into a net evil. We should not remain trapped within copyright after we have outgrown the need for its shelter, but should instead escape its confines and seek the common good in the common law.

ACKNOWLEDGMENTS

I'd like to thank everyone who helped bring this book to fruition, though I'll count myself lucky if I remember them all. Chapman University supported the initial research and writing that went into *Intellectual Privilege*; the Mercatus Center at George Mason University, through a team headed by Jerry Brito and including Ted Bolema, Robert E. Raffety, and Corrie Schwab, helped polish and publish the book. I thank Jim Harper, Richard A. Epstein, Tim Lee, Sam Bayer, Brian W. Carver, David J. Previn, Elizabeth Knoll, and Stephan Kinsella for commenting on draft versions of the text; Gil Milbauer and Donna G. Matias for eagle-eyed proofreading; Christine Song for research help; and the many various commentators on the portions of the book that I posted at the *Intellectual Privilege, Agoraphilia,* and *Technology Liberation Front* blogs. My fellow academics have helped me in more ways, great and small, that I can fully credit; herewith follows a partial list of those who helped on particular points: Oren Bracha, Kenneth D. Crews, Lawrence Greenberg, Shubha Gosh, Howard C. Analwalt, and Eric Goldman. If I forgot to give you proper credit, please excuse my oversight. I hasten to add, with regard to those whom I did remember to name, that I alone bear the blame for any of the book's errors, omissions, or eccentricities. Lastly, I thank my readers, without whom all my efforts would mean little.

EARLIER APPEARANCES OF MATERIAL IN THIS BOOK

Several chapters of this book are adaptations or revisions of articles I had previously published with various journals and organizations. Chapter 3 largely derives from material first published in my paper "Escape from Copyright: Market Success vs. Statutory Failure in the Protection of Expressive Works," *University of Cincinnati Law Review* 69 (2001): 741–806, particularly 760–74. An earlier version of a portion of chapter 4—the description of a Hollywood executive's view of copyright—appeared as "Towards a Copyriot Act—and Away from It, Again," *Cato Unbound: The Future of Copyright* (June 2008),

http://www.cato-unbound.org/2008/06/16/tom-w-bell/towards-a
-copyriot-act-and-away-from-it-again/.

Chapter 5 comes largely from "Copyright as Intellectual ~~Property~~
Privilege," *Syracuse Law Review* 58 (2007): 523–46 (invited). A small
bit comes from "Authors' Welfare: Copyright as a Statutory Mechanism
for Redistributing Rights," *Brooklyn Law Review* 69 (2003): 229–80.
Most of chapter 6 comes from edited portions of my paper "Escape
from Copyright," particularly pages 780–87. Portions also come from
"Copyright as Intellectual ~~Property~~ Privilege" and from "Indelicate
Imbalancing in Copyright and Patent Law," in *Copy Fights: The Future
of Intellectual Property in the Information Age*, ed. Adam Thierer and
Wayne Crews (Washington, DC: Cato Institute, 2002), 1–16.

Most of chapter 7 comes from edited portions of "Fair Use vs. Fared
Use: The Impact of Automated Rights Management on Copyright's Fair
Use Doctrine," *North Carolina Law Review* 76 (1998): 557–619. Chapter
8 derives primarily from "Codifying Copyright's Misuse Doctrine,"
Utah Law Review 2007, 573–86. Chapter 9 comes primarily from
"Escape from Copyright," 794–98; and from "Fair Use vs. Fared Use."

Much of the material in chapter 10 comes from a reworked passage of
"Escape from Copyright," 801–3. The material on blockheaded authors
made up part of "The Specter of Copyism v. Blockheaded Authors:
How User-Generated Content Affects Copyright Policy," *Vanderbilt
Journal of Entertainment & Technology Law* 10 (2008): 841–61. I first
wrote about "We Celebrate Your Birthday" at *A Free Birthday Song,
Agoraphilia* (blog), November 11, 2006, http://agoraphilia.blogspot.
com/2006/11/free-birthday-song.html. My conclusion borrows liberally from "Escape from Copyright," 803–5.

NOTES

Introduction: Copyright on the Third Hand

1. U.S. Const. art. I, § 8, cl. 8.

2. Id. at art. I, § 8, cl. 18; preamble.

Chapter 1: What Is Copyright?

1. See Marybeth Peters, Register of Copyrights, "In the Matter of Mechanical and Digital Phonorecord Delivery Rate Adjustment Proceeding," Memorandum Opinion, Docket No. RF 2006–1 (October 16, 2006), http://www.copyright.gov/docs/ringtone-decision.pdf. This memorandum rules that cell phone ringtones qualify as digital phone record deliveries as defined in 17 U.S.C. § 115 (2012).

2. For a general discussion of how copyright affects freedom of expression, see Neil Weinstock Netanel, *Copyright's Paradox* (Oxford: Oxford University Press, 2008).

3. Ibid.

4. Granted, the First Amendment plays a vital role in preventing lawmakers and prosecutors from exercising the property rights they hold in such things as public parks in a way that would violate our freedoms of expression. We can certainly understand such puzzles, however, as raising questions about the proper use of property held by the government for the benefit of the people. In other words, principles from the law of trusts, as well as from the law of property, should control in such cases.

5. Eldred v. Ashcroft, 537 U.S. 186, 221 (2003).

6. The term "statist" is not a simple pejorative: it serves to distinguish this particular form of positivism from alternatives. For an explanation of the difference between statist legal positivism and natural legal positivism, see Randy E. Barnett, *The Structure of Liberty: Justice and the Rule of Law* (Oxford: Oxford University Press, 1998), 18–22.

7. "State" here means "an administrative body that credibly claims an exclusive right on the initiation of coercion within a particular geographic area," a definition derived from Max Weber's classic one: "A compulsory political organization with a continuous organization . . . will be called a 'state' if and in so far as its administrative staff successfully upholds a claim to the *monopoly* of the *legitimate* use of physical force in the enforcement of its order" (emphasis in the original). Max Weber, *The Theory of Social and Economic Organization*, trans. A. M. Henderson and Talcott Parsons, ed. Talcott Parsons (New York: Oxford University Press, 1947), 154.

8. U.S. Const. art. I, § 8, cl. 8.

9. For examples, compare the following cases. Feist Publications, Inc. v. Rural Telephone Service Co., 499 U.S. 340, 349 (1991); Campbell v. Acuff-Rose Music, Inc., 510 U.S. 569, 575 (1994); Fogerty v. Fantasy, Inc., 510 U.S. 517, 527 (1994); and Harper & Row Publishers, Inc. v. Nation Enterprises, 471 U.S. 539, 549 (1985) all quote the promotion of both "Science and useful Arts" as copyright's goals. Metro-Goldwyn-Mayer Studios, Inc. v. Grokster, Ltd., 545 U.S. 913, 961 (2005) (justices Breyer, Stevens, and O'Connor, concurring) cites only "useful Arts." Golan v. Holder, 132 S. Ct. 873, 888 (2012) and *Eldred*, 537 U.S. at 193 cite only "Science."

10. U.S. Const. art. I, § 8, cl. 8.

11. See, for example, In re Bergy, 596 F.2d 952, 958 (C.C.P.A. 1979); Robert A. Kreiss, "Accessibility and Commercialization in Copyright Theory," *UCLA Law Review* 43 (1995): 7n21; Lydia Pallas Loren, "Redefining the Market Failure Approach to Fair Use in an Era of Copyright Permission Systems," *Journal of Intellectual Property Law* 5 (1997): 3n2; William F. Patry, "The Failure of the American Copyright System: Protecting the Idle Rich," *Notre Dame Law Review* 72 (1997): 911n18.

12. See, for example, Graham v. John Deere Co., 383 U.S. 1, 6 (1966).

13. See, for example, Malla Pollack, "Unconstitutional Incontestability? The Intersection of the Intellectual Property and Commerce Clauses of the Constitution: Beyond a Critique of *Shakespeare Co. v. Silstar Corp.*," *Seattle University Law Review* 18 (1995): 282–83. Although I have for many years advocated a similarly broad reading, I now believe that I erred in arguing that "this more generous reading . . . slightly reduces (but certainly does not eliminate) suspicions that the extraordinarily broad scope of contemporary copyright law transgresses constitutional limits." Tom W. Bell, "Escape from Copyright: Market Success vs. Statutory Failure in the Protection of Expressive Works," *University of Cincinnati Law Review* 69 (2001): 743n3. Having more recently developed a theory that calls for interpreting the Constitution in favor of individual liberties and against federal powers, I would argue that I formerly misread "and" in the copyright clause. See Tom W. Bell, "Graduated Consent Theory, Explained and Applied" (Research Paper No. 09-13, Legal Studies Research Paper Series, Chapman University School of Law, March 11, 2009), available at http://ssrn.com/abstract=1357825. That conjunction, properly understood, requires copyright to promote the progress of both the sciences and the useful arts. If it fails in either one, we must judge copyright legislation unconstitutional.

14. See the review of eighteenth-century usage in Malla Pollack, "What Is Congress Supposed to Promote? Defining 'Progress' in Article I, Section 8, Clause 8 of the United States Constitution, or Introducing the Progress Clause," *Nebraska Law Review* 80 (2001): 791n178.

15. Copyright Act of 1790, 1 Stat. 124 (1790), § 1, reprinted in Copyright Office, Library of Congress, Bulletin No. 3 (Revised), *Copyright Enactments: Laws Passed in the United States since 1783 Relating to Copyright* (1973), 22.

16. William Hill Brown, *The Power of Sympathy* (Boston, MA: Isaiah Thomas, 1789), dedication page. For the historical context of Brown's novel, see Patricia Crain, "Print and Everyday Life in the Eighteenth Century," in *Perspectives on American Book History: Artifacts and Commentary*, ed. Scott E. Casper, Joanne D. Chaison, and Jeffrey D. Groves (Amherst, MA: University of Massachusetts Press, 2002), 74.

17. In America from 1640 to 1790, imprints of practical and instructional genres such as government works (7,182), sermons (3,192), almanacs (1,977), schoolbooks (1,085), and academic dissertations (323) greatly outnumbered imprints of poetry (1,854), hymnals (254), psalm books (253), satires (201), plays (111), and novels (38). Hugh Amory, "Appendix One: A Note on Statistics," in *A History of the Book in America*, vol. 1, *The Colonial Book in the Atlantic World*, ed. Hugh Amory and David D. Hall (Cambridge: Cambridge University Press, 2000), 511. See also the description of the typical contents of libraries and private collections in eighteenth-century America provided in Julie Hedgepeth Williams, *The Significance of the Printed Word in Early America: Colonists' Thoughts on the Role of the Press* (Westport, CT: Greenwood Publishing, 1999).

18. For an argument on behalf of this interpretive approach, see Tom W. Bell, "Graduated Consent in Contract and Tort Law: Toward a Theory of Justification," *Case Western Reserve Law Review* 61 (2010): 17–83.

19. I here set aside the possibility that the interstate commerce clause might alone empower federal lawmakers to create copyright-like protections for purely expressive works. If copyrights could be excused solely as exercises of the power to regulate interstate commerce, after all, why would the Constitution include the copyright clause?

20. See Edward C. Walterscheid, "The Remarkable—and Irrational—Disparity between the

Patent Term and the Copyright Term," *Journal of the Patent and Trademark Office Society* 83 (2001): 265.

21. Eldred v. Ashcroft, 537 U.S. 186, 212–13 (2003).

22. Id. at 215.

23. Id. at 204.

24. The Supreme Court has explained that it will uphold a law under the rational basis test "if there is any conceivable state of facts that could provide a rational basis" for the law. Beach Communications v. FCC, 508 U.S. 307, 313 (1993). "Moreover, because we never require a legislature to articulate its reasons for enacting a statute, it is entirely irrelevant for constitutional purposes whether the conceived reason for the challenged distinction actually motivated the legislature." Id. at 315.

25. Feist Publications, Inc. v. Rural Telephone Service Co., 499 U.S. 340, 345 (1991) (quoting Melville B. Nimmer and David Nimmer, *Nimmer on Copyright*, vol. 1 (1990), § 1.08[C][1]).

26. Id. at 359.

27. 17 U.S.C. § 101 (2012).

28. "A timespan appropriately 'limited' as applied to future copyrights does not automatically cease to be 'limited' when applied to existing copyrights." Eldred v. Ashcroft, 537 U.S. 186, 199 (2003).

29. To wit: "The Congress shall have Power . . . To promote the Progress of Science and useful Arts, by securing for limited Times to Authors . . . the exclusive Right to their . . . Writings." U.S. Const. art. I, § 8, cl. 8. Those who do not include "and useful Arts" will, of course, attribute only twenty-four words about copyright to the Constitution.

30. This is my count. My calculations cover only 17 U.S.C. §§ 101–805 and 1001–1010 (2012), comprising chapters 1–8 and 10 of title 17 of the U.S. Code. I thus excluded, as not properly within the scope of copyright, chapter 9 (concerning the protection of semiconductor chips), chapter 11 (concerning unfixed musical recordings and videos), chapter 12 (concerning copyright protection and management systems), and chapter 13 (concerning original designs *qua* vessel hulls). I also excluded appendices A–L, which, though they may pertain to copyright, have not been codified in title 17 of the U.S. Code.

31. 17 U.S.C. § 102(1)–(8) (2012).

32. For the definition of literary works for the purposes of copyright law, see id. § 101.

33. To the contrary, the Copyright Office counsels, "Mere listings of ingredients as in recipes, formulas, compounds or prescriptions are not subject to copyright protection." US Copyright Office, "Recipes" (Form Letter 122), accessed August 3, 2009, http://www.loc.gov/copyright /fls/fl122.pdf. Interestingly, recipes apparently represent the oldest known subject matter of IP. See Steven L. Nichols, "Comment: Hippocrates, the Patent-Holder: The Unenforceability of Medical Procedure Patents," *George Mason Law Review* 5 (1997): 233–34, which reports that c. 500 BC the Greek colony of Sybarius, in southern Italy, afforded patent-like privileges to recipe holders.

34. But see Kecofa B.V. v. Lancôme Parfums et Beauté et Cie S.N.C., Case No. C04/327HR (Supreme Court of the Netherlands, June 16, 2006), which held that perfume may be copyrighted under Dutch law.

35. Lotus Development Corp. v. Borland Intern., Inc., 49 F.3d 807, 815 (1st Cir. 1995). Affirmed by 516 U.S. 233 (1996). Note that because the court affirmed in an equally divided opinion, its holding binds only the First Circuit.

36. See, for example, Nichols v. Universal Pictures, 45 F.2d 119 (2d Cir. 1930); Sheldon v. Metro-Goldwyn Pictures Corp., 81 F.2d 49 (2d Cir. 1936).

37. Baker v. Selden, 101 U.S. 99 (1879).

38. 17 U.S.C. § 101 (2012). This section also defines pictorial, graphic, and sculptural works.

39. For a description of how the fashion industry generates innovation despite the lack of *sui generis* protection for clothing designs, see Kal Raustiala and Christopher Sprigman, "The Piracy Paradox: Innovation and Intellectual Property in Fashion Design," *Virginia Law Review* 92 (2006): 1687–777. For a description of furniture as "largely untouched by the scheme of the copyright law," see Craig Joyce et al., eds., *Copyright Law*, 5th ed. (Newark, NJ: LexisNexis, 2001), 200. For an explanation of why patent law (and, by extension, copyright law) has had little effect on new car designs, see Michael E. Peters, "Note, When Patent and Trademark Law Hit the Fan: Potential Effects of *Vornado Air Circulation Systems, Inc. v. Duracraft Corp.* on Legal Protection for Industrial Design," *Temple Environmental Law & Technology Journal* 15 (1996): 126. US copyright in architectural works arguably extends only to habitable structures, "such as houses and office buildings," as well as to "structures that are used, but not inhabited, by human beings, such as churches, pergolas, gazebos, and garden pavilions." H.R. Rep. No. 735, 101st Cong., 2d Sess. 20 (1990). According to that interpretation, copyright law would not cover structures not intended for human occupancy, such as bridges, highway interchanges, and dams. Although in theory such structures could qualify as patentable inventions, in practice patent law appears to have no influence on the creativity evinced in their design.

40. For many examples, see Kal Raustiala and Christopher Sprigman, *The Knockoff Economy: How Imitation Sparks Innovation* (Oxford: Oxford University Press, 2012).

41. 17 U.S.C. § 105 (2012).

42. Id. § 103(a): "Protection for a work employing preexisting material in which copyright subsists does not extend to any part of the work in which such material has been used unlawfully."

43. Id. § 102(a).

44. Id. § 411.

45. See, for example, US Copyright Office, "Form CO," accessed January 14, 2013, http://www.copyright.gov/forms/formco2d.pdf.

46. 17 U.S.C. § 410 (2012) describes the limited scope of examination by the register of copyrights.

47. See US Copyright Office, "Copyright Office Fees," July 2009, accessed January 14, 2013, http://www.copyright.gov/docs/fees.html.

48. 17 U.S.C. § 408(a) (2012) describes the permissibility of registration.

49. Id. § 412.

50. Id. § 408(f).

51. Sheldon v. Metro-Goldwyn Pictures Corp., 81 F.2d 49, 54 (2d Cir. 1936).

52. 17 U.S.C. § 401 (2012) describes the means and ends of putting notice of copyright on copies of protected works. See also id. § 402, which describes similar rules with regard to phone records.

53. Christopher Sprigman, "Reform(aliz)ing Copyright," *Stanford Law Review* 57 (2004): 485–568; William M. Landes and Richard A. Posner, "Indefinitely Renewable Copyright," *University of Chicago Law Review* 70 (2003): 471–518; Lawrence Lessig, *The Future of Ideas: The Fate of the Commons in a Connected World* (New York: Random House, 2001), 250–52.

54. 17 U.S.C. § 302(a) (2012).

55. Id. § 302(b), (c).

56. See id. §§ 303–4.

57. Copyright Act of 1790, 1 Stat. 124 (1790), § 1, in Copyright Office, *Copyright Enactments*, 22.

58. Digital Performance Right in Sound Recordings Act of 1995, 109 Stat. 336 (1995), § 2, codified at 17 U.S.C. § 106(6) (2012). Even more recent amendments expand copyright rights by making actionable the import or export of any work that violates one of the six rights specified in § 106. Prioritizing Resources and Organization for Intellectual Property (PRO-IP) Act of 2008, 122 Stat. 4256 (2008), § 105(b), codified at 17 U.S.C. § 602(a) (2012).

59. Id. § 114(a), moreover, clarifies the intention behind that lacuna: "The exclusive rights of the owner of copyright in a sound recording . . . do not include any right of performance under section 106(4)."

60. *Internet Streaming of Radio Broadcasts: Balancing the Interests of Sound Recording Copyright Owners with Those of Broadcasters, Hearing Before the Subcomm. on Courts, the Internet, and Intellectual Property of the H. Comm. on the Judiciary*, 108th Cong. 82–83 (July 15, 2004) (statement of David O. Carson, General Counsel, Copyright Office), http://www.copyright.gov/docs/carson071504.pdf.

61. See, for example, *The Performance Rights Act and Parity among Music Delivery Platforms, Hearing Before the Committee on the Judiciary, U.S. Senate*, 111th Cong., 1st Sess. (August 4, 2009) (statement of Marybeth Peters, Register of Copyrights), http://www.copyright.gov /docs/regstat070509.html. The register of copyrights argues for expanding public performance rights in sound recordings because "our treatment of the public performance right for sound recordings falls short of prevailing international norms."

62. 17 U.S.C. § 107 (2012).

63. Id. § 109.

64. On that question, compare Lee v. A.R.T. Co., 125 F.3d 580 (7th Cir. 1997), which held that § 106(2) rights did not reach unauthorized mounting of lawfully acquired prints on decorative tiles, with Mirage Editions, Inc. v. Albuquerque A.R.T. Co., 856 F.2d 1341 (9th Cir. 1988), which held that a similar practice did violate § 106(2) rights.

65. 17 U.S.C. § 111(c)–(d) (2012) specifies the compulsory licensing of secondary transmissions by cable systems; § 112(e) provides for the compulsory licensing of certain ephemeral recordings; § 114(d)(2), (e)–(f) relates to the compulsory licensing of public performances of sound recordings via digital audio transmissions; § 115 describes compulsory licensing for the making and distribution of phone records; § 118(b)(3), (d) provides that the librarian of Congress may establish a binding schedule of rates and terms for the use of certain copyrighted works by public broadcasting entities.

66. Id. § 201(d).

67. Ronald A. Cass and Keith N. Hylton, *Laws of Creation: Property Rights in the World of Ideas* (Cambridge, MA: Harvard University Press, 2013).

68. 17 U.S.C. §§ 203, 304(c), and 304(d) (2012).

69. See id. §§ 203(a)(5), 304(c)(5), both of which say, "Termination . . . may be effected notwithstanding any agreement to the contrary, including an agreement to make a will or to make any future grant."

70. See, for example, Restatement (Second) of Contracts § 208 (1979), which describes the narrow conditions under which a court might refuse to enforce a contract on grounds of unconscionability and the relatively constrained termination of rights effectuated in such cases.

71. 17 U.S.C. § 501(a) (2012).

72. Id. § 501(b).

73. Restatement (Second) of Torts § 158 (1965) defines liability for intentional intrusions on land.

74. See, for example, Nichols v. Universal Pictures, 45 F.2d 119 (2d Cir. 1930).

75. See, for example, Steinberg v. Columbia Pictures, 663 F. Supp. 706 (S.D.N.Y. 1987).

76. See Ty, Inc. v. GMA Accessories, Inc., 132 F.3d 1167, 1169–70 (7th Cir. 1997); *Steinberg*, 663 F. Supp. at 714.

77. See Towler v. Sayles, 76 F.3d 579, 583–84 (4th Cir. 1996); Selle v. Gibb, 741 F.2d 896, 904 (7th Cir. 1984).

78. See *Towler*, 76 F.3d at 584; *Selle*, 741 F.2d at 900–901; *Steinberg*, 663 F. Supp at 711.

79. See, for example, Bouchat v. Baltimore Ravens, Inc., 241 F.3d 350, 356 (4th Cir. 2000); Gaste v. Kaiserman, 863 F.2d 1061, 1066 (2d Cir. 1988).

80. See, for example, *Ty*, 132 F.3d at 1170; Ferguson v. NBC, 584 F.2d 111 (5th Cir. 1978).

81. Computer Associates International, Inc. v. Altai, Inc., 982 F.2d 693 (2d Cir. 1992).

82. Compare *Selle*, 741 F.2d, which analyzes alleged infringement of musical works, with Gross v. Seligman, 212 F. 930 (2d Cir. 1914), which concerns graphic works.

83. Douglas Lichtman and William M. Landes, "Indirect Liability for Copyright Infringement: An Economic Perspective," *Harvard Journal of Law & Technology* 16 (2003): 395–410.

84. "The Copyright Act does not expressly render anyone liable for infringement committed by another." Sony Corp. v. Universal City Studios, Inc., 464 U.S. 417, 434 (1984). But see the discussion of how amendments to the act have recognized secondary liability in certain narrow contexts in Lichtman and Landes, "Indirect Liability," 401–2.

85. See, for example, Metro-Goldwyn-Mayer Studios, Inc. v. Grokster, Ltd., 545 U.S. 913, 930 (2005).

86. See *Sony*, 464 U.S. at 442.

87. See *Grokster*, 545 U.S. at 934.

88. 17 U.S.C. § 502 (2012).

89. Id. § 504.

90. Id. § 505.

91. Id. §§ 601–3.

92. Id. § 512(h).

93. Id. § 504(d).

94. See id. § 503(a)—a provision that codifies the PRO-IP Act of 2008.

95. Id. § 506(b) provides for the forfeiture and destruction of criminally infringing works and the means of their production; § 509 provides for the seizure and forfeiture to the United States (as opposed to the party suffering infringement) of criminally infringing works and the means of their production.

96. Id. § 506(a)(1).

97. Id. § 106A.

98. Id. at chap. 12, §§ 1201–5.

99. Id. at chap. 13, §§ 1301–32.

100. Id. § 106A(e).

101. Id. § 106A(a).

102. Id. §§ 1203–4.

103. Id. § 1301(a)(1).

104. Id. § 1301(b)(2), which defines "useful article" as it is used in chapter 13 of the Copyright Act.

105. Id. § 101, which defines "pictorial, graphic, and sculptural works."

106. See Feist Publications, Inc. v. Rural Telephone Service Co., 499 U.S. 340 (1991).

107. Authors must register their works in order to vindicate their rights in court, however. 17 U.S.C. § 411 (2012).

108. See id. § 301(a).

109. See Cal. Civ. Code § 980(a) (2013). See also § 981, which provides for joint ownership of unfixed works, and § 982, which provides for the transfer of ownership in unfixed works.

110. See N.Y. Penal Law §§ 275.15, 275.20 (2013). Though they do not expressly state as much, the criminal statutes of California and Illinois arguably have sufficient breadth to outlaw the same behavior. See Cal. Penal Code § 653h (2013); Ill. Code Ann. § 5/16-7 (2012).

111. Wheaton v. Peters, 33 U.S. (8 Pet.) 591, 663 (1834).

112. "There is no historical justification whatsoever for the claim that copyright was recognized as a common law right of an author." Howard B. Abrams, "The Historic Foundation of American Copyright Law: Exploding the Myth of Common Law Copyright," *Wayne Law Review* 29 (1983): 1128. See also pp. 1129–33.

113. Melville B. Nimmer and David Nimmer, *Nimmer on Copyright*, vol. 1 (2013), § 2.02.

114. See Capitol Records, Inc. v. Naxos, Inc., 4 N.Y.3d 540, 560 (N.Y. 2005): "In the realm of sound recordings, it has been the law in this state for over 50 years that, in the absence of federal statutory protection, the public sale of a sound recording otherwise unprotected by statutory copyright does not constitute a publication sufficient to divest the owner of common-law copyright protection."

115. See La Cienega Music Co. v. ZZ Top, 53 F.3d 950, 953 (9th Cir. 1995).

116. See Rowe v. Golden West Television Productions, 184 N.J. Super 264, 269 (App. Div. 1982): "Common law copyright protection is afforded under New Jersey law to 'literary property' which . . . has been embodied in some 'material form.'" See also Falwell v. Penthouse International, Ltd., 521 F. Supp. 1204, 1207 (W.D. Va. 1981): "The existence of common law copyright protection for the spoken word has not been established by any court."

117. See, for example, Estate of Hemingway v. Random House, Inc., 23 N.Y.2d 341, 348 (N.Y. Ct. App. 1968): "Conceivably, there may be limited and special situations in which an interlocutor brings forth oral statements from another party which both understand to be the unique intellectual product of the principal speaker, a product which would qualify for common-law copyright if such statements were in writing. Concerning such problems, we express no opinion; we do no more than raise the questions, leaving them open for future consideration." Nimmer and Nimmer say that whether the common law protects unfixed works is "by no means free from doubt." Nimmer and Nimmer, *Nimmer on Copyright*, vol. 1, § 2.02.

118. Richard A. Epstein, *Simple Rules for a Complex World* (Cambridge, MA: Harvard University Press, 1995).

119. Arthur R. Hogue, *Origins of the Common Law* (Bloomington: Indiana University Press, 1966), 5.

120. Ibid., 190. Strike the word "royal," and you'll find Hogue's definition entirely compatible with my own.

121. Richard A. Posner, *The Problems of Jurisprudence* (Cambridge, MA: Harvard University Press, 1990), 247.

122. *Black's Law Dictionary*, 6th ed. (1990), s.v. "common law."

123. For a description of the origins of the law qua nomos, see Friedrich A. Hayek, *Law, Legislation and Liberty* (Chicago: University of Chicago Press, 1973), vol. 1, chap. 4.

124. "In determining whether conduct is negligent, the customs of the community, or of others

under like circumstances, are factors to be taken into account." Restatement (Second) of Torts § 295A (1965).

125. For a definition of adverse use, see Restatement of Property § 458 (1944).

126. See Restatement (Second) of Contracts §§ 219–21 (1981): § 219 defines "usage" as "habitual or customary practice," § 220 specifies when usage shapes interpretation of an agreement, and § 221 specifies when usage supplements or qualifies an agreement.

127. In US law reference to natural rights provided a check on custom as well as on positive law. Richard H. Helmholz, "The Law of Nature and the Early History of Unenumerated Rights in the United States," *University of Pennsylvania Journal of Constitutional Law* 9 (2007): 401–21. Natural rights also played a similar role in English law from a much earlier era. Helmholz, "Natural Law and Human Rights in English Law: From Bracton to Blackstone," *Ave Maria Law Review* 3 (2005): 1–22.

128. See Epstein, *Simple Rules for a Complex World*. His catalog of simple but sufficient rules also includes the constitutional requirement that just compensation be paid for public takings of private property.

129. The idea "that we are all born with certain natural rights, as reflected largely in the English common law," is embodied in the Constitution. Roger Pilon, "*Town of Castle Rock v. Gonzales*: Executive Indifference, Judicial Complicity," *Cato Supreme Court Review* 2004–2005, 105. Even skeptics of natural right jurisprudence acknowledge its powerful influence on the common law. For example, Cass R. Sunstein observes that "the common law categories were taken as a natural rather than social construct." Sunstein, "Lochner's Legacy," *Columbia Law Review* 87 (1987): 879.

130. See, for example, Paul H. Rubin, "Why Is the Common Law Efficient?," *Journal of Legal Studies* 6 (1977): 51–63; George L. Priest, "The Common Law Process and the Selection of Efficient Rules," *Journal of Legal Studies* 6 (1977): 65–82; Todd Zywicki, "The Rise and Fall of Efficiency in the Common Law: A Supply-Side Analysis," *Northwestern University Law Review* 97 (2003): 1551–633. Zywicki, in particular, attributes the efficiency of the common law to competitive processes, the majority of which have been long since disappeared, that influenced its early evolution. Zywicki, "Rise and Fall of Efficiency," 1581–613. Daniel Klerman disagrees that competition could have had that effect: "There is no reason to believe that competition among courts should have led to efficient law because plaintiffs, who chose the forum, had no incentive to prefer efficient law." Klerman, "Jurisdictional Competition and the Evolution of the Common Law," *University of Chicago Law Review*, 74 (2007): 1183.

131. Tom W. Bell, "Graduated Consent Theory" (see n. 13).

132. For instance, "The natural law's recognition of the inherent right to freedom did actually play a role in American case law. It was not a nullity. It meant, for example, that a master could not kill his slave and pretend that he was only destroying a chattel. He must stand trial for murder." Helmholz, "Law of Nature," 411.

133. For a description of how the "electorate of law" shapes the common law, see Barnett, *Structure of Liberty*, 124–27 (see n. 6).

134. Unlike statutory law, however, the common law does not offer sui generis protection to anti-circumvention technologies; hence the perceived need for title I of the Digital Millennium Copyright Act, 17 U.S.C. §§ 1201–5 (2012).

135. U.S. Const., preamble.

136. U.S. Const. art. I, § 8, cl. 8.

Chapter 2: Copyright in Public Policy

1. White-Smith Music Publishing Co. v. Apollo Co., 209 U.S. 1, 19 (1908) (Justice Holmes, concurring). See also Jane C. Ginsburg, "Copyright without Walls," *Representations* 42 (1993): 59, where Ginsburg argues that copyright law "has traditionally presumed a world in which, but for copyright, unauthorized reproductions would be pervasive and unremediable."

2. Copyright Act of 1976, 17 U.S.C. §§ 101–1332 (2012).

3. See 17 U.S.C. § 106 (2012) which sets forth the exclusive rights enjoyed by copyright holders.

4. See id. §§ 201–5, which defines rules of copyright ownership and transfer.

5. See William M. Landes and Richard A. Posner, "An Economic Analysis of Copyright Law," *Journal of Legal Studies* 18 (1989): 326.

6. The Copyright Act covers only *fixed* expressive works, granted. See 17 U.S.C. § 102(a) (2012). It doubtless stimulates the production of unfixed works indirectly, however, as when a jazz musician extemporizes during a performance in order to convince listeners to buy a recorded version of the unfixed work.

7. See Landes and Posner, "Economic Analysis of Copyright Law," 327.

8. That label hardly suffices to establish the proper scope of copyright, of course; I intend no more than irony.

9. Commentators often refer to this as a "deadweight loss." See, for example, William W. Fisher III, "Property and Contract on the Internet," *Chicago-Kent Law Review* 3 (1998): 1236; Julie E. Cohen, "Copyright and the Perfect Curve," *Vanderbilt Law Review* 53 (2000): 1801. To clarify the cause of that loss, I prefer the label "nonholders' opportunity costs."

10. See, for example, Landes and Posner, "Economic Analysis of Copyright Law," 326, which characterizes seeking for this balance as "the central problem of copyright law." But also see chapter 6, where I argue that copyright policy cannot strike a delicate balance between public and private interests, and Christopher S. Yoo, "Copyright and Product Differentiation," *NYU Law Review* 79 (2004): 212–80. Yoo argues that the economics of product differentiation suggests that the access-incentives tradeoff is not so intractable as generally believed.

11. More generally, the author would need to sell sufficient quantities at any price (P) sufficient to cover average costs (AC).

12. I considered, for instance, adding a variety of average cost curves to illustrate how works with different production costs fare under a given level of copyright restriction.

13. See, for example, Fisher, "Property and Contract on the Internet," 1238–39. Fisher argues that price discrimination can both increase copyright holders' profits and decrease nonholders' opportunity costs.

14. See, for example, Yoo, "Copyright and Product Differentiation," 231–35. Yoo criticizes the standard model as deficient on a number of grounds.

15. For an explanation of the ubiquity of monopolistic competition, see David D. Friedman, *Price Theory: An Intermediary Text* (Cincinnati, OH: South-Western, 1986), 244–45.

16. See Karl Marx and Friedrich Engels, *Manifesto of the Communist Party* (1848), in *The Marx-Engels Reader*, 2nd ed., ed. Robert C. Tucker (New York: W.W. Norton, 1978), 473.

17. Both examples assume that the copyright holder cannot distinguish between potential customers with such exactitude—i.e., price-discriminate—as to be able to offer a market for such unpaying uses.

18. This analysis does not assume that all users willing to pay above MC and below AC will infringe; or, more precisely, it includes moral qualms and the like among a consumer's

potential marginal costs. For a copyright maximalist, the marginal cost of infringing a copyright might equal infinity.

19. This assumes that the marginal costs of the producer at least roughly equal those of the average consumer. That is not an unjustified assumption in a digital environment—though, as discussed in the prior note, some consumers may have very different marginal costs curves.

20. That holds especially true of digital works. Works in other media may prove more difficult to copy without authorization. Stephen Breyer, who was later appointed a justice of the Supreme Court, describes such an effect in the book publishing industry. See Breyer, "The Uneasy Case for Copyright: A Study of Copyright in Books, Photocopies, and Computer Programs," *Harvard Law Review* 84 (1970): 281–351.

21. Strictly speaking, lawmakers should think in terms of how would-be infringers perceive the marginal costs of infringement. In the long run, though, would-be infringers will probably figure out the real risks of infringement.

22. William M. Landes and Richard A. Posner, *The Economic Structure of Intellectual Property Law* (Cambridge, MA: Harvard University Press, 2003), 71–72.

23. See Aronson v. Quick Point Pencil Co., 440 U.S. 257 (1979), which held that enforcing a contract requiring royalty payments for an unpatented invention did not contravene federal policy.

Chapter 3: Copyright, Philosophically

1. For example, "The D.C. Circuit spoke too broadly when it declared copyrights 'categorically immune from challenges under the First Amendment.'" Eldred v. Ashcroft, 537 U.S. 186, 221 (2003), quoting Eldred v. Reno, 239 F.3d 372, 375 (D.C. Cir. 2001).

2. See state copyright statutes reprinted in Copyright Office, *Copyright Enactments,* 1–21 (see chap. 1, n. 15).

3. An Act for the Encouragement of Literature and Genius (Connecticut Copyright Act) § 7, Acts and Laws of the State of Connecticut (Sherman & Law) (passed January 1783, repealed 1812), reprinted in Copyright Office, *Copyright Enactments*, 3. See also An Act for the Encouragement of Literature and Genius (Georgia Copyright Act) § IV, A Digest of the Laws of the State of Georgia (Watkins & Watkins) (passed February 3, 1786), reprinted in Copyright Office, *Copyright Enactments*, 17–18, and An Act to Promote Literature (New York Copyright Act) § IV, Laws of the State of New York, passed by the legislature of said State at their ninth session (Loudon & Loudon) (passed April 29, 1786), reprinted in Copyright Office, *Copyright Enactments*, 19, 21, which is the same but for minor grammatical differences.

4. H. Jefferson Powell, "The Original Understanding of Original Intent," *Harvard Law Review* 98 (1985): 898–99.

5. United States v. Texas, 507 U.S. 529, 534 (1993), quoting Isbrandtsen Co. v. Johnson, 343 U.S. 779, 783 (1952).

6. Astoria Federal Savings and Loan Association v. Solimino, 501 U.S. 104, 108 (1991).

7. United States v. Texas, 507 U.S. at 534.

8. Norfolk Redevelopment and Housing Authority v. Chesapeake & Potomac Telephone Co., 464 U.S. 30, 35 (1983), quoting Fairfax's Devisee v. Hunter's Lessee, 11 U.S. (7 Cranch) 603 (1813).

9. See Fogerty v. Fantasy, Inc., 510 U.S. 517, 533 (1996), which interprets § 505 of the Copyright Act against the backdrop of the US rule that litigants generally pay their own attorneys' fees.

10. For an explanation of how an appreciation of natural rights illuminates and legitimizes

constitutional principles, see Barnett, *Structure of Liberty*, 20–22, 25–26 (see chap. 1, n. 6); for a description of how common-law processes discover natural rights, refine them, and make them concrete, see ibid., 108–31.

11. James Madison to Thomas Jefferson, October 17, 1788, in *The Republic of Letters: The Correspondence Between Thomas Jefferson and James Madison*, ed. James Morton Smith, vol. 1, 1776–1790 (New York: W. W. Norton, 1995), 566.

12. See state copyright statutes reprinted in Copyright Office, *Copyright Enactments*, 1–21. Delaware was the only state to have no such statute. See ibid., 21.

13. Connecticut's original copyright act justifies itself on the grounds that "it is perfectly agreeable to the principles of natural equity and justice, that every author should be secured in receiving the profits that may arise from the sale of his works." Connecticut Copyright Act, Preamble, in Copyright Office, *Copyright Enactments*, 1. Massachusetts's act justifies itself in part on the grounds that "the legal security of the fruits of . . . study and industry . . . is one of the natural rights of all men," and New Hampshire's and Rhode Island's acts use similar language. An Act for the Purpose of Securing to Authors the Exclusive Right and Benefit of Publishing Their Literary Productions, for Twenty-One Years (Massachusetts Copyright Act), Preamble, Acts and laws of the Commonwealth of Massachusetts 236 (Edes & Sons) (passed March 17, 1783), reprinted in Copyright Office, *Copyright Enactments*, 4; An Act for the Encouragement of Literature and Genius, and for Securing to Authors the Exclusive Right and Benefit of Publishing Their Literary Productions, for Twenty Years (New Hampshire Copyright Act), Preamble, The Perpetual Laws of the State of New-Hampshire, from July 1776, to the session in December, 1788, continued into 1789, 161–62 (Melcher) (passed November 7, 1783, repealed 1842), reprinted in Copyright Office, *Copyright Enactments*, 8; An Act for the Purpose of Securing to Authors the Exclusive Right and Benefit of Publishing Their Literary Productions, for Twenty-One Years (Rhode Island Copyright Act), § 1, At the general assembly of the governor and company of the State of Rhode Island and Providence-Plantations, begun and holden at East-Greenwich on the 4th Monday of December, 1783, pp. 6–7 (Carter) (passed December 1783), reprinted in Copyright Office, *Copyright Enactments*, 9. North Carolina's act justifies itself in part on the grounds that "nothing is more strictly a man's own than the fruit of his study." An Act for Securing Literary Property (North Carolina Copyright Act), Preamble, Laws of the State of North-Carolina, pp. 563–64 (Edenton, Hodge & Wills) (passed November 19, 1785), reprinted in Copyright Office, *Copyright Enactments*, 15. Georgia's justifies itself in part on grounds of "principles of natural equity and justice," and New York's uses similar language. Georgia Copyright Act, Preamble, in Copyright Office, *Copyright Enactments*, 17; New York Copyright Act, Preamble, in Copyright Office, *Copyright Enactments*, 19.
 New Jersey's act also comes close to using the language of natural rights: it justifies the privileges it creates as "perfectly agreeable to the principles of equity." An Act for the Promotion and Encouragement of Literature (New Jersey Copyright Act), Preamble, Acts of the seventh general assembly of the State of New Jersey, at a session begun at Trenton, on the 22d day of October, 1782, and continued by adjournments, being the second sitting, chap. 21, p. 47 (Collins) (passed May 27, 1783, repealed 1799), reprinted in Copyright Office, *Copyright Enactments*, 6.

14. See Mary Helen Sears and Edward S. Irons, "The Constitutional Standard of Invention—The Touchstone for Patent Reform," *Utah Law Review* 1973, 667–73. Sears and Irons review historical evidence that the Founders had a strong aversion to monopolies in general. During the ratification debates, that aversion roused widespread objection to the inclusion of the copyright and patent clause in the proposed Constitution. See Edward C. Walterscheid, "To Promote the Progress of Science and Useful Arts: The Background and Origin of the Intellectual Property Clause of the United States Constitution," *Journal of Intellectual Property Law* 2 (1994): 54–56.

15. Maryland Declaration of Rights art. XXXIX (1776), quoted in Richard L. Perry, ed., *Sources of Our Liberties: Documentary Origins of Individual Liberties in the United States*

and Bill of Rights, rev. ed. (Chicago: American Bar Foundation, 1978), 350; see also North Carolina Declaration of Rights art. XXII (1776), quoted in Perry, *Sources of Our Liberties*, 355–56: "Perpetuities and monopolies are contrary to the genius of a free State, and ought not to be allowed."

16. See Paul Goldstein, *Copyright's Highway: From Gutenberg to the Celestial Jukebox* (New York: Hill & Wang, 1994), 51; Harry R. Warfel, *Noah Webster: Schoolmaster to America* (New York: Macmillan, 1936), 55–58, 132–35, 184–85; Karl Fenning, "The Origin of the Patent and Copyright Clause of the Constitution," *Georgetown Law Journal* 17 (1929): 115. Goldstein credits the origins of US copyright law to Webster's lobbying. Warfel describes Webster's lobbying efforts and observes that "Webster unquestionably is the father of copyright legislation in America." Warfel, *Noah Webster,* 58. Fenning credits the state statutes to "the efficient urging of Noah Webster."

17. For a review of state copyright terms, see Francine Crawford, "Pre-constitutional Copyright Statutes," *Bulletin of the Copyright Society of the U.S.A.* 23 (1975): 21–23. Maximum copyright terms varied between fourteen and twenty-eight years. For a summary of the types of works covered by the state copyright laws, see ibid., 18–21. See also Massachusetts Copyright Act § 2, in Copyright Office, Copyright Enactments, 4; New Hampshire Copyright Act § 1, in Copyright Office, *Copyright Enactments*, 8; Rhode Island Copyright Act § 1, in Copyright Office, *Copyright Enactments*, 9.

18. Connecticut's, New Jersey's, Georgia's, and New York's acts limited coverage to works authored by "inhabitants" or "residents" of the United States. See Connecticut Copyright Act § 1, in Copyright Office, Copyright Enactments, 2; New Jersey Copyright Act § 1, in Copyright Office, *Copyright Enactments*, 7; Georgia Copyright Act § 1, in Copyright Office, Copyright Enactments, 17; New York Copyright Act § 1, in Copyright Office, *Copyright Enactments*, 19. Massachusetts's and New Hampshire's acts limited coverage to works authored by "subjects" of the United States. Massachusetts Copyright Act § 2, in Copyright Office, *Copyright Enactments*, 4; New Hampshire Copyright Act § 1, in Copyright Office, *Copyright Enactments*, 8. Rhode Island's, Pennsylvania's, Virginia's, and North Carolina's acts limited coverage to works authored by "citizens." Rhode Island Copyright Act § 1, in Copyright Office, *Copyright Enactments*, 9; Pennsylvania Act of 1784 for the Encouragement and Promotion of Learning by Vesting a Right to the Copies of Printed Books in the Authors or Purchasers of Such Copies, During the Time Therein Mentioned (Pennsylvania Copyright Act), § III, Laws enacted in the second sitting of the eighth general assembly of the Commonwealth of Pennsylvania, which commenced the 13th day of Jan., 1784, ch. 125, pp. 306–8 (Bradford) (passed March 15, 1784), reprinted in Copyright Office, *Copyright Enactments*, 10; An Act Securing to Authors of Literary Works an Exclusive Property Therein for a Limited Time (Virginia Copyright Act), § I, Acts passed at a General Assembly of the Commonwealth of Virginia, pp. 8–9 (Dunlap & Hayes) (passed October 1785), reprinted in Copyright Office, *Copyright Enactments*, 14; North Carolina Copyright Act § 1, in Copyright Office, *Copyright Enactments*, 15. Maryland and South Carolina, the notable exceptions in this list of states limiting coverage to inhabitants, residents, subjects, or citizens, made no claims about copyright's natural status. See An Act Respecting Literary Property, (Maryland Copyright Act), Laws of Maryland, made and passed, at a session of assembly, begun and held at the city of Annapolis on Monday the 21st of April, 1783, ch. 24 (Green) (passed April 21, 1783), reprinted in Copyright Office, *Copyright Enactments*, 5; An Act for the Encouragement of Arts and Sciences (South Carolina Copyright Act), Acts, Ordinances, and Resolves of the General Assembly of the State of South Carolina, passed in the year 1784, pp. 49–51 (Miller) (passed March 26, 1784), reprinted in Copyright Office, *Copyright Enactments*, 11.

19. See Maryland Copyright Act § II, in Copyright Office, *Copyright Enactments*, 5; New Jersey Copyright Act § 1, in Copyright Office, *Copyright Enactments*, 6–7; Pennsylvania Copyright Act § III, in Copyright Office, *Copyright Enactments*, 10; North Carolina Copyright Act § 1, in Copyright Office, *Copyright Enactments*, 15. Massachusetts's, New Hampshire's, and Rhode Island's acts limited remedies to works "not yet printed." Massachusetts Copyright Act § 3, in Copyright Office, *Copyright Enactments*, 4; New

Hampshire Copyright Act § 2, in Copyright Office, *Copyright Enactments*, 8; Rhode Island Copyright Act § 2, in Copyright Office, *Copyright Enactments*, 9.

20. See Connecticut Copyright Act § 1, in Copyright Office, *Copyright Enactments*, 1–2; Georgia Copyright Act § 1, in Copyright Office, *Copyright Enactments*, 17.

21. See New Hampshire Copyright Act § 1, in Copyright Office, *Copyright Enactments*, 8; Rhode Island Copyright Act § 1, in Copyright Office, *Copyright Enactments*, 9.

22. For a general overview of registration requirements, see Crawford, "Pre-constitutional Copyright Statutes," 23–25.

23. See North Carolina Copyright Act § 1, in Copyright Office, *Copyright Enactments*, 15–16.

24. Massachusetts Copyright Act § 3, in Copyright Office, *Copyright Enactments*, 4; New Hampshire Copyright Act § 1, in Copyright Office, *Copyright Enactments*, 8.

25. Connecticut's, South Carolina's, Georgia's, and New York's copyright acts provided penalties for copyrighted works that were either unreasonably priced or not supplied in sufficient numbers. See Connecticut Copyright Act § 5, in Copyright Office, *Copyright Enactments*, 1–2; South Carolina Copyright Act § 4, in Copyright Office, *Copyright Enactments*, 11, 13; Georgia Copyright Act § III, in Copyright Office, *Copyright Enactments*, 17–18; New York Copyright Act § III, in Copyright Office, *Copyright Enactments*, 19–20. See also North Carolina Copyright Act § II, in Copyright Office, *Copyright Enactments*, 15–16, which provided penalties for setting "an unreasonable price" on a copyrighted work.

26. See Walterscheid, "To Promote the Progress of Science and Useful Arts," 10, 37. Walterscheid cites the practices of the various states as an influence on the Constitutional Convention. For a description of Webster's proximity to the Convention, close and continuing contact with many of the delegates, and reputation as an authority on matters of public concern, see Richard M. Rollins, *The Long Journey of Noah Webster* (Philadelphia: University of Pennsylvania Press, 1980), 51–52.

27. Rollins, *Long Journey*, 38–41.

28. *Journals of the Continental Congress*, 1774–1789, ed. Gaillard Hunt (Washington, DC: 1922 [1783]), 24:180.

29. Ibid., 24:326.

30. U.S. Const. art. I, § 8, cl. 8.

31. See Connecticut Copyright Act, preamble, in Copyright Office, *Copyright Enactments*, 1, and New York Copyright Act, preamble, in Copyright Office, *Copyright Enactments*, 19, both of which suggest that copyright may encourage people "of learning and genius to publish their writings"; Georgia Copyright Act, preamble, in Copyright Office, *Copyright Enactments*, 17; Massachusetts Copyright Act, preamble, in Copyright Office, *Copyright Enactments*, 4, which refers to "the efforts of learned and ingenious persons in the various arts and sciences"; Maryland Copyright Act, preamble, in Copyright Office, *Copyright Enactments*, 5; New Jersey Copyright Act, preamble, in Copyright Office, *Copyright Enactments*, 6, which calls for copyright to accomplish the "embellishment of human nature, the honour of the nation, and the general good of mankind"; New Hampshire Copyright Act, preamble, in Copyright Office, *Copyright Enactments*, 8; Rhode Island Copyright Act, preamble, in Copyright Office, *Copyright Enactments*, 9; Pennsylvania Copyright Act, in Copyright Office, *Copyright Enactments*, 10, which is entitled in part "An Act for the Encouragement and Promotion of Learning"; South Carolina Copyright Act, in Copyright Office, *Copyright Enactments*, 11; and North Carolina Copyright Act, preamble, in Copyright Office, *Copyright Enactments*, 15, which calls for copyright "to encourage genius, to promote useful discoveries, and to the general extension of arts and commerce."

32. James Madison, Federalist No. 43, in *The Federalist Papers*, ed. Clinton Rossiter (New York: Penguin, 1961), 272.

33. See H.R. Rep. No. 52-1494, at 2 (1892).

34. For a discussion of the paucity of evidence from sources other than Madison's comments, see Patry, "Failure of the American Copyright System," 912 (see chap. 1, n. 11). For a description of the paucity of evidence from the Convention, see Walterscheid, "To Promote the Progress of Science and Useful Arts," 23–54. See also William F. Patry, *Copyright Law and Practice* (Washington, DC: Bureau of National Affairs, 1994), 1:23–24. For information on the absence of debate in state ratifying conventions, see Walterscheid, "To Promote the Progress of Science and Useful Arts," 56. Finally, for a review of all the evidence, see Fenning, "Origin of the Patent and Copyright Clause," 114: the copyright clause "apparently aroused substantially no controversy either in the Convention or among the States adopting the Constitution."

35. Madison, Federalist No. 43, 271–72.

36. Any argument that Madison's rhetoric, regardless of its sincerity, shaped the original understanding of the Constitution must face the same *expressio unius* counterargument set forth at the end of the last subsection.

37. Millar v. Taylor, (1769) 98 Eng. Rep. 201.

38. Donaldson v. Becket, (1774) 98 Eng. Rep. 257 (H.L.). The US Supreme Court later reached a similar conclusion, holding that no federal common-law copyright exists and that all federal copyright "originated, if at all, under the acts of Congress." Wheaton v. Peters, 33 U.S. (8 Pet.) 591, 663 (1834).

39. For example, "The right of property in a slave is distinctly and expressly affirmed in the Constitution." Scott v. Sandford, 60 U.S. 393, 451 (1856). But, according to the Constitution, "neither slavery nor involuntary servitude . . . shall exist within the United States, or any place subject to their jurisdiction." U.S. Const. amend. XIII, § 1.

40. Thomas Jefferson to James Madison, July 31, 1788, in *Republic of Letters*, vol. 1, *1776–1790* (New York: W. W. Norton, 1995), 545.

41. Madison to Jefferson, October 17, 1788, 566 (see n. 11).

42. It is also noteworthy that Jefferson did not raise a natural rights argument either.

43. Madison later made his views on the proper subject matter for property rights, and the need to defend them from monopolies, more clear and public:

> That is not a just government, nor is property secure under it, where arbitrary restrictions, exemptions, and monopolies deny to part of its citizens that free use of their facilities, and free choice of their occupations which not only constitute their property in the general sense of the word, but are the means of acquiring property strictly so called.

James Madison, "Property," in *The Mind of the Founder: Sources of the Political Thought of James Madison*, ed. Marvin Meyers, rev. ed. (Hanover, NH: University Press of New England, 1981), 186–87.

44. See Powell, "Original Understanding," 888–94 (see n. 4). For reactions to Powell's analysis, compare Charles A. Lofgren, "The Original Understanding of Original Intent?," in *Interpreting the Constitution: The Debate over Original Intent*, ed. Jack N. Rakove (Boston: Northwestern University Press, 1990), 117, with Jack N. Rakove, "The Original Intention of Original Understanding," *Constitutional Commentary* 13 (1996): 159–86. Lofgren faults Powell for misusing historical evidence and for ignoring the interpretive understandings of the members of the state ratifying conventions, while Rakove argues that historical evidence does not demonstrate that the Founders thought the intent of the ratifying conventions counted, and agrees with Powell that the members of the Constitutional Convention gave no sign that they thought their intentions should aid in interpreting the Constitution.

45. See Powell, "Original Understanding."

46. See Richard A. Epstein, "Liberty versus Property? Cracks in the Foundations of Copyright Law," *San Diego Law Review* 42 (2005): 4. Epstein argues that critiques of Locke's theory make it "necessary to recast this theory in more consequentialist terms. Once that is done, the gulf between property rights in tangibles and property rights in intangibles is far narrower than [critics of applying Locke's theory to copyright] believe."

47. John Locke, *The Second Treatise of Government*, in *Two Treatises of Government*, ed. Peter Laslett, rev. ed. (Cambridge: Cambridge University Press, 1963 [1690]).

48. Ayn Rand, "Patents and Copyrights," in *Capitalism: The Unknown Ideal* (New York: Signet, 1967), 130–34. For an argument against Rand, see Timothy Sandefur, "A Critique of Ayn Rand's Theory of Intellectual Property Rights," *Journal of Ayn Rand Studies* 9 (2007): 139–61. Herbert Spencer, The Principles of Ethics (Indianapolis: Liberty Fund, 1978), 2:121. Lysander Spooner, *A Letter to Scientists and Inventors, on the Science of Justice, and Their Right of Perpetual Property in Their Discoveries and Inventions*, in *The Collected Works of Lysander Spooner*, ed. Charles Shively (Weston, MA: M & S Press, 1971), 3:68. For a review of these theorists' arguments, an explanation of why they rely on Lockean labor-based moral desert theory, and a critique, see Tom G. Palmer, "Are Patents and Copyrights Morally Justified? The Philosophy of Property Rights and Ideal Objects," *Harvard Journal of Law & Public Policy* 13 (1990): 817–66.

49. See Adam D. Moore, "A Lockean Theory of Intellectual Property," *Hamline Law Review* 21 (1997): 65–108; Wendy J. Gordon, "A Property Right in Self-Expression: Equality and Individualism in the Natural Law of Intellectual Property," *Yale Law Journal* 102 (1993): 1533–609; Alfred C. Yen, "Restoring the Natural Law: Copyright as Labor and Possession," *Ohio State Law Journal* 51 (1990): 517–59. See also the exploration of the uses and limits of the Lockean justification of intellectual property in Justin Hughes, "The Philosophy of Intellectual Property," *Georgetown Law Journal* 77 (1988): 296–331.

50. Epstein observes, "It is easy to imagine how a system of property rights is natural, in the sense that it does not take any state agency to mark off the rights in question," but concludes, "That solution . . . is not possible with copyright." Epstein, "Liberty versus Property," 20.

51. Epstein objects:

> We do have a system of nonwispy copyrights at the present. While one might oppose their creation, the rights in question are capable of sale or licensing, are protected against confiscation and infringement, and are capable of valuation. One might as well give the same dubious description to ordinary contract rights, for which the government cannot take an assignment unless it is prepared to compensate the assignor for the loss of his entitlement.

Ibid., 21. But to say that copyright rights, like contract rights, can be *defined* is neither to say that they qualify as *tangible* nor, more pointedly, that they fit very well into Locke's theory.

52. For an argument from irony, consider this: the text that allegedly inspired a natural rights view of copyright among the Founders, Locke's *Second Treatise of Government*, appears not to have been copyrighted.

53. See Ronan Deazley, *Rethinking Copyright: History, Theory, Language* (Cheltenham, UK: Edward Elgar, 2006), 143–44n32. Deazley reads Locke's correspondence to indicate that "Locke himself did not consider that his theory of property extended to intellectual properties such as copyrights and patents."

54. Locke, *Second Treatise of Government*, 328–29 (chap. 5, § 27). Emphasis in the original.

55. Ibid., 315 (chap. 1, § 6).

56. "Every one as he is *bound to preserve himself*, and not to quit his Station wilfully." Ibid.

57. Epstein, "Liberty versus Property," 11.

58. Ibid., 15.

59. Ibid., 17–18.

60. Ibid., 18.

61. Ibid., 28.

62. John Locke, "Observations on the Printing Act under Consideration in Parliament in 1694," in *The Life of John Locke*, by Peter King (London, 1830), 1:386.

63. See 17 U.S.C. §§ 501–11 (2012), which defines remedies for copyright infringement.

64. "A system of intellectual property rights is not compossible with a system of property rights to tangible objects, especially one's own body, the foundation of the right to property in alienable objects." Tom G. Palmer, "Intellectual Property: A Non-Posnerian Law and Economics Approach," *Hamline Law Review* 12 (1989): 281. See also Tom G. Palmer, "Are Patents and Copyrights Morally Justified?," 827. Here Palmer critiques the Lockean argument for intellectual property rights on the grounds that such "rights" "restrict others' uses of their own bodies in conjunction with resources to which they have full moral and legal rights." And see Douglas G. Baird, "Common Law Intellectual Property and the Legacy of *International News Service v. Associated Press*," *University of Chicago Law Review* 50 (1983): 414. Baird explains, "Granting individuals exclusive rights to . . . information . . . conflicts with other rights in a way that granting exclusive rights to tangible property does not."

65. Locke, *Second Treatise of Government*, 309 (chap. 2, § 4).

66. Though originalists do not always take care to do so, one ought to distinguish between original meaning and original intent. Justice Antonin Scalia explains, "What I look for in the Constitution is precisely what I look for in a statute: the original meaning of the text, not what the original draftsmen intended." Scalia, *A Matter of Interpretation: Federal Courts and the Law* (Princeton, NJ: Princeton University Press, 1997), 38. Scalia searches for original meaning in the writings of Founders who attended the Constitutional Convention, such as Madison and Hamilton, only "because their writings, like those of other intelligent and informed people of the time, display how the text of the Constitution was originally understood." He gives "equal weight" to pieces by John Jay and Jefferson, even though neither man attended the Convention. Ibid. What is the problem with original intent? The untrustworthiness of the records of what transpired during the Constitutional Convention and the states' ratifying conventions, not to mention the problems with ascribing intentions to deliberative bodies, should alone discourage attempts to divine the Constitution's original intent. With regard to copyright in particular, a near-vacuum of recorded debate utterly frustrates the search for original intent. For a description of the historical record of these debates, see Walterscheid, "To Promote the Progress of Science and Useful Arts," 23–54 (see n. 14).

67. U.S. Const. art. I, § 8, cl. 8.

68. See, for example, Scalia, *A Matter of Interpretation*, 37–41.

69. Barnett, *Structure of Liberty*, 22. Emphasis in the original.

70. See ibid., 170, where Barnett describes social relations between humans and vampires.

71. Ibid., 64–65.

72. Ibid., 64, 67.

73. Ibid., 67.

74. Hayek, *Law, Legislation and Liberty*, 1:99 (see chap. 1, n. 123).

75. Ibid., 169n7.

76. Ibid., 72.

77. David Hume, *A Treatise of Human Nature*, ed. Lewis Amherst Selby-Bigge (Oxford:

Clarendon, 1896 [1739]), book III, part II, § VIII, available through The Online Library of Liberty (Liberty Fund), http://oll.libertyfund.org/?option=com_staticxt&staticfile=show .php%3Ftitle=342&chapter=55231&layout=html&Itemid=27.

78. Felix S. Cohen, "Transcendental Nonsense and the Function Approach," *Columbia Law Review* 35 (1935): 836–37.

79. Epstein, "Liberty versus Property," 18.

80. See, for example, Bruce Benson, *The Enterprise of Law: Justice without the State* (San Francisco: Pacific Research Institute for Public Policy, 1990); Harold J. Berman, *Law and Revolution: The Formation of the Western Legal Tradition* (Cambridge, MA: Harvard University Press, 1983).

81. See Benson, *Enterprise of Law*.

82. See the discussion in chapters 2 and 3. See also Alex Kozinski and Christopher Newman, "What's So Fair about Fair Use?," *Bulletin of the Copyright Society of the U.S.A.* 46 (1999): 519–20; and Mark A. Lemley, "Romantic Authorship and the Rhetoric of Property," review of *Shamans, Software, and Spleens: Law and the Construction of the Information Society*, by James Boyle, *Texas Law Review* 75 (1997): 879–95.

83. Fox Film Corp. v. Doyal, 286 U.S. 123, 127 (1932). See also L. Ray Patterson, "Copyright and the 'Exclusive Right' of Authors," *Journal of Intellectual Property Law* 1 (1993): 5. "There is . . . no reason for confusion as to either the source or the nature of copyright. The authoritative pronouncements that copyright is the grant of a limited statutory monopoly are too many and too clear."

Chapter 4: Copyright in Everyday Life

1. John Tehranian, "Infringement Nation: Copyright Reform and the Law/Norm Gap," *Utah Law Review* (2007), 543–48.

2. Ibid., 547.

3. 15 U.S.C. § 333(a)(2)(A) (2012).

4. Id. § (a)(1)(A).

5. Adam Smith, *The Theory of Moral Sentiments*, 6th ed. (1790) (Library of Economics and Liberty, 2000), part 2, § 2, chap. 3, ¶ 21, http://www.econlib.org/Library/Smith/smMS2.html.

6. See Patricia Louise Loughlan, "'You Wouldn't Steal a Car': Intellectual Property and the Language of Theft," *European Intellectual Property Review* 29 (2007): 401–5, available at http://papers.ssrn.com/sol3/papers.cfm?abstract_id=1120585.

7. See Restatement (Second) of Torts § 525 (1977).

8. See Restatement (Second) of Contracts §§ 241–43 (1980).

9. See id. § 90(1).

10. See id. §§ 159–64.

11. See, for example, Cal. Bus. & Prof. Code § 17500 (2013), which prohibits false advertising, and see 15 U.S.C. § 1125(a) (2012), which prohibits unfair competition.

12. Strictly speaking, to sell your own expression as another's would qualify as passing off whereas to sell another's expressive work as your own, as described in the text, would constitute *reverse* passing off. Either kind of passing off can harm consumers by fooling them into buying unwanted goods or services. Passing off expressive works could harm competitors by besmirching their good names, while the reverse passing off of expressive works could deceitfully lure away customers and make them doubt the originality of the copied author.

13. See Thomas Bender and David Sampliner, "Poets, Pirates, and the Creation of American Literature," *New York University Journal of International Law and Politics* 29 (1997): 255–70.

14. See Tom W. Bell, "Authors' Welfare: Copyright as a Statutory Mechanism for Redistributing Rights," *Brooklyn Law Review* 69 (2003): 229–80.

15. For example, "'The touted 'new paradigm' that the Internet gurus tell us we Luddites must adopt sounds to me like old-fashioned trafficking in stolen goods." *The Future of Digital Music: Is There an Upside to Downloading?, Hearings on Copyright Issues and Digital Music on the Internet Before the Senate Judiciary Comm.*, 106th Cong. (2000) (statement of Lars Ulrich, drummer, Metallica).

Chapter 5: The Language of Copyright, an Intellectual ~~Property~~ Privilege

1. For example, *Black's Law Dictionary* calls it "the right of literary property as recognized and sanctioned by positive law." *Black's Law Dictionary*, 6th ed. (1990), s.v. "copyright."

2. For example, *Black's Law Dictionary* also describes copyright as a "privilege." Ibid.

3. See, for example, Eldred v. Ashcroft, 537 U.S. 186, 233 (2003) (Justice Stevens, dissenting); Sony Corp. v. Universal City Studios, Inc., 464 U.S. 417, 421 (1984); Watson v. Buck, 313 U.S. 387, 404 (1941); Bobbs-Merrill Co. v. Straus, 210 U.S. 339, 346 (1908), which explains that "copyright property under the Federal law is wholly statutory"; Creative Technology v. Aztech Systems PTE, 61 F.3d 696, 708 (9th Cir. 1995), which calls copyright "a privilege bestowed by our government upon the author in order to reward creativity"; Williams & Wilkins Co. v. United States, 203 Ct. Cl. 74, 89 (1973); Martinetti v. Maguire, 16 F. Cas. 920, 922 (Cal. Cir. 1867).

4. U.S. Const. art. I, § 8, cl. 8.

5. Patent Act of 1952, 35 U.S.C. §§ 101–376 (2012); Copyright Act of 1976, 17 U.S.C. §§ 101–1332 (2012).

6. See 17 U.S.C. §§ 501–13 (2012), which defines copyright infringement and describes the remedies afforded for infringement.

7. See Palmer, "Are Patents and Copyrights Morally Justified?," 855 (see chap. 3, n. 48); Baird, "Common Law Intellectual Property," 414 (see chap. 3, n. 64).

8. See, for example, Locke, *Second Treatise of Government,* 309 (chap. 2, § 4, lines 3–7) (see chap. 3, n. 47), where Locke explains that in nature all men enjoy "a *State of perfect Freedom* to order their Actions, and dispose of their Possessions, and Persons as they think fit, within the bounds of the Law of Nature, without asking leave, or depending upon the Will of any other Man" (emphasis in the original). See also Thomas Paine, *The Rights of Man* (1791) (New York: Heritage Press, 1961), 39. Paine includes among the natural rights "all those rights of acting as an individual for [one's] own comfort and happiness, which are not injurious to the natural rights of others."

9. Some theoretical models, such as the one presented in chapter 3, suggest that we might suffer an underproduction of expressive works absent the copyright privilege, whereas others, such as the one that will be presented in chapter 11, suggest that we would escape that fate.

10. See 17 U.S.C. § 503 (2012), which provides for the impounding and disposition of infringing articles; id. § 509, which sets up seizure and forfeiture remedies.

11. See id. § 502, which grants the power to issue injunctions against infringement.

12. *Black's Law Dictionary*, s.v. "privilege."

13. See 17 U.S.C. § 501 (2012), which defines actionable infringement; id. § 502, which provides for injunctions against infringement; id. § 504, which provides for awards of damages and profits in copyright infringement cases.

14. See *Black's Law Dictionary*, s.v. "privilege."

15. See Wesley Newcomb Hohfeld, "Some Fundamental Legal Conceptions as Applied in Judicial Reasoning," *Yale Law Journal* 23 (1913): 36.

16. "A 'liberty' considered as a legal relation . . . must mean, if it have any definite content at all, precisely the same thing as *privilege*." Ibid. Later, Hohfeld explains that he prefers to rely on "privilege" because "liberty" "is far more likely to be used in the sense of physical or personal freedom (i.e., absence of physical [*sic*] restraint), as distinguished from a legal relation." Ibid., 43.

17. See Lewis C. Cassidy, "Privilege: Its Past and Present Content," *Mississippi Law Journal* 2 (1929–1930): 326. Cassidy reviews the standard meaning of "privilege," noting, "Conceding . . . the service which has been rendered legal science by the classifications of Professor Hohfeld . . . [his usage] has not as a whole fully commended itself to eminent present-day jurists."

18. For a criticism of Hohfeld's characterization of a liberty as identical to a privilege, see Judith Jarvis Thomson, *The Realm of Rights* (Cambridge, MA: Harvard University Press, 1990), 53–54. Hohfeld's usage, Thomson explains, would have us say that when someone possesses a liberty to do something, such as travel to another state, we mean nothing more than that he has no duty *not* to travel to the other state. Instead, Thomson argues, we mean that other persons have "a duty toward him to not interfere with his doing of it in some appropriately chosen set of ways."

19. See Jessica Litman, "Lawful Personal Use," *Texas Law Review* 85 (2007): 1903–7. Litman uses "copy liberty" to describe certain limits, within copyright law, on copyright holders' powers.

20. For a contrasting approach, see Wendy J. Gordon, "An Inquiry into the Merits of Copyright: The Challenges of Consistency, Consent, and Encouragement Theory," *Stanford Law Review* 41 (1989): 1343–468. Gordon applies Hohfeldian terminology to the Copyright Act, concluding that "because the section 106 grant includes an entitlement 'to do' the enumerated physical acts, creators have a *privilege* to use their creations in the manners specified" (emphasis in the original). Ibid., 1366.

21. Hohfeld, "Some Fundamental Legal Conceptions," 32.

22. For example, "Rights of all sorts restrict what individuals can do with their bodies and property." Moore, "Lockean Theory of Intellectual Property" (see chap. 3, n. 49). See also Gordon, "Inquiry into the Merits of Copyright," 1423.

23. For an explanation of why rights to persons and tangible property carry special authority, see Palmer, "Are Patents and Copyrights Morally Justified?," 855–61. For examples of common-law rights carrying special legal weight, see United States v. Texas, 507 U.S. 529, 534 (1993), which explains the presumption that statutes do not contradict common-law rights; Astoria Federal Savings and Loan Association v. Solimino, 501 U.S. 104, 108 (1991), which explains that statutes operate against a background of common-law principles; Norfolk Redevelopment and Housing Authority v. Chesapeake & Potomac Telephone Co., 464 U.S. 30, 35 (1983), which explains that clear and explicit statutory language is required to repeal the common law. See also U.S. Const. amend. IX, which protects the rights "retained by the people."

24. Adam Mossoff, "Who Cares What Jefferson Thought about Patents? Reevaluating the Patent 'Privilege' in Historical Context," *Cornell Law Review* 92 (2007): 967–76.

25. See Harrison v. Sterry, 9 U.S. (5 Cranch) 289, 298 (1809), which refers to the "privilege to contracts." As for trial by jury, James Madison explains that "trial by jury cannot be considered a natural right, but a right resulting from a social compact . . . as essential to secure the liberty of the people as any one of the pre-existing rights of nature." 1 Annals of Cong. 454 (1789). As for habeas corpus, see Corfield v. Coryell, 6 F. Cas. 546, 552 (C.C.E.D. Pa. 1823) (No. 3, 230), which includes among those "privileges deemed to be fundamental" such rights as habeas corpus.

26. Mossoff, "Who Cares What Jefferson Thought," 969. Mossoff later cites "the omnipresent references to patents as privileges in the late eighteenth and early nineteenth centuries." Ibid., 975–76.

27. Ibid., 971–75.

28. See Locke, *Second Treatise of Government*, 402 (chap. 11, § 142, lines 1–20). Locke describes "the *Bounds* which the trust that is put in them by the Society, and the Law of God and Nature, have *set to the Legislative* Power of every Commonwealth, in all Forms of Government" (emphasis in the original). See also Paine, *Rights of Man*, 39, which notes that "every civil right has for its foundation some natural right pre-existing in the individual," but describes such rights only as "those which relate to security and protection."

29. "Intellectual property rights create large patterns of interference in the freedom of others because abstract objects are a crucial kind of resource.... The analogy between intellectual property rights and other kinds of property rights is only superficial." Peter Drahos, *A Philosophy of Intellectual Property* (Sudbury, MA: Dartmouth, 1996), 212.

30. See, for example, Fox Film Corp. v. Doyal, 286 U.S. 123, 128 (1932), which calls copyright "property derived from a grant by the United States"; and Green v. Biddle, 21 U.S. (8 Wheat.) 1, 57 (1823). See also Justin Hughes, "Copyright and Incomplete Historiographies: Of Piracy, Propertization, and Thomas Jefferson," *Southern California Law Review* 79 (2006): 1004–46; Adam Mossoff, "Is Copyright Property?," *San Diego Law Review* 42 (2005): 36–37.

31. Edmund Sanders and Jube Shiver Jr., "Digital TV Copyright Concerns Tentatively Resolved by Group," *Los Angeles Times*, April 26, 2002 (quoting Valenti's speech before a congressional committee).

32. Doug Bedell, "Piracy Enforcement Flounders with Rise of MP3," *Dallas Morning News*, August 11, 1999 (quoting Rosen).

33. See, for example, Frank H. Easterbrook, "Intellectual Property Is Still Property," *Harvard Journal of Law & Public Policy* 13 (1990): 108–18; Yen, "Restoring the Natural Law" (see chap. 3, n. 49); Rand, "Patents and Copyrights," 130–34.

34. See *Black's Law Dictionary*, s.v. "property," which defines property as "in the strict legal sense, an aggregate of rights which are guaranteed and protected by government." See also O. Lee Reed, "What Is 'Property'?," *American Business Law Journal* 41 (2004): 471–72.

35. See, for example, Kaiser Aetna v. United States, 444 U.S. 164, 176 (1979), which describes the right to exclude as "one of the most essential sticks in the bundle of rights that are commonly characterized as property"; Florida Prepaid Postsecondary Educational Expense Board v. College Savings Bank, 527 U.S. 627, 673 (1999), which describes the right as "the hallmark of a protected property interest"; Thomas W. Merrill, "Property and the Right to Exclude," *Nebraska Law Review* 77 (1998): 731, which says the right is "a necessary and sufficient condition of identifying the existence of property." But see Adam Mossoff, "What Is Property? Putting the Pieces Back Together," *Arizona Law Review* 45 (2003): 371–443. Mossoff criticizes the view that exclusion is the *sine qua non* of property, and argues for also defining property in terms of acquisition, use, and disposal.

36. "The right to exclude in intellectual property entitlements exists by legal fiat. It is solely a creation of the law with no natural counterpart in the actual facts of how people interact in the world." Mossoff, "Is Copyright Property?," 39. Notably, however, Mossoff argues that the orthodox view of property focuses too narrowly on exclusivity, and that a broader view of property's attributes might allow it to encompass copyright. Ibid., 40–42.

37. 18 U.S.C. § 106 (2012) specifies that "the owner of copyright under this title has the exclusive right to do and to authorize any of" six uses of a work. But it states that the exclusive rights defined in § 106 come only "subject to sections 107 through 122" of the act.

38. "Copyright lawyers of all stripes agree that copyright includes a free zone in which individuals may make personal use of copyrighted works without legal liability.... [But] differ-

ently striped copyright lawyers will differ vehemently on whether a particular personal use is lawful or infringing." Litman, "Lawful Personal Use," 1872.

39. See, for example, 17 USC § 107 (2012), which defines fair use; id. § 111(c)–(d), which mandates the compulsory licensing of secondary transmissions by cable systems; id. § 112(e), which provides for the compulsory licensing of certain ephemeral recordings; id. § 114(d)(2), (e)–(f), which relates to the compulsory licensing of public performances of sound recordings via digital audio transmissions; id. § 115, which describes compulsory licensing for the making and distribution of phone records; id. § 118(b)(3), (d), which stipulates that the librarian of Congress may establish a binding schedule of rates and terms for the use of certain copyrighted works by public broadcasting entities.

40. For a summary of patent law's experimental use and shop right doctrines, see Simone A. Rose, "On Purple Pills, Stem Cells, and Other Market Failures: A Case for a Limited Compulsory Licensing Scheme for Patent Property," *Howard Law Journal* 48 (2005): 614n170.

41. See *Black's Law Dictionary*, s.v. "use."

42. See, for example, Mossoff, "What Is Property?," 381, 385, 390–403.

43. Authors who keep their works unpublished of course enjoy special use rights, even in a state of nature. They find it hard to profit from such secret works, however. The Copyright Act thus allows authors to both publish their works and profit from them.

44. 17 U.S.C. § 114(a), which denies the holders of sound recordings the exclusive right to public performances of their works.

45. See id. § 201 (2012), which describes the ownership and transfer of copyrights.

46. Id. §§ 203, 304(c), and 304(d). These sections also allow certain members of dead authors' estates to exercise termination rights—see id. §§ 203(a)(1)–(2) and 304(c)–(d), which reference parties defined in § 304(a)(1)(C). Those termination rights come with strings attached, granted. See id. §§ 203(a)(3), 304(c)(3), and 304(d)(2), which specify that termination rights last for only five years; id. §§ 203(a)(3) and 304(c)(1), (3), which provide that termination rights do not arise before thirty-five years after the grant; id. §§ 203(a)(4), 304(c)(4), and 304(d)(1), which limit the form and timing of the notice of termination. Nonetheless, termination rights remain very real.

47. See, for example, Restatement (Second) of Contracts § 208 (1979), which describes comparatively narrow conditions under which a court might refuse to enforce a contract on grounds of unconscionability, and the relatively constrained termination of rights effectuated in such cases.

48. 17 U.S.C. §§ 203(a)(5) and 304(c)(5) (2012). See also id. § 304(d)(1), which incorporates the conditions of § 304(c)(5) by reference. But see id. §§ 203(b)(4), 304(c)(6)(D), and 304(d)(1), which allow for the enforcement of a post-termination grant or of an agreement to make such a grant if the grant or agreement occurs between certain parties and after proper notice of termination has been given.

49. See also Davis v. Blige, 505 F.3d 90 (2d Cir. 2007), which held that, while a copyright co-owner can license exclusive rights in the co-owned work without the permission of other co-owners, a copyright co-owner's retroactive licensing of such rights cannot preclude co-owners from suing the licensee for infringement. As William F. Patry points out, the opinion "broadly eliminates one of the central tenets of the 1976 Act: the alienability of one co-owner's rights without the permission of the other co-author(s)." Patry, "Second Circuit Goes to the Dark Side," *Copyright Blog*, October 8, 2007, http://williampatry.blogspot.com /2007/10/second-circuit-goes-to-dark-side.html.

50. See Lydia Pallas Loren, "Building a Reliable Semicommons of Creative Works: Enforcement of Creative Commons Licenses and Limited Abandonment of Copyright," *George Mason Law Review* 14 (2007): 321–22. Loren interprets cases and commentary to hold that copyright owners cannot abandon only a portion of their rights. See also Robert

A. Kreiss, "Abandoning Copyrights to Try to Cut Off Termination Rights," *Missouri Law Review* 58 (1993): 111–23. Kreiss argues that the Copyright Act's termination provisions should limit the effectiveness of an abandonment made before the vesting of any contingent reversionary rights.

51. Epstein, "Liberty versus Property," 20 (see chap. 3, n. 46). Epstein goes on to defend copyright on consequentialist grounds, saying, "On balance, as with tangible objects, the pairing of liberty and property seems to survive, even if it does not exactly prosper." Ibid., 24.

52. Ronan Deazley, professor of copyright law at the University of Glasgow, reads Locke's correspondence to indicate that "Locke himself did not consider [that] his theory of property extended to intellectual properties such as copyrights and patents," and instead recognized that it could exist only grace of parliamentary action. Deazley, *Rethinking Copyright*, 144n32 (see chap. 3, n. 53).

53. See 35 U.S.C. § 154(a)(2) (2012), which specifies the limits of a patent term; 17 U.S.C. § 302 (2012), which specifies the limits of a copyright term. But see Eldred v. Ashcroft, 537 U.S. 186, 199–218 (2003), which upholds the constitutionality of a retroactive copyright term extension.

54. *Arguments Before the Committees on Patents on S. 6330 and H.R.19853*, 59th Cong. 116 (1906) (statement of Samuel L. Clemens [Mark Twain, pseud.], author).

55. Mark Twain, "Copyright," in *Mark Twain's Speeches* (New York: Harper & Brothers, 1910), 324–27. See also 144 Cong. Rec. 9946, 9952 (1998): a statement of Mary Bono, that "Sonny [Bono] wanted the term of copyright protection to last forever."

56. U.S. Const. art. I, § 8, cl. 8. The Constitution authorizes Congress to secure for only "limited Times" authors' rights.

57. U.S. Const. amend. V.

58. See Reed, "What Is 'Property'?," 473–83.

59. Thomas F. Cotter, "Do Federal Uses of Intellectual Property Implicate the Fifth Amendment?" *Florida Law Review* 50 (1998): 532. Cotter observes that the issue "has evoked wildly differing responses, ranging from the view that virtually all government uses of intellectual property constitute takings to the view that virtually none of them do."

60. Zoltek Corp. v. United States, 442 F.3d 1345 (Fed. Cir. 2006), rehearing denied, 464 F.3d 1335, 1350 (Fed. Cir. 2006), *certiorari* denied, 127 S. Ct. 2936, 168 L. Ed. 2d 262 (2007), held that patent infringement by the federal government does not constitute a taking under the Fifth Amendment.

61. Notably, most commentary arguing that copyright takings merit compensation under the Fifth Amendment predates *Zoltek*. See, for example, Laurie Messerly, "'Taking' Away Music Copyrights: Does Compulsory Licensing of Music on the Internet Violate the Fifth Amendment's Takings Clause?" (Center for Individual Freedom policy paper, 2002), accessed September 19, 2009, http://www.cfif.org/htdocs/legal_issues/legal _activities/policy_papers/copyright.htm; Eugene Volokh, "Sovereign Immunity and Intellectual Property," *Southern California Law Review* 73 (2000): 1163n5; Cotter, "Do Federal Uses of Intellectual Property Implicate the Fifth Amendment?," 532. But see Adam Mossoff, "Patents as Constitutional Private Property: The Historical Protection of Patents under the Takings Clause," *Boston University Law Review* 87 (2007): 689–724. Mossoff, writing after the Federal Circuit decided *Zoltek* but before the Supreme Court denied *certiorari*, admits that "most agree that the status of patents as constitutional private property is far from clear," but attributes that to a misunderstanding of patent law's history. Ibid., 695.

62. *Zoltek*, 127 S. Ct.

63. Ruckelshaus v. Monsanto Co., 467 U.S. 986, 1001 (1984).

64. U.S. Const. art. I, § 8, cl. 8.

65. See, for example, Madhavi Sunder, "IP3," *Stanford Law Review* 59 (2006): 315n325; Craig Anthony "Tony" Arnold, "The Reconstitution of Property: Property as a Web of Interests," *Harvard Environmental Law Review* 26 (2002): 331–41; Jeff C. Dodd, "Rights in Information: Conversion and Misappropriation Causes of Action in Intellectual Property Cases," *Houston Law Review* 32 (1995): 465–66. Dodd calls the "web of relationships" school of thought "one of the oldest theories of property."

66. Arnold, "Reconstitution of Property," 333.

67. Ibid., 335.

68. See Hughes, "Copyright and Incomplete Historiographies," 997 (see n. 30); Alfred C. Yen, "*Eldred*, the First Amendment, and Aggressive Copyright Claims," *Houston Law Review* 40 (2003): 678.

69. "Piracy is rampant and . . . surveys show the prevailing attitude toward copyright is one of either incomprehension or disrespect." James Gibson, "Once and Future Copyright," *Notre Dame Law Review* 81 (2005): 230. See also Andrew P. Lycans, "Cyberdemons: Regulating a Truly World-Wide Web," review of *Beyond Our Control? Confronting the Limits of Our Legal System in the Age of Cyberspace*, by Stuart Biegel, *Michigan Law Review* 101 (2003): 1941. Lycans admits that "the prevailing social norms in cyberspace do reflect a belief that copyright laws somehow do not apply there," but argues that "this does not mean that society should abandon copyright law on the web as it now stands because of these social norms."

70. Arnold, "Reconstitution of Property," 363.

71. Drahos, *Philosophy of Intellectual Property*, 215. Drahos advocates "property instrumental-ism" and observes, "Property cannot, in an instrumentalist theory of property, operate as a fundamental value or right, for this would push the theory in proprietary directions."

72. "The property instrumentalism we are developing proposes a limited negative metaphysical thesis: there are not natural rights of property. This thesis has a corollary. Property instrumentalism embraces a radical skepticism about the nature of property." Ibid., 216.

73. This untoward consequence of creating a special copyright right should surprise no one, however. As Randy E. Barnett warned, we should "temper our enthusiasm for recognizing rights. For the background rights that define justice serve also to legitimate the use of force or violence to secure compliance. *The more rights we recognize the more violence we legitimate*" (emphasis in the original). Barnett, *Structure of Liberty*, 200 (see chap. 1, n. 6).

74. It is not a case of unfair competition law, of course, since no entity can justly claim the exclusive right to sell goods or services under the mark "property"; I speak here only by analogy.

75. See the description of the views of copyright expressed by Internet users who exchange music files in Michael W. Carroll, "Whose Music Is It Anyway? How We Came to View Musical Expression as a Form of Property," *University of Cincinnati Law Review* 72 (2004): 1406–7. Also, "Many believe that 'information wants to be free' since the majority of the public fails to respect copyright law and instead ignores it." Laura N. Gasaway, "The New Access Right and Its Impact on Libraries and Library Users," *Journal of Intellectual Property Law* 10 (2003): 291.

76. See Deazley, *Rethinking Copyright*, 144; Drahos, *Philosophy of Intellectual Property*, 211. Drahos warns that the expansion of intellectual property rights "threatens the core of nega-tive liberty." But see Hughes, "Copyright and Incomplete Historiographies," 1046–67. Hughes disputes the propitiation analysis of trends in copyright policy.

77. See U.S. Const., preamble, which specifies the government's aim to "promote the gen-eral Welfare," in contrast to that of special interests; id. at art. I, § 8, cl. 8, which permits copyrights only "To promote the Progress of Science and useful Arts, by securing for lim-ited Times to Authors" rights to their writings; id. at art. II, § 1, cl. 9, which specifies that the president shall take an oath or affirmation to uphold the Constitution; id. at art. VI,

cl. 3, which specifies that senators and representatives shall take such an oath also; id. at
amends. I–VII, which protect certain common-law and natural rights; id. at amend. IX,
which, notwithstanding those enumerated rights, protects those "retained by the people."

Chapter 6: Copyright Politics: Indelicately Imbalanced

1. See, for example, Sony Corporation v. Universal City Studios, Inc., 464 U.S. 417, 429
    (1984); American Geophysical Union v. Texaco, Inc., 60 F.3d 913, 917 (2nd Cir. 1994);
    Recording Industry Association v. Copyright Royalty Tribunal, 662 F.2d 1, 17 (D.C. Cir.
    1981); David Nimmer et al., "The Metamorphosis of Contract into Expand," *California
    Law Review* 87 (1999): 19.

2. Note that copyright policy aims at offsetting not just private interests against public ones,
    but, more precisely, the select private interests of copyright holders against both (1) the many
    private parties who suffer violation of their common-law rights under copyright and (2) the
    public's interest in the positive externalities generated by free access to expressive works.

3. U.S. Const., preamble.

4. Id. at art. I, cl. 8, § 8.

5. Copyright Act of 1790, 1 Stat. 124 (1790), § 1, reprinted in Copyright Office, *Copyright
    Enactments*, 22 (see chap. 1, n. 15). For a discussion of the subtleties in the terms provided
    under this and subsequent copyright acts, see Patry, "Failure of the American Copyright
    System," 915–23 (see chap. 1, n. 11).

6. An Act to Amend the Several Acts Respecting Copyrights, 4 Stat. 436 (February 3, 1831),
    §§ 1–2, reprinted in Copyright Office, *Copyright Enactments*, 27. The act retroactively
    extended by fourteen years copyrights still in their first term as of its effective date. Id. § 16.

7. Copyright Act of 1909, 17 U.S.C. § 23 (1909) (repealed 1978). The act retroactively
    extended by fourteen years copyrights extant at its effective date. Id. § 24.

8. 17 U.S.C. § 302(a) (2012). The act gave works authored anonymously, pseudonymously, or
    for hire a term the lesser of publication plus seventy-five years or creation plus one hun-
    dred years. Id. § 302(c). It retroactively extended to seventy-five years copyrights extant at
    its effective date. Id. § 304(a), (b).

9. Sonny Bono Copyright Term Extension Act, Pub. L. No. 105–298, 112 Stat. 2827 (1998),
    codified at 17 U.S.C. § 302(a)–(b) (2012). Works made anonymously, pseudonymously,
    or for hire get a copyright term lasting the lesser of publication plus 95 years or cre-
    ation plus 120 years. Id. § 302(c). The amendment applies retroactively to copyrights
    that originated under the 1976 act. Id. § 302(a)–(c). It retroactively extends to 95 years
    copyrights extant at its effective date that had originated under the 1909 act. Id. § 304
    (a)–(b).

10. Professor James Boyle has quite rightly observed that in some respects the graph overstates
    the effective copyright term under the early acts, which imposed formalities limiting or
    completely prohibiting copyrights in many works, and that the graph thus understates the
    effective increase in copyright terms under recent acts. James Boyle, "Tom Bell Thinks ©
    Extensions Are Mickey Mouse," *The Public Domain* (blog), August 7, 2009, http://www
    .thepublicdomain.org/2009/08/07/tom-bell-thinks-©-extensions-are-mickey-mouse/.
    I lack the data necessary to trace the effective median copyright term per copyrightable
    work over time, however.

11. See Eldred v. Ashcroft, 537 U.S. 186, 204 (2003): "Guided by text, history, and precedent,
    we cannot agree with petitioners' submission that extending the duration of existing copy-
    rights is categorically beyond Congress' authority under the Copyright Clause."

12. See U.S. Const. art. I, § 8, cl. 8, which empowers Congress "To promote the Progress of
    Science and useful Arts, by securing for limited Times to Authors . . . the exclusive Right to
    their . . . Writings."

13. Id.

14. Copyright Act of 1790, 1 Stat. 124 (1790), § 1, in Copyright Office, *Copyright Enactments*, 22.

15. Act of April 29, 1802, chap. 15, 2 Stat. 171 (1802), § 2, reprinted in Copyright Office, *Copyright Enactments*, 24–25.

16. An Act to Amend the Several Acts Respecting Copyrights, 4 Stat. 436 (February 3, 1831), § 1, in Copyright Office, *Copyright Enactments*, 27.

17. An Act Supplemental to an Act Entitled "An Act to Amend the Several Acts Respecting Copyright," Approved February Third, Eighteen Hundred and Thirty-One, 11 Stat. 138 (August 18, 1856), reprinted in Copyright Office, *Copyright Enactments*, 33.

18. An Act Supplemental to an Act Entitled "An Act to Amend the Several Acts Respecting Copyright," Approved February Third, Eighteen Hundred and Thirty-One, and to the Acts in Addition Thereto and Amendment Thereof, 13 Stat. 540, § 1 (March 3, 1865), reprinted in Copyright Office, *Copyright Enactments*, 34.

19. An Act to Revise, Consolidate, and Amend the Statutes Relating to Patents and Copyrights, 16 Stat. 212 (July 8, 1870), § 86, reprinted in Copyright Office, *Copyright Enactments*, 36–7. A subsequent act temporarily moved the registration of engravings, cuts, or prints not connected with the fine arts from the Copyright Office to the Patent Office. An Act to Amend the Law Relating to Patents, Trademarks, and Copyrights, 18 Stat. 78 (June 18, 1874), § 3, reprinted in Copyright Office, *Copyright Enactments*, 47–8. This purely administrative move apparently had no effect on the copyrightability of such works, however. See also An Act to Transfer Jurisdiction over Commercial Prints and Labels, for the Purpose of Copyright Registration, to the Register of Copyrights, 54 Stat. 51 (July 31, 1939), reprinted in Copyright Office, *Copyright Enactments*, 99, which repeals the act of June 18, 1874, and refers throughout to copyrights registered in the Patent Office.

20. Act of Aug. 24, 1912, ch. 356, 37 Stat. 488 (1912), reprinted in Copyright Office, *Copyright Enactments*, 87.

21. Act of July 17, 1952, Pub. L. No. 82-575, 66 Stat. 752 (1952), reprinted in Copyright Office, *Copyright Enactments*, 127.

22. The Sound Recording Act, Pub. L. No. 92-140, 85 Stat. 391 (1971), § (a), reprinted in Copyright Office, *Copyright Enactments*, 135-M, amending 17 U.S.C. § 102.

23. Pub. L. No. 96-517, 94 Stat. 3015, 3028 (1980), amending 17 U.S.C. § 101.

24. The Architectural Works Copyright Protection Act, Pub. L. No. 101-650, 701–706, 104 Stat. 5089, 5133 (1990), amending 17 U.S.C. § 102(8).

25. See An Act Providing for the Public Printing and Binding and the Distribution of Public Documents, 28 Stat. 608, § 52 (January 12, 1895), reprinted in Copyright Office, *Copyright Enactments*, 55. A subsequent act modified but did not clearly expand the scope of this exception. See An Act to Permit the Printing of Black-and-White Illustrations of United States and Foreign Postage Stamps for Philatelic Purposes, 52 Stat. 6 (January 27, 1938), which in § 1 provides that the United States may secure copyrights in black-and-white illustrations of its postage stamps and in § 2 exempts from criminal sanctions the reproduction of stamp images for collecting purposes.

26. 17 U.S.C. § 106A (2012) creates attribution and integrity rights for authors of works of visual art.

27. 17 U.S.C. §§ 1301–32 (2012).

28. 17 U.S.C. §§ 1201–5 (2012) sets up civil and criminal penalties for a variety of acts that might interfere with the effectiveness of copyright management systems.

29. Copyright Act of 1790, 1 Stat. 124 (1790), § 1, in Copyright Office, *Copyright Enactments*, 22. The act grants to copyright owners "the sole right and liberty of printing, reprinting,

publishing and vending" covered works. But see id. §§ 2, 23, which provides a remedy against unauthorized printing, reprinting, publishing, or *importation* of copyrighted works.

30. 17 U.S.C. § 106 (2012).

31. Copyright Act of 1790, 1 Stat. 124 (1790), § 2, in Copyright Office, *Copyright Enactments*, 23. This section provides for the forfeiture of infringing copies to the copyright owner, "who shall forthwith destroy the same," and for payment "of fifty cents for every [infringing] sheet which shall be found in his or their possession," payable in equal halves to the copyright owner and the United States.

32. 17 U.S.C. § 503 (2012) provides the civil remedies of impounding and disposition of infringing articles and devices used in infringing works. See also id. §§ 506(b), 509, which provides similar remedies in criminal cases.

33. Id. § 504.

34. Id. § 505.

35. Id. §§ 601–3.

36. Id. § 512(h).

37. Id. § 506 calls for criminal punishments in certain cases as provided under 18 U.S.C. § 2319 (2012), which sets forth applicable fines and prison terms. See also 17 U.S.C. §§ 506(b) and 509 (2012), which provide in criminal cases for the seizure and forfeiture to the United States of infringing items and devices used to infringe.

38. Copyright Act of 1790, 1 Stat. 124 (1790), in Copyright Office, *Copyright Enactments*, 22–24. The word count is my estimate.

39. 17 U.S.C. §§ 101–803, 1001–1332 (2012). The word count is my estimate.

40. Id. § 119.

41. Id. § 121. See also id. § 110(8)–(9), which allows, under certain conditions, for the performance of literary works for disabled persons.

42. Id. § 512. Note that, strictly speaking, § 512 does not limit rights under the Copyright Act, but rather the remedies for infringement.

43. See also id. at 111(a)–(b), (e), which allows secondary transmissions embodying performances or displays of a work under certain conditions; id. § 112, which allows transmitting organizations to make ephemeral recordings under certain conditions; id. § 113(c), which allows advertisements, commentaries, and news reports to distribute or display useful articles embodying copyrighted works; id. § 114(a)–(c), which limits rights in sound recordings so as to safeguard copyrights in the underlying works thus recorded; id. § 114(d), which defines rights in sound recordings so as to allow their performance via digital audio transmission under certain conditions; id. § 120(b), which allows alterations of buildings embodying copyrighted works.

44. See id. § 108, which allows reproduction by libraries and archives under certain conditions; id. § 110(1)–(4), (6), (10), which allows nonprofit entities to perform or display works under certain conditions; id. § 110(7), which allows the performance of nondramatic musical works to promote sales; id. § 117, which excuses functionally necessary or archival copying of computer programs; id. § 120(a), which allows representations of architectural works constructed in public places and alterations of buildings embodying copyrighted works. See also id. § 513, which provides for the determination of reasonable license fees charged by performing rights societies. Note that, strictly speaking, § 513 does not limit rights under the Copyright Act, but rather the remedies for infringement.

45. See id. § 107, which codifies the fair use doctrine.

46. See id. § 109, which codifies the first-sale doctrine.

47. With regard to the codification of the fair use doctrine, see Harper & Row, Publishers, Inc.

v. Nation Enterprises, 471 U.S. 539, 549 (1985), which states that § 107 was "intended to restate the [preexisting] judicial doctrine of fair use, not to change, narrow, or enlarge it in any way," quoting H.R. Rep. No. 94-1476, p. 66 (1976), reprinted in 1976 U.S.C.C.A.N. at 5680. See also S. Rep. No. 473, 94th Cong., 1st Sess. 62 (1976), which makes the same statement. With regard to the codification of the first sale doctrine, see Paul Goldstein, *Goldstein on Copyright*, 2nd ed. 2005 supp., vol. 2, § 5.6.1 at 5:106–108, which credits Bobbs-Merrill Co. v. Straus, 210 U.S. 339 (1908), the leading case in a long line of decisions, as the holding that Congress codified in the Copyright Act of 1909, chap. 320, § 41, 35 Stat. 1075, 1084 (1909). The Copyright Revision Act of 1976, Pub. L. No. 94-553, 90 Stat. 2541, replaced § 41 with 17 U.S.C. § 109 (2012), the current codification of the first-sale doctrine, without substantially altering it. With regard to the first-sale doctrine, moreover, federal lawmakers have repeatedly trimmed back the judicial exception that they earlier codified. See The Record Rental Amendment of 1984, Pub. L. No. 98-450, 98 Stat. 1727 (October 4, 1984), codified as amended at 17 U.S.C. § 109(b) (2012), which excludes sound recordings from the scope of the first-sale doctrine; The Computer Software Rental Amendments Act of 1990, Pub. L. No. 101-650, Tit. VIII § 804, 104 Stat. 5136 (December 1, 1990), codified at 17 U.S.C. § 109(b) (2012), which excludes computer programs from the scope of the first-sale doctrine.

48. Seminal works on public choice theory include James M. Buchanan and Gordon Tullock, *The Calculus of Consent: Logical Foundations of Constitutional Democracy* (Ann Arbor: University of Michigan Press, 1962); Mancur Olson Jr., *The Logic of Collective Action: Public Goods and the Theory of Groups* (Cambridge, MA: Harvard University Press, 1965).

49. For a description of the interest group dynamics affecting copyright legislation, see Jessica Litman, "Copyright and Information Policy," *Law and Contemporary Problems* 55 (1992): 187–95. For a description of the legislative processes through which commercial interests shaped the 1976 Copyright Act, see Jessica Litman, "Copyright, Compromise, and Legislative History," *Cornell Law Review* 72 (1987): 865–79.

50. For a description calling questions about the optimality of copyright's *quid pro quo* "vacuous," see Ejan Mackaay, "Economic Incentives in Markets for Information and Innovation," *Harvard Journal of Law & Public Policy* 13 (1990): 906.

51. See Friedrich A. Hayek, *Individualism and the Economic Order* (Chicago: University of Chicago Press, 1948), 77–78, which explains that the knowledge essential for central planning does not exist in concentrated form.

52. See Buchanan and Tullock, *Calculus of Consent; Olson, Logic of Collective Action.*

53. Douglas Hedencamp, "Free Mickey Mouse: Copyright Notice, Derivative Works, and the Copyright Act of 1909," *Virginia Sports and Entertainment Law Journal* 2 (2003): 256.

54. "Walt Disney failed to place his name in the copyright notices of the first few Mickey Mouse films. This forfeited the copyrights in those films, as well as the copyright in the original incarnation of Mickey Mouse." Ibid., 255. See also Lauren Vanpelt, "Mickey Mouse—A Truly Public Character" (Student Paper in Advanced Copyright, Arizona State University College of Law, Spring 1999), http://www.public.asu.edu/~dkarjala/public domain/Vanpelt-s99.html.

55. Joseph Menn, "Disney's Rights to Mickey Mouse May Be Wrong," *Los Angeles Times*, August 22, 2008, http://articles.latimes.com/2008/aug/22/business/fi-mickey22.

56. Copyright Act of 1976, Pub. L. No. 94-553, § 302, 90 Stat. 2541, 2572–73 (codified as amended in 17 U.S.C.).

57. Sonny Bono Copyright Term Extension Act, Pub. L. No. 105-298, 112 Stat. 2827 (1998) (codified in scattered sections of 17 U.S.C.).

58. Compare 17 U.S.C. § 304(a) (2012), which describes the term of copyrights in their first term as of January 1, 1978, with id. § 304(b), which describes the term of copyrights, such as the copyright presumed to exist in *Steamboat Willie*, in their second term as of January 1, 1978.

59. For evidence of Disney's lobbying efforts, see Jessica Litman, *Digital Copyright* (Amherst, NY: Prometheus Press, 2000), 23.

60. It seems safe to say that we do not face that particular problem. To the contrary, exhausted from being bombarded with music in public spaces, some have called for an annual "No Music Day." Michael White, "Who'll Stop the Ring Tones?," *New York Times*, November 18, 2007.

61. See, for example, Steven E. Siwek, "Copyright Industries in the U.S. Economy: The 2003–2007 Report" (Economists Incorporated, prepared for the International Intellectual Property Alliance, Washington, DC, June 2009), http://www.iipa.com/pdf/IIPASiwek Report2003-07.pdf. Siwek reports that US copyright industries had growth rates well above that of the US economy as a whole during the studied period. Compare with Eric H. Smith, foreword to ibid., 1–2: "Economic reports such as this are but one piece of evidence that governments should use to justify far more effective legal and enforcement regimes to promote and foster the growth of the content-based industries in their national economies."

62. See Pierre Breese, "Olfactory Measurement Methods Linked to Sensory Analysis, Designation and Comparison Tools for Use by the Legal Expert," *Seminars in Food Analysis* 3 (1998): 114–18; US Copyright Office, "Recipes" (see chap. 1, n. 33); Raustiala and Sprigman, "Piracy Paradox" (see chap. 1, n. 39); Joyce et al., *Copyright Law*, 200 (see same note); Peters, "Note, When Patent and Trademark Law Hit the Fan," 126 (see same note); H.R. Rep. No. 735, 101st Cong., 2d Sess. 20 (1990).

63. Although some of the works listed here could in theory win design patent coverage under US law, "the patent process has proved too rigid, slow, and costly for the fast-moving, short-lived products of mass consumption, and too strict in excluding the bulk of all commercial designs on grounds of obviousness." J. H. Reichman, "Legal Hybrids between the Patent and Copyright Paradigms," *Columbia Law Review* 94 (1994): 2460.

64. See Epstein, *Simple Rules for a Complex World* (see chap. 1, n. 118).

Chapter 7: Fair Use vs. Fared Use

1. See David Stipp, "The Electric Kool-Aid Management Consultant," *Fortune* (October 16, 1995), 160, 166. Stipp characterizes "information wants to be free" as the "cyberhacker rallying cry," and attributes it to Stewart Brand, founder of the *Whole Earth Catalog*.

2. In defense of Brand (see previous note), he actually came fairly close to my interpretation of the epigram in an early formulation of his now-widespread dictum: "Information wants to be free because it has become so cheap to distribute, copy and recombine—too cheap to meter. It wants to be expensive because it can be immeasurably valuable to the recipient." Stewart Brand, *The Media Lab: Inventing the Future at M.I.T.* (New York: Viking, 1987), 202.

3. See, for example, American Geophysical Union v. Texaco, Inc., 60 F.3d 913 (2d Cir. 1994); Princeton University Press v. Michigan Document Services, Inc. 99 F.3d 1381 (6th Cir. 1996).

4. I disavow the view that "if a market is physically available, imposing infringement liability on all copiers will not discourage desirable use of copyrighted works." Wendy J. Gordon and Daniel Bahls, "The Public's Right to Fair Use: Amending Section 107 to Avoid the 'Fared Use' Fallacy," *Utah Law Review* (2007), 621. Gordon and Bahls evidently mean something quite different by "fared use" from what I mean here, or from what I meant in my earlier writings on the topic, where I explain, "Technical prowess alone does not justify . . . censorship. . . . Public policy and copyright law pose additional hurdles, and . . . quite high ones." Bell, "Fair Use vs. Fared Use: The Impact of Automated Rights Management on Copyright's Fair Use Doctrine," *North Carolina Law Review* 76 (1998): 591. Nonetheless, I continue to agree with Gordon's caution, "A refusal to license must not automatically justify a right to fair use; markets can function only if owners

have a right to say 'no' as well as 'yes.'" Wendy J. Gordon, "Fair Use as Market Failure: A Structural and Economic Analysis of the *Betamax* Case and Its Predecessors," *Columbia Law Review* 82 (1982): 1634.

5. The relevant part reads, "The fair use of a copyrighted work . . . for purposes such as criticism, comment, news reporting, teaching (including multiple copies for classroom use), scholarship, or research, is not an infringement of copyright." 17 U.S.C. § 107 (2012).

6. See, for example, Eldred v. Ashcroft, 537 U.S. 186, 220 (2003), which describes fair use as one of copyright law's "built-in First Amendment accommodations."

7. I thank law professor and copyright scholar Jane C. Ginsburg for first bringing this point to my attention, during a conversation in the winter of 1996.

8. 17 U.S.C. § 107 (2012).

9. Richard A. Posner, *Economic Analysis of Law*, 3rd ed. (Boston: Little, Brown, 1986), 6.

10. See Landes and Posner, "Economic Analysis of Copyright Law," 357–58 (see chap. 2, n. 5); Gordon, "Fair Use as Market Failure," 1613–23.

11. Gordon, *Fair Use as Market Failure*, 1601.

12. American Geophysical Union v. Texaco, Inc., 60 F.3d 913, 931 (2d Cir. 1994). See also Princeton University Press v. Michigan Document Services, Inc., 99 F.3d 1381, 1387n4 (6th Cir. 1996).

13. Courts and commentators have given a variety of formulations to what sort of *quid* will balance the *quo* of copyright's statutory monopoly. For example, compare the following two cases. Feist Publications, Inc. v. Rural Telephone Service Co., Inc., 499 U.S. 340, 349–50 (1991): "The primary objective of copyright is not to reward the labor of authors, but 'to promote the Progress of Science and useful Arts.' To this end, copyright assures authors the right to their original expression, but encourages others to build freely upon the *ideas and information conveyed by* a work" (emphasis added). Sony Corporation v. Universal City Studios, Inc., 464 U.S. 417, 429 (1984): "The monopoly privileges that Congress may authorize are neither unlimited nor primarily designed to provide a special private benefit. Rather, the limited grant . . . . is intended to motivate the creative activity of authors and inventors by the provision of a special reward, and to allow the public access to the products of their genius *after the limited period of exclusive control* has expired" (emphasis added). Also compare Robert A. Kreiss, "Accessibility and Commercialization in Copyright Theory," *UCLA Law Review* 43 (1995): 20. Kreiss argues, "The constitutional goals of copyright are the advancement of learning and knowledge. The means to achieve those ends is the incentive system which induces authors *to create and disseminate their works*" (emphasis added). For a general discussion about how US copyright law strives to achieve a balance between incentives and access, see Goldstein, *Goldstein on Copyright*, 2nd ed. 2005 supp., vol. 1, § 1.14.

14. See Dennis S. Karjala, "Federal Preemption of Shrinkwrap and On-Line Licenses," *University of Dayton Law Review* 22 (1997): 521; Pierre N. Leval, "Toward a Fair Use Standard," *Harvard Law Review* 103 (1990): 1110, which describes fair use as "a necessary part" of the copyright monopoly; Laura N. Gasaway et al., "Amicus Advocacy: Brief *Amicus Curiae* of Eleven Copyright Law Professors in *Princeton University Press v. Michigan Document Services, Inc.,*" *Journal of Intellectual Property Law* 2 (1994): 203; L. Ray Patterson, "Free Speech, Copyright, and Fair Use," *Vanderbilt Law Review* 40 (1987): 2, which argues that fair use is "necessary for the partial fulfillment of the constitutional purpose of copyright—the promotion of learning."

15. The Copyright Act of 1976 specifies that courts "shall include" its nonexhaustive list of factors when weighing the fair use defense. 17 U.S.C. § 107 (2012). As Congress explained when codifying fair use in § 107, "the endless variety of situations and combinations of circumstances that can arise in particular cases precludes the formulation of exact rules in the statute." H.R. Rep. No. 94-1476, 94th Cong., 2d Sess. 66 (1976), reprinted in 1976 U.S.C.C.A.N. 5659, 5680.

16. Dellar v. Samuel Goldwyn, Inc., 104 F.2d 661, 662 (2d Cir. 1939). Far from being an out-dated dictum, this quotation has been found "in nearly every major treatise, casebook, or law review article on the subject of fair use." Linda J. Lacey, "Of Bread and Roses and Copyrights," *Duke Law Journal* (1989), 1544n58. See also Nimmer and Nimmer, *Nimmer on Copyright*, vol. 4, § 13.05 (see chap. 1, n. 113).

17. Ronald H. Coase, "The Institutional Structure of Production," in *Essays on Economics and Economists* (Chicago: University of Chicago Press, 1994), 11.

18. For a general discussion of the effect of reduced transaction costs on the optimal distribu-tion of resources, see Ronald H. Coase, "The Problem of Social Cost," *Journal of Law & Economics* 3 (1960): 1–44.

19. See Mark Stefik, "Trusted Systems," *Scientific American* (March 1997), 78–79, 81; Mackaay, "Economic Incentives," 880 (see chap. 6, n. 50).

20. See Goldstein, *Copyright's Highway*, 217 (see chap. 3, n. 16). Goldstein argues that uncom-pensated use dilutes market signals about consumer demand for copyrighted works.

21. American Geophysical Union v. Texaco, Inc., 60 F.3d 913, 931 (2d Cir. 1994). See also Princeton University Press v. Michigan Document Services, Inc., 99 F.3d 1381, 1387n4 (6th Cir. 1996), which quotes *American Geophysical*.

22. Campbell v. Acuff-Rose Music, Inc., 510 U.S. 569, 592 (2005).

23. "The fair use of a copyrighted work . . . for purposes such as criticism, comment, . . . schol-arship, or research, is not an infringement of copyright." 17 U.S.C. § 107 (2012).

24. See Alex Kozinski and Christopher Newman, "What's So Fair about Fair Use?," *Bulletin of the Copyright Society of the U.S.A.* 46 (1999): 513–30.

25. "We should not make it easy for musicians to exploit existing works and then later claim that their rendition was a valuable commentary on the original." *Campbell*, 510 U.S. at 599 (Justice Kennedy, concurring).

26. Id. at 579.

27. For evidence from the field that copyright holders simply want money, not the power to censor, consider that the court in *Princeton University Press v. Michigan Document Services, Inc.*, a case involving the right to reproduce articles in course packs, reported only one instance of a publisher refusing to license copies, and then only because "the excerpt was so large that the publisher would have preferred that students buy the book itself." 99 F.3d 1381, 1388 (6th Cir. 1996). See also the discussion of how and why the litigants in *Campbell* finally settled their dispute in Bell, "Fair Use vs. Fared Use," 597.

Chapter 8: Codifying Misuse

1. See 17 U.S.C. § 106(1) (2012), which gives the owner of a copyright the exclusive right to reproduce it.

2. See, for example, Video Pipeline, Inc. v. Buena Vista Home Entertainment, Inc., 342 F.3d 191, 206 (3d Cir. 2003); Bond v. Blum, 317 F.3d 385, 397–98 (4th Cir. 2003); DSC Communications Corp. v. Pulse Communications, Inc., 170 F.3d 1354, 1368 (Fed. Cir. 1999); Alcatel USA, Inc. v. DGI Technologies, Inc., 166 F.3d 772, 792 (5th Cir. 1999); Practice Management Information Corp. v. American Medical Association, 121 F.3d 516, 520 (9th Cir. 1997); Lasercomb America, Inc. v. Reynolds, 911 F.2d 970, 976 (4th Cir. 1990). See also Rosemont Enterprises, Inc. v. Random House, Inc., 366 F.2d 303, 311 (2d Cir. 1966) (Chief Justice Lumbard, concurring), which recognizes that the doctrine of unclean hands should bar the enforcement of a copyright used to "restrict the dissemina-tion of information about persons in the public eye even though those concerned may not welcome the resulting publicity."

3. See Goldstein, *Goldstein on Copyright*, vol. 2, 3rd ed. 2006 supp., § 11.6 at 11:42.

4. See United States v. Loew's, Inc., 371 U.S. 38, 50 (1962), which states that "the principles underlying our *Paramount Pictures* decision have general application to tying arrangements involving copyrighted products"; United States v. Paramount Pictures, Inc., 334 U.S. 131, 158 (1948), which approved an injunction on certain copyright licensing practices on the grounds that the practices "add to the monopoly of the copyright in violation of the principle of the patent cases involving tying clauses"; *Lasercomb*, 911 F.2d at 976, which explains that "no United States Supreme Court decision has firmly established a copyright misuse defense in a manner analogous to the establishment of the patent misuse defense."

5. See Copyright Act of 1976, 17 U.S.C. §§ 101–1332 (2012).

6. See Goldstein, *Goldstein on Copyright*, vol. 2, 3rd ed. 2006 supp., § 11.6 at 11:40; Mark A. Glick, Lara A. Reymann, and Richard Hoffman, *Intellectual Property Damages: Guidelines and Analysis* (Hoboken, NJ: John Wiley & Sons, 2003), 297; Ralph Jonas et al., "Copyright and Trademark Misuse," in *ABA Section of Antitrust Law, Intellectual Property Misuse: Licensing and Litigation* (Chicago: American Bar Association, 2000), 165.

7. See note 2 for a list of federal circuits that have recognized the defense. See also International Motor Contest Association v. Staley, 434 F. Supp. 2d 650, 664 (N.D. Iowa 2006), which notes the absence of "a single Circuit Court of Appeals decision expressly rejecting such a defense as a *matter of law*."
   Several circuits have yet, however, to expressly recognize the validity of the copyright misuse defense. See Garcia-Goyco v. Law Environmental Consultants, Inc., 428 F.3d 14, 21n7 (1st Cir. 2005), which observes that the First Circuit "has not yet recognized misuse of a copyright as a defense to infringement"; Telecom Technical Services v. Rolm Co., 388 F.3d 820, 831 (11th Cir. 2004), which notes that "this circuit has not recognized, but has not rejected, misuse as a defense for infringement suits"; Data General Corp. v. Grumman Systems Support Corp., 36 F.3d 1147, 1170 (1st Cir. 1994); BellSouth Advertising & Publishing Corp. v. Donnelley Information Publishing, 999 F.2d 1436, 1439 n.5, 1446 (11th Cir. 1993) (en banc); United Telephone Co. v. Johnson Publishing Co., Inc., 855 F.2d 604, 612 (8th Cir. 1988).

8. See Ty, Inc. v. Publications International Ltd., 292 F.3d 512, 517 (7th Cir. 2002).

9. See Goldstein, *Goldstein on Copyright*, vol. 2, 3rd ed. 2006 supp., § 11.6 at 11:38.

10. See 35 U.S.C. § 271(d) (2012).

11. See, for example, Nimmer and Nimmer, *Nimmer on Copyright*, vol. 4, § 13.09[A] (see chap. 1, n. 113); Glick, Reymann, and Hoffman, *Intellectual Property Damages*, 297–304; Goldstein, *Goldstein on Copyright*, vol. 2, 3rd ed. 2006 supp., § 11.6 at 11:36–11:43; Brett Frischmann and Dan Moylan, "The Evolving Common Law Doctrine of Copyright Misuse: A Unified Theory and Its Application to Software," *Berkeley Technology Law Journal* 15 (2000): 871–900; Kathryn Judge, "Note, Rethinking Copyright Misuse," *Stanford Law Review* 57 (2004): 915–23.

12. See Nimmer and Nimmer, *Nimmer on Copyright*, vol. 4, § 13.09[A][2][a]. Nimmer and Nimmer explain that courts "have long held that a patentee who uses his patent privilege contrary to the public interest by violating the antitrust laws will be denied the relief of a court of equity in a patent infringement action."

13. See National Cable Television Association v. Broadcast Music, Inc., 772 F. Supp. 614, 652 (D.D.C. 1991), which explains that "failure to show violation of the antitrust laws makes it more difficult to conclude that [copyright owners] have misused their copyrights."

14. For one of the few opinions to address the viability of a copyright misuse defense associated with a violation of the antitrust laws, see Electronic Data Systems Corp. v. Computer Associates International, Inc., 802 F. Supp. 1463 (N.D. Tex. 1992). See also Nimmer and Nimmer, *Nimmer on Copyright*, vol. 4, § 13.09[A][2][a]. Nimmer and Nimmer state that

"some courts have indicated that a copyright owner would be denied relief in an infringement action, if he is in violation of the antitrust laws."

15. Lasercomb America, Inc. v. Reynolds, 911 F.2d 970, 978 (4th Cir. 1990).

16. See Alcatel USA, Inc. v. DGI Technologies, Inc., 166 F.3d 772, 793–94 (5th Cir. 1999), which held that the plaintiff engaged in copyright misuse by licensing its software on condition that it be used only with the plaintiff's hardware. See also Practice Management Information Corp. v. American Medical Association, 121 F.3d 516, 520–21 (9th Cir. 1997); *Lasercomb*, 911 F.2d at 977–79. But see Costar Group, Inc. v. Loopnet, Inc., 164 F. Supp. 2d 688, 708 (D. Md. 2001), which rejected the misuse defense where the plaintiff had attempted by license to "restrict licensees from distributing photographs and data over which, by its own admission, it has no claim of ownership."

17. Bond v. Blum, 317 F.3d 385, 397–98 (7th Cir. 2003); Video Pipeline, Inc. v. Buena Vista Home Entertainment, Inc., 342 F.3d 191 (3d. Cir. 2003). In *Video Pipeline*, the court recognized that a copyright owner might commit misuse by trying to enforce a license that prohibits criticism of copyright-restricted works, though it affirmed that the licenses in question had not gone that far.

18. In Assessment Technologies, LLC v. WIREdata, Inc., 350 F.3d 640, 647 (7th Cir. 2003), the court explained that it constitutes misuse "to use an infringement suit to obtain property protection, here in data, that copyright law clearly does not confer." See also A&M Records, Inc. v. Napster, Inc., 239 F.3d 1004, 1026 (9th Cir. 2001); *Lasercomb*, 911 F.2d at 979. In *Lasercomb*, the court stated that "the misuse arises from Lasercomb's attempt to use its copyright . . . to control competition in an area outside the copyright."

19. See Nimmer and Nimmer, *Nimmer on Copyright*, vol. 4, § 13.09[A][2][b], which suggests that the copyright misuse defense could include "contracts that eliminate the fair use or first sale defenses"; Lydia Pallas Loren, "Slaying the Leather-Winged Demons in the Night: Reforming Copyright Owner Contracting with Clickwrap Misuse," *Ohio Northern University Law Reveiw* 30 (2004): 516–19, which discusses the recent trend toward expanding the misuse doctrine to protect public policy concerns.

20. See *Lasercomb*, 911 F.2d at 979n22.

21. See Donald S. Chisum, *Chisum on Patents*, 2000 ed. 2005 supp., vol. 6, § 19.04[4], 19-537-38. Chisum reads Supreme Court case law "to assume that a patent owner could not, even after complete [sic] abandonment and dissipation, recover monetary relief for infringing acts occurring prior to such dissipation." See also James B. Kobak Jr., "The Misuse Defense and Intellectual Property Litigation," *Journal of Science & Technology Law* 1 (1995): 25, ¶ 21. Kobak states that "when misuse is purged, damages or royalties can be recovered only for the period post-purge."

22. See Jonas et al., *Copyright and Trademark Misuse*, 189.

23. See In re Napster, Inc. Copyright Litigation, 191 F. Supp. 2d 1087, 1108 (N.D. Cal. 2002). The court evidently read too much into the precedents it quoted, which, while stating that no remedies should be afforded during misuse, did not say that rights should be retroactively enforced.

24. Glick, Reymann, and Hoffman, *Intellectual Property Damages*, 303. See also Altera Corp. v. Clear Logic, Inc., 424 F.3d 1079, 1090 (9th Cir. 2005); Association of American Medical Colleges v. Princeton Review, Inc., 332 F. Supp. 2d 11, 17–20 (D.D.C. 2004); Novell, Inc. v. CPU Distrib., Inc., No. H-97-2326, 2000 U.S. Dist. LEXIS 9952, at *15–16 (S.D. Tex. May 15, 2000).

25. Electronic Data Systems Corp. v. Computer Associates International, Inc., 802 F. Supp. 1463, 1466 (N.D. Tex. 1992).

26. See Video Pipeline, Inc. v. Buena Vista Home Entertainment, Inc., 342 F.3d 191, 204 (3d Cir. 2003): "To defend on misuse grounds, the alleged infringer need not be subject to the purported misuse."

27. See Lasercomb America, Inc. v. Reynolds, 911 F.2d 970, 979 (4th Cir. 1990): "The fact that appellants here were not parties to one of Lasercomb's standard license agreements is inapposite to their copyright misuse defense. The question is whether Lasercomb is using its copyright in a manner contrary to public policy."

28. See Glick, Reymann, and Hoffman, *Intellectual Property Damages*, 302–3.

29. *Lasercomb*, 911 F.2d at 980.

30. Atari Games Corp. v. Nintendo, Inc., 975 F.2d 832, 846 (Fed. Cir. 1992).

31. Alcatel USA, Inc. v. DGI Technologies, Inc., 166 F.3d 772, 794 (5th Cir. 1999).

32. See Altera Corp. v. Clear Logic, Inc., 424 F.3d 1079, 1090 (9th Cir. 2005); Davidson & Associates, Inc. v. Internet Gateway, Inc., 334 F. Supp. 2d 1164, 1182–83 (E.D. Mo. 2004).

33. See, for example, PRC Realty Systems, Inc. v. National Association of Realtors, Nos. 91-1125, 91-1143, 1992 U.S. App. LEXIS 18017, at *38 (4th Cir. August 4, 1992), which affirmed the reward of damages for breach of contract while reversing, on grounds of misuse, remedies for copyright infringement; Tamburo v. Calvin, No. 94 C 5206, 1995 U.S. Dist. LEXIS 3399, at *15–19 (N.D. Ill. March 17, 1995), which granted a motion to dismiss a copyright infringement claim on the grounds of misuse, but granted leave to amend the contract and other claims.

34. See, for example, *Alcatel*, 166 F.3d at 792–94, which neglects to rule on the enforceability of contract; Practice Management Information Corp. v. American Medical Association, 121 F.3d 516, 520–21 (9th Cir. 1997), which allows the misuse defense without addressing the viability of the copyright holder's other potential common-law claims; *Lasercomb*, 911 F.2d at 979.

35. See 35 U.S.C. § 271(d) (2012).

36. See Rosemont Enterprises, Inc. v. Random House, Inc., 366 F.2d 303, 311 (2d Cir. 1966) (Chief Justice Lumbard, concurring).

37. See 17 U.S.C. § 107(a) (2012), which specifies that fair use includes certain enumerated uses and that determinations of fair use shall include certain enumerated factors, without precluding courts from protecting other uses or considering other factors.

38. See Goldstein, *Goldstein on Copyright*, vol. 2, 3rd ed. 2006 supp., § 11.6 at 11:38.

39. In re Napster, Inc. Copyright Litigation, 191 F. Supp. 2d 1087, 1108 (N.D. Cal. 2002).

40. But see Judge, "Note, Rethinking Copyright Misuse," 948–49. Judge argues that even under the *In re Napster* court's approach, "A variety of factors . . . reduce the estimated cost to a consumer of using the misused copyright" and this "represents a significant shift away from patent misuse and toward a remedy better suited to effectuate the purpose of copyright misuse."

41. U.S. Const. amend. I: "Congress shall make no law . . . abridging the freedom of speech, or of the press."

42. See Eldred v. Ashcroft, 537 U.S. 186, 219 (2003), which included fair use among copyright law's "built-in First Amendment accommodations."

43. Section 106A(a) gives "the owner of a work of visual art" the right to "claim authorship of that work," 18 U.S.C. § 106A(a)(1)(A) (2012); to disavow misattributions of authorship, id. § 106A(a)(1)(B); to disavow authorship to his or her works that have suffered modifications that "would be prejudicial to his or her honor or reputation," id. § 106A(a)(2); and to protect his or her works from specified sorts of harm, id. § 106A(a)(3).

44. Notably, the same person who enjoys rights under § 106—a painter not creating a work for hire, for example—might also enjoy rights under § 106A.

45. Similar reasoning suggests that lawmakers might also find it worthwhile to expand the defense to bar misuses of the rights that the Digital Millennium Copyright Act created to protect systems that themselves protect copyrighted works—see 17 U.S.C. § 1201 (2012)—

and copyright management information—see 17 U.S.C. § 1202 (2012). For an argument on behalf of that sort of extension, see Dan L. Burk, "Anti-circumvention Abuse," *UCLA Law Review* 50 (2003): 1095–140. For a case suggesting that judges, at least, have hesitated to take up that call, see 321 Studios v. Metro-Goldwyn-Mayer Studios, Inc., 307 F. Supp. 2d 1085, 1101–3 (N.D. Cal. 2004), which holds that the misuse defense does not apply to anticircumvention provisions of the Digital Millennium Copyright Act, 17 U.S.C. § 1201 (2012).

46. Sentence 3 thus says only that a court *may* remedy breach of contract.

47. See 17 U.S.C. § 107 (2012), which codifies the fair use defense.

48. Assuming it finds such a clause enforceable, a court should take that clause to provide an effective counterargument to any defense asserted under § 107(b).

49. Indeed, in light of that contract, § 107(b) would give *anyone* a defense to *any* copyright claim concerning BugFest brought by its copyright owner, ThinSkin.

50. See 17 U.S.C. §§ 502–5 (2012). See also id. § 506, which provides for criminal penalties against copyright infringers; id. § 509, which provides for the seizure and forfeiture of illegal copies and copying equipment.

51. See Restatement (Second) of Contracts §§ 344–56 (1979), which specify a variety of rules for awarding monetary relief for breach of contract; id. § 356, which specifies when the party breaching a contract may owe liquidated damages; id. § 359, which defines when courts should award injunctive relief for breach of contract.

Chapter 9: Deregulating Expressive Works

1. See 17 U.S.C. § 106 (2012), which defines the exclusive rights of copyright holders.

2. See id. § 801–3, which establishes powers and duties of copyright arbitration royalty panels. See also id. § 107, which effectively sets a price of zero for the fair use of copyrighted works.

3. See id. § 505; Fogerty v. Fantasy, Inc., 510 U.S. 517 (1994).

4. See Friedrich Kessler, "Contracts of Adhesion—Some Thoughts about Freedom of Contract," *Columbia Law Review* 43 (1943): 630. Kessler describes adhesion contracts as "private legislation." This metaphor tends to mislead, however, because it overemphasizes citizens' power to shape legislation, underestimates consumers' power to choose between and thus shape contracts, and ignores the fact that so-called "private legislation" does not fundamentally rely on coercive state power. See Richard A. Epstein, "Notice and Freedom of Contract in the Law of Servitudes," *Southern California Law Review* 55 (1982): 1359. Here, Epstein argues that contrary to "private legislation" arguments, "freedom of contract and private property . . . define domains in which individuals may establish both the means and the ends for themselves, to pursue as they see fit (so long as they do not infringe upon the rights of third parties)," and that "private property is an institution that fosters individualized, if not eccentric, preferences; it does not stamp them out."

5. See Sony Corp. v. Universal City Studios, Inc., 464 U.S. 417, 429 (1984): "As the text of the Constitution makes plain, it is *Congress* that has been assigned the task of defining the scope of the limited monopoly that should be granted to authors or to inventors in order to give the public appropriate access to their work product" (emphasis added).

6. See Pacific & Southern Co. v. Duncan, 572 F. Supp. 1186, 1196 (N.D. Ga. 1983), which found that a television station had abandoned its copyright in news broadcasts because it evinced an intent to do so by destroying copies thereof; affirmed in relevant part, 744 F.2d 1490, 1500 (11th Cir. 1984); Hadady Corp. v. Dean Witter Reynolds, Inc., 739 F. Supp. 1392, 1399 (C.D. Cal. 1990), which found that a notice limiting copyright to a two-day period effectuated abandonment after that time. See also National Comics Publications, Inc. v. Fawcett Publications, Inc., 191 F.2d 594, 598 (2d Cir. 1951), which asserted in dicta that a copyright's holder may abandon it "by some overt act which manifests his purpose

to surrender his rights in the 'work,' and to allow the public to copy it"; modified, 198 F.2d 927 (2d Cir. 1952).

7. *Intellectual Property and the National Information Infrastructure: The Report of the Working Group on Intellectual Property Rights,* US Department of Commerce, Information Infrastructure Task Force, September 1995, 16; Kreiss, "Abandoning Copyrights," 92 (see chap. 5, n. 50); Henry H. Perritt Jr., "Property and Innovation in the Global Information Infrastructure," *University of Chicago Legal Forum* 1996, 292n119. See also Goldstein, *Goldstein on Copyright,* 2nd ed. 2005 supp., vol. 2, § 9.3, which describes how abandonment functions as a defense to copyright infringement; Nimmer and Nimmer, *Nimmer on Copyright,* vol. 4, § 13.06 (see chap. 1, n. 113).

8. Notwithstanding that consensus, it bears noting that the Copyright Act nowhere specifically permits abandonment and perhaps even implicitly disallows it. See Kreiss, "Abandoning Copyrights," 98. Kreiss offers five powerful arguments, however, why no one can reasonably take the act to forbid abandonment. Ibid., 98–101, 117–18. One of these proves especially relevant to the argument that we should allow an exit from copyright: "Personal freedom, including the freedom to control or dispose of one's own property . . . underlies the notion that an author can abandon his copyrights." Ibid., 100.

9. To grasp the scope of the uncertainty, compare the following authorities. On the one hand, see Metro-Goldwyn-Mayer, Inc. v. Showcase Atlanta Cooperative Productions, Inc., 1981 Copyright L. Dec. (CCH) ¶ 25,314 (N.D. Ga. 1981), which rejects the concept of "limited abandonment" of copyright; Paramount Pictures Corp. v. Carol Publishing Group, 11 F. Supp. 2d 329, 337 (S.D.N.Y. 1998) (which quotes *Showcase*); Richard Feiner & Co. v. H.R.I. Industries, 10 F. Supp. 2d 310, 313 (S.D.N.Y. 1998) (which quotes *Showcase* and Nimmer and Nimmer, *Nimmer on Copyright*); and Nimmer and Nimmer, *Nimmer on Copyright,* vol. 4, § 13.06, which states that "the law does not recognize a limited abandonment, such as an abandonment only in a particular medium, or only as regards a given mode of presentation." On the other hand, see Micro Star v. Formgen, 154 F.3d 1107, 1114 (9th Cir. 1998), which suggests that copyright rights may be partially abandoned; Goldstein, *Goldstein on Copyright,* 2nd ed. 2005 supp., vol. 2, § 9.3 at 9:12-1 (which cites *Micro Star*); and Kreiss, "Abandoning Copyrights," 96, which argues for allowing the abandonment of select copyright rights for select periods.

10. See 17 U.S.C. § 203 (2012), which provides that any grant, other than by will, of a transfer or license made on or after January 1, 1978, of a copyrighted work not made for hire may be terminated by the author upon certain conditions notwithstanding any agreement to the contrary. See also id. § 304(c), which provides much the same with regard to any grant of a transfer or license of a renewal of copyright or any right under it executed before January 1, 1978. In effect, these provisions mean it is impossible for an author to make an enforceable promise to not terminate a transfer or license of copyright.

11. Law professor and copyright scholar Robert A. Kreiss gives this question extensive consideration. See Kreiss, "Abandoning Copyrights," 111–23. He answers it with a qualified yes, but at the same time he defends abandonment in general as a matter of personal freedom and autonomy. See ibid., 100–01. These principles directly conflict with the act's termination provisions, which embody a paternalistic restraint on authors' freedom of contract. Kreiss defends his interpretation on the grounds that in particular circumstances the termination provisions protect authors from the hazards of imbalanced negotiations with copyright grantees. See ibid., 114–15. Policy considerations in fact argue against extending termination's scope, however. First, whatever the benefits of termination in traditional contexts, it generally proves useless to authors considering abandonment. The public to whom such authors "grant" their works does not, after all, enjoy overwhelming bargaining power. Kreiss would, in all fairness, bar only the abandonment of contingent reversionary rights effectuated under bargaining pressure and in conjunction with a grant of present rights. See ibid., 121–23. But even that goes too far because, secondly and more fundamentally, termination in fact hurts most authors by decreasing the present value of their grants and erodes their bargaining power by denying them the right to credibly offer nonterminable

grants. Kreiss appears to have a zero-sum view of bargains between authors and grantees: "If a copyright grantee receives a grant and also negotiates for the abandonment of other copyrights, one can presume that the abandonment is designed for the benefit of the grantee." Ibid., 123. But one can also presume that such an abandonment benefits the grantor! Termination makes no economic sense even in traditional contexts, much less in the context of abandonment.

12. Ideally, a copyright holder should be able to effectuate complete, immediate, and permanent abandonment by placing both all extant copyright rights and any contingent reversionary rights into the public domain.

13. For a detailed discussion of such legal strategies, see Bell, "Escape from Copyright," 788–93 (see chap. 1, n. 13).

14. U.S. Const. art. VI, § 8.

15. See Nimmer and Nimmer, *Nimmer on Copyright*, vol. 1, § 1.01[B]. Nimmer and Nimmer explain that courts have had little need to refer to the supremacy clause because they "may simply turn to the explicit statutory language." Stanford law professor and copyright scholar Paul Goldstein makes a similar case: "Arguably, section 301 has entirely displaced constitutional preemption doctrine under the supremacy clause in cases involving state protection of copyright subject matter." Goldstein, *Goldstein on Copyright*, 2nd ed. 2001 supp., vol. 3, § 15.3.3 at 15:35.

16. The court's discussion of supremacy clause preemption in Goldstein v. California, 412 U.S. 546, 567–71 (1973) proves unhelpful, since that case concerned solely a California criminal statute and not a common-law claim. But see Fantastic Fakes, Inc. v. Pickwick International, Inc., 661 F.2d 479, 483 (5th Cir. 1981) (dictum): "It is possible to hypothesize situations where application of particular state rules of [contract] construction would so alter rights granted by the copyright statutes as to invade the scope of copyright or violate its policies." See also Tom W. Bell, "Misunderestimating *Dastar*: How the Supreme Court Unwittingly Revolutionized Copyright Preemption," *Maryland Law Review* 65 (2006): 206–45, which argues that the Dastar court unwittingly revived implied supremacy clause copyright preemption.

17. 17 U.S.C. § 301 (2012).

18. See H.R. Rep. No. 1476, 94th Cong., 2d Sess. 62, reprinted in 1976 U.S. Code Cong. & Admin. News 5659, at 79. This report states that the first-sale doctrine set forth in § 109 "does not mean that conditions on future disposition of copies or phone records, imposed by a contract between their buyer and seller, would be unenforceable between the parties as a breach of contract, but it does mean that they could not be enforced by an action for infringement of copyright." See also American International Pictures, Inc. v. Foreman, 576 F.2d 661, 664 (5th Cir. 1978); United States v. Wise, 550 F.2d 1180, 1187n10 (9th Cir.); Bobbs-Merrill Co. v. Straus, 210 U.S. 339 (1908). In *Bobbs-Merrill* the court expressed willingness to uphold a valid contract claim despite the applicability of the first-sale doctrine.

19. Dastar Corp. v. Twentieth Century Fox Film Corp., 539 U.S. 23 (2003).

20. See id. at 37: "The phrase 'origin of goods' in [§ 43(a) of] the Lanham Act . . . refers to the producer of the tangible goods that are offered for sale, and not to the author of any idea, concept, or communication embodied in those goods. To hold otherwise would be akin to finding that § 43(a) created a species of perpetual patent and copyright, which Congress may not do."

21. Fogerty v. Fantasy, Inc., 510 U.S. 517 (1994).

22. Id. at 535n19, quoting Lieb v. Topstone Industries, Inc., 788 F.2d 151, 156 (3d Cir. 1986).

23. Garcia-Goyco v. P.R. Highway Authority, 275 F. Supp. 2d 142 (D.Ct. Puerto Rico 2003) awarded attorney's fees under § 505 due to copyright misuse; affirmed on other grounds, 428 F.3d 14 (1st Cir. 2005). Although the lower court never expressly invoked

the misuse doctrine, the court of appeals explained, "We understand the district court to have held that [attorney's] fees were justified because (1) the plaintiffs misused the copyright." Id. at 21.

24. Assessment Technologies, LLC v. Wire Data, Inc., 361 F.3d 434, 437 (7th Cir. 2004) held attorney's fees appropriate under § 505 where the plaintiff's conduct "came close" to copyright misuse.

25. The only court to evidently find otherwise, Lasercomb America, Inc. v. Reynolds, 911 F.2d 970 (6th Cir. 1990), in fact offers the exception proving the rule. Because *Lasercomb* largely pioneered the copyright misuse defense, it declined to award attorney's fees under § 505 because of the "obscurity" of the defense. Id. at 979n22. Now that the defense has become more well known, that particular reason for denying an award of attorney's fees carries much less weight.

26. See *Fogerty*, 510 U.S. at 533.

Chapter 10: Uncopyright and Open Copyright

1. The copyright notice requirement was largely struck from the Copyright Act by the Berne Convention Implementation Act of 1988, Pub. L. No. 100-568, 102 Stat. 2853 (October 31, 1988), effective March 1, 1989.

2. "Registration is not a condition of copyright protection," according to 17 U.S.C. § 408(a) (2012). But see id. § 411(a), which provides that a copyright owner cannot in general bring suit for infringement before having at least applied for registration; id. § 412, which limits some remedies in some cases to registered works.

3. Id. § 401(a) provides merely that such notice "may be placed on publicly distributed copies" of a work.

4. But see id. §§ 401(d), 402(d), which provides that attaching a copyright notice to published works will generally bar a defense of innocent infringement in mitigation of actual or statutory damages; id. § 405(b), which describes limits to the liability of an innocent infringer of a copyrighted work published before March 1, 1989, without an attached copyright notice.

5. For a call to reverse that presumption by reimposing copyright registration requirements, see Sprigman, "Reform(aliz)ing Copyright" (see chap. 1, n. 53).

6. For a fuller description of the problem, and some proposed solutions, see Jason Mazzone, "Copyfraud," *NYU Law Review* 81 (2003): 1026–100.

7. 17 U.S.C. § 402(b)(1) (2012).

8. See Project Gutenberg at http://www.gutenberg.org/wiki/Main_Page.

9. Among the many licenses it offers, Creative Commons includes a "Public Domain Dedication." See http://creativecommons.org/licenses/publicdomain/. I salute that effort, but here offer a more direct approach to the problem.

10. Samuel Johnson, quoted in James Boswell, *The Life of Samuel Johnson* (1791) (Everyman's Library, 1993), 641.

11. Johnson's biographer certainly realized "blockheaded" authors exist; he characterized Johnson's opinion as "strange," attributed it to his "indolent disposition," and, immediately following the "no man but a blockhead" quotation, critically commented that "numerous instances to refute this will occur to all who are versed in the history of literature." Boswell, *Life of Samuel Johnson*, 641.

12. See David Byrne, "The Fall and Rise of Music," *Wired*, January 2008, 127.

13. See U.S. Const. art I, § 8, cl. 8.

14. That is not to say that copyright has nothing to offer authors driven by nonmonetary incentives. Authors who seek fame, in particular, may find copyright useful. It is only to say that, even for such authors, copyright may offer more privileges than necessary.

15. With regard to Linux operating system software, of course, they already have. See, for example, Jem Matzan, "The Gift Economy and Free Software," Linux.com, June 5, 2004, http://www.linux.com/articles/36554.

16. For a detailed analysis of the song's copyrighted status, see Robert Brauneis, "Copyright and the World's Most Popular Song," *Journal of the Copyright Society of the U.S.A.* 56 (2009): 335–426, available at http://papers.ssrn.com/sol3/papers.cfm?abstract_id =1111624.

17. Such a performance would not qualify as a public one, and thus would not fall within the copyright holder's rights. See 17 U.S.C. § 106(4) (2012).

18. Kevin Underhill, "Happy Birthday to You: The Lawsuit," *Forbes*, June 15, 2013, http://www .forbes.com/sites/kevinunderhill/2013/06/15/happy-birthday-to-you-the-lawsuit/.

19. For a trenchant critique of the breadth of the right of publicity, see White v. Samsung Electronics America, Inc., 989 F.2d 1512, 1521 (9th Cir. 1993) (denial of motion for rehearing) (Judge Kozinski, dissenting).

20. Dastar Corp. v. Twentieth Century Fox Film Corp., 539 U.S. 23 (2003).

21. That provision provides that anyone who uses any mark or misleading description which "is likely to cause confusion . . . as to the affiliation, connection, or association of such person with another person, or as to the origin, sponsorship, or approval of his or her goods, services, or commercial activities by another person . . . shall be liable in a civil action by any person who believes that he or she is or is likely to be damaged by such act." 15 U.S.C. § 1125(a)(1)(A) (2012).

22. 539 U.S. at 32.

23. See, for example, Twentieth Century Fox Film Corp. v. Dastar Corp., 2003 U.S. Dist. LEXIS 21194, 68 U.S.P.Q.2d (BNA) 1536 (C.D. Cal. October 14, 2003) (deciding the case on remand).

24. See, for example, Keane v. Fox Television Stations, Inc., 297 F. Supp. 2d 921, 935 (S.D. Tex. 2005, which dismissed the plaintiff's Lanham Act claim on the grounds that § 43(a) of the act does not forbid the reverse passing off of mere ideas.

25. That provision provides that anyone who "in commercial advertising or promotion, misrepresents the nature, characteristics, qualities, or geographic origin of his or her or another person's goods, services, or commercial activities, shall be liable in a civil action by any person who believes that he or she is or is likely to be damaged by such act." 15 U.S.C. § 1125(a)(1)(B) (2012).

26. *Dastar*, 539 U.S. at 38.

27. In Baden Sports, Inc. v. Molten USA, Inc., 556 F.3d 1300, 1307 (9th Cir. 2009), the court held that "authorship, like licensing status, is not a nature, characteristic, or quality, as those terms are used in Section 43(a)(1)(B) of the Lanham Act." In Sybersound Records, Inc. v. UAV Corp., 517 F.3d 1137, 1144 (9th Cir. 2008), the court held that misrepresentations about a work's copyright licensing status fall outside the scope of § 43(a)(1)(B).

28. Granted, an uncopyright notice might lead to confusion if attached to a work that reenters copyright due to the vesting of a contingent reversionary interest, or due to the curing of copyright misuse. As an argument against using uncopyright notices, however, that is little stronger than the argument that the marginal problem of expired copyrights should preclude the use of copyright notices. In addition, good-faith reliance on an erroneous uncopyright notice might mitigate the penalties for infringement. See the description of the scope and effect of an innocent infringement defense in Nimmer and Nimmer, *Nimmer on Copyright*, vol. 4, § 13.08 (see chap. 1, n. 113). See also the description of how an innocent infringer might have laches defense in ibid., vol. 3, § 12.06.

Chapter 11: Outgrowing Copyright

1. Other legal academics do not appear to have grappled with the question of how copyright (or patent) policy should react to market growth. Economists have, though; see Michele Boldrin and David K. Levine, "IP and Market Size," (unpublished manuscript, June 22, 2005), http://www.dklevine.com/papers/scale22.pdf. Boldrin and Levine argue, as I do, that the optimal level of patent or copyright restriction decreases as the size of the market for patented or copyrighted works increases. They do so for distinctly different reasons than I do, however. Their model, based on a model relatively standard in the economic literature, shows that general demand for the labor of "idea workers"—the sort of workers who create inventions and expressions—increases more rapidly than does the market for patents or copyrights. That labor constraint increases the monopoly rents afforded by patents and copyrights, thereby decreasing the need for patent or copyright privileges.

2. Here, as elsewhere, my focus is on US copyright law. Much of the analysis will, however, apply to copyright policy generally.

3. I neglected to consider this factor when, in an earlier paper, I briefly addressed the question of the effect of market growth on copyright policy. See Bell, "Authors' Welfare," 267–69 (see chap. 4, n. 14). I now regard that argument as incompletely developed; hence this effort.

4. A copyright plaintiff must establish that the defendant both had access to the restricted work and created a substantial similar version of it. See Amini Innovation Corp. v. Anthony California, Inc., 439 F.3d 1365, 1368 (Fed. Cir., 2006); Shaw v. Lindheim, 919 F.2d 1353, 1356 (9th Cir. 1990).

5. I thank economist and law professor David Friedman for bringing this factor to my attention. See David Friedman, June 8, 2007, comment on Tom W. Bell, "When Markets Outgrow Copyrights," *Agoraphilia* (blog), June 4, 2007, http://agoraphilia.blogspot.com /2007/06/when-markets-outgrow-copyrights.html#9009387265935622973.

6. See Patrick Frater, "Inside China's New Trade Deal," *Hollywood Reporter*, March 9, 2012, http://www.hollywoodreporter.com/news/china-new-trade-deal-298200.

7. See United States v. Paramount Pictures, Inc., 334 U.S. 131, 158 (1948).

8. See Michael Abramowicz, "An Industrial Organization Approach to Copyright Law," *William & Mary Law Review* 46 (2004): 109. "Because the number of copyrighted works, and indeed the rate at which copyrighted works are produced, is growing over time . . . copyright generally should become less strict over time," argues Abramowicz, though with some caveats.

9. The proliferation of cell-phone cameras and high-powered sound-engineering software provide two salient examples. For a discussion of decreasing production and distribution costs in the music industry, see Amanda M. Witt, "Burned in the USA: Should the Music Industry Utilize Its American Strategy of Suing Users to Combat Online Piracy in Europe?," *Columbia Journal of European Law* 11 (2005): 409–10.

10. Indeed, "Copying technology has improved over time and is likely to continue to improve as computer technology becomes ever more commonplace in portable devices." Abramowicz, "Industrial Organization Approach," 109.

11. Indeed, sometimes consuming the work once may suffice to satisfy a consumer's demand for it. See Sanjay Sood and Xavier Drèze, "Brand Extensions of Experiential Goods: Movie Sequel Evaluations," *Journal of Consumer Research* 33 (2006): 353.

12. See Patrick McNutt, "Public Goods and Club Goods," in *Encyclopedia of Law and Economics*, ed. Boudewijn Bouckaert and Gerrit de Geest (Cheltenham, UK: Edward Elgar, 1999), 928, available at http://encyclo.findlaw.com/0750book.pdf.

13. See ibid., 929.

14. Copyright owners may have an incentive to try to extend their statutory privileges within the consumer household, such as by implementing automated rights management

schemes that limit reuse of a work, or by claiming licenses that limit fair use—17 U.S.C. § 107 (2012)—or the scope of the first sale doctrine—id. § 109.

15. In some cases, authors retain the copyrights in the works they create. In other cases, other parties buy those rights. In either event, authors benefit from increases in copyright profits.

16. Yoo, "Copyright and Product Differentiation," 239.

17. See Edward Chamberlin, *The Theory of Monopolistic Competition* (Cambridge, MA: Harvard University Press, 1933) 111–12.

18. Interestingly, Yoo seems to come to the opposite conclusion, arguing that as the size of a market for copyrighted works grows, its competitiveness likewise increases. Yoo, "Copyright and Product Differentiation," 266. He does not evidently consider markets so large as to support the sort of specialization described here, though.

19. Nicholas Negroponte, founder of the Massachusetts Institute of Technology's Media Lab and an early observer of this phenomenon, argued that it would ultimately result in the "Daily Me." See Nicholas Kristof, "The Daily Me," *New York Times*, March 18, 2009, http://www.nytimes.com/2009/03/19/opinion/19kristof.html.

20. See Chris Anderson, "The Long Tail," *Wired*, October 2004, http://www.wired.com/wired/archive/12.10/tail.html.

21. See Kylie J. Veale, "Internet Gift Economies: Voluntary Payment Schemes as Tangible Reciprocity," *First Monday*, Nov. 28, 2003.

22. Robert E. Rector, "How Poor Are America's Poor? Examining the 'Plague' of Poverty in America" (Backgrounder #2064, Heritage Foundation, Washington, DC, August 24, 2007), http://www.heritage.org/Research/Welfare/bg2064.cfm.

23. I'm happy to pass on the question, as I consider it unanswerable. See chapter 6, where I argue that it is impossible for policymakers to strike such a balance.

24. Adam Smith, *An Inquiry into the Nature and Causes of the Wealth of Nations*, ed. Edwin Cannan (New York: Modern Library, 1937), 3–12.

25. Ibid., 7–8.

26. Specifically, Smith points to three reasons why the division of labor promotes efficient production: it increases each laborer's skill; it saves time otherwise spent "passing from one species of work to another"; and it encourages industrialization. Ibid., 7.

27. Market growth blesses copyright holders with savings because, as described above, the average costs of producing copies of expressive works decline with every additional copy made and distributed.

28. The parallel also recurs in Smith's observation that markets must grow to a certain size before producers can reap the benefits of the division of labor. Ibid., 17–18.

29. See U.S. Const. art I, § 8, cl. 8.

Conclusion: The Packet-Switched Society

1. True to its roots and its meaning everywhere but in contemporary US mass media, "liberal" here means not "left-wing" but rather "free."

2. See Epstein, *Simple Rules for a Complex World* (see chap. 1, n. 118).

3. For descriptions of spontaneous orders, see Barnett, *Structure of Liberty*, 44–62 (see chap. 1, n. 6); Friedrich A. Hayek, *Law, Legislation and Liberty*, 1:35–54 (see chap. 1, n. 123).

4. See, for example, Eli M. Noam, "Beyond Auctions: Open Spectrum Access," in *Regulators' Revenge: The Future of Telecommunications Deregulation,* ed. Tom W. Bell and Solveig Singleton (Washington, DC: Cato Institute, 1998), 113.

5. See, for example, David R. Hughes and Dewayne Hendricks, "Spread-Spectrum Radio," *Scientific American,* April 1998, 94.

6. For a discussion about how network bottlenecks facilitate control by third parties, see David G. Post, "Anarchy, State, and the Internet: An Essay on Law-Making in Cyberspace," *Journal of Online Law* (June 1995), art. 3, ¶¶ 25–31.

INDEX

Page numbers in *italics* indicate figures; the letter n following a page number indicates a note.

A

abandoned works, 137, 138–139, 140, 204–206nn6–12

Abramowicz, Michael, 209n8

Abrams, Howard B., 177n112

acquisition of copyright, 95

adhesion contracts, 136, 204n4

Alcatel USA, Inc. v. DGI Technologies, Inc. (1999), 126, 202n16, 203n34

alienation
    of copyright rights, 24, 26–27, 94–95, 191n49
    of property rights, 94–95
    See also termination rights

American Geophysical Union v. Texaco, Inc. (1994), 117, 119

"American Rule," 140

anonymous and pseudonymous works, 24

antitrust laws, 201n14

architectural structures, habitable, 174n39

architectural structures, uninhabited, 22

Arnold, Tony, 97

Aronson v. Quick Point Pencil Co. (1979), 180n23

artists, moral rights of, 104, 129, 195n17, 203nn43–44

Assessment Technologies, LLC v. WIREdata, Inc. (2003), 202n18

Astoria Federal Savings and Loan Association v. Solimino (1991), 189n23

Atari Games Corp. v. Nintendo, Inc. (1992), 126

attorney's fees, award of, 140, 206–207nn23–25

authorship
    "blockheaded" authorship, 146–150, *148*, *149*
    citizenship/residence, 63, 182n18
    constitutional requirement, 19
    discouraged by expenses, *148*
    discouraged by unauthorized use, *50*
    expenses, 147, *148*, 157
    misdescriptions of, 83–84
    nonmonetary incentives, 147, 150, 208n14
    promoted by common law, 135
    public-domain works, 146–150
    termination power, 26–27, 137, 205nn10–11
    visual arts, 30, 129, 203nn43–44

automated rights management schemes, 209n14

automobile design, 22, 174n39

B

Baden Sports, Inc. v. Molten USA, Inc. (2009), 208n27

Bahls, Daniel, 198n4

Baird, Douglas G., 186n64

Baker v. Selden (1879), 21

Barnett, Randy E., 4, 59–60, 68, 72–73, 193n73

Bell, Tom W., on supremacy clause, 206n16

Berne Convention Implementation Act (1988), 207n1

Black's Law Dictionary

common law, 35
copyright, 188nn1–2
privilege, 90–91
property, 190n34
"blockheaded" authorship, 146–150,
 148, 149
Bobbs-Merrill Co. v. Straus (1908),
 188n3, 197n47, 206n18
Boldrin, Michele, 209n1
Bono, Mary, 192n55
Bono, Sonny, 192n55, 194n9
Boyle, James, 194n10
Brand, Stewart, 198nn1–2
breach of contract, 204n51
Breyer, Stephen, 180n20
Brown, William Hill, 16
Burk, Dan L., 203n45

C

cable systems, compulsory licensing,
 175n65, 191n39
California
 public performance protection,
 177n110
 restrictions for unfixed expressive
 works, 32
Campbell v. Acuff-Rose Music, Inc.
 (2005), 119
Capitol Records, Inc. v. Naxos, Inc.
 (2005), 177n114
car designs, 22, 174n39
Carroll, Michael W., 193n75
Cass, Ronald A., 26
Cassidy, Lewis C., 189n17
cell phone ringtones, 11, 171n1
censorship, barred by fair use,
 119–120
Chisum, Donald S., 202n21
circuit-switched networks, 167–168
civil rights
 fundamental, 91–92
 safeguarding natural rights, 92,
 190n28
co-owners of copyright, 24, 177n109,
 191n49
Coase, Ronald, 118

Cohen, Felix S., 74
common law and common-law
 rights
 abandoned works, 137, 138–140
 bird's-eye view, 34–38
 community standards in, 35,
 177n124
 in contracts, 35, 178n126
 vs. copyright, 34–38
 as copyright alternative, 38–39,
 133–135
 copyright as statutory exception
 to, 67–68, 90–91
 copyright as violation of, 2, 11–15,
 90–91
 copyright protections under,
 32, 34, 65–66, 84, 138–139,
 177n114, 177nn116–117
 decentralized and adaptive structure, 135–136
 definitions, 35, 177n120
 development, 35–36, *36*
 fundamental principles, 37
 natural rights and, 37, 178n129,
 180n10
 origins in custom, 35
 promoting authorship, 135
 promoting economic efficiency,
 37, 178n130
 special legal weight, 91, 189n23
 sui generis protection, 178n134
 "common-law copyright," 33–34,
 177n112
compensation for takings, 96
compulsory licensing, 26, 175n65,
 191n39
*Computer Associates International,
 Inc. v. Altai, Inc.* (1992), 28
computer software, 20, 28, 150,
 196n44, 196n47
Computer Software Rental
 Amendments Act (1990), 197n47
Connecticut
 Founding-Era copyright act,
 61, 181n13, 182n18, 183n25,
 183n31

digital works, production costs, 53, 180nn19–20
disabled persons, adapted works for, 104, 196n41
Disney, Walt, 197n54
See also Walt Disney Company
Dodd, Jeff C., 193n65
Donaldson v. Becket (1774), 65
Drahos, Peter, 97, 190n29, 193nn71–72, 193n76
duration of copyright
anonymous and pseudonymous works, 24
constitutional limitations, 19–20, 96
Copyright Act (1790), v, 24, 102, *103*
Copyright Act (1831), 102, *103*, 194n6
Copyright Act (1909), 102, *103*, 194n7, 194n9
Copyright Acts (1962–74), *103*
Copyright Act (1976), 102, *103*, 106, 194nn8–9
Copyright Act (current), 22–24
copyright's imbalance, 102, *103*
copyright's indelicacy, *107*
expansion, 102, *103*
first term *vs.* second term, 106, 197n58
joint works, 24
retroactive changes, 18, 19–20, 102, 106, *107*, 194nn6–9, 194n11
state copyright acts, 182n17
trends, 102, *103*
works made for hire, 24
dynamic works, 25

E

economics of copyright
common law's promotion of economic efficiency, 37, 178n130
complications, quibbles, and criticism, 47, 179nn12–14
copyright holders' revenues, 54–55
effect of market growth, 157, 158–161, 209n1
fair use costs, 116
infringement discouraging authorship, 49–50, *50*, 52
justification for copyright, 157
marginal costs to infringers, 52–55, *55*, 180n21
market power, 48
monopoly profits, 47–48, 55, 162
nonholders' opportunity costs, 45, *46*, 47, 52, 179n9, 179n13
policy implications, 108, 198n61
policy ramifications, 163–164
price discrimination, 158, 161, 179n13, 179n17
public policy path, *42*
standard economic model, 45–47, *46*
statutory *vs.* common law, 56–57
supply and demand, 158
technology's impact on production costs, 148–149, *149*, 150, 160, 209n9
See also market failure
Eldred v. Ashcroft (2003), 18, 173n28, 199n6, 203n42
Electronic Data Systems Corp. v. Computer Associates International, Inc. (1992), 201n14
Engels, Friedrich, 49–50
Epstein, Richard A.
common-law principles, 4, 34, 37, 178n128
on copyright and natural rights, 95
on copyright's capabilities, 185n51
critiques of Locke, 70, 185n46
defense of copyright, 68, 192n51
on freedom of contract, 204n4
on necessity of state power, 74
on private property, 204n4
on property rights, 185n46, 185n50
utilitarian analysis of copyright, 70

fraud, expressive, 83–84
freedom of contract, 72, 204n4
Friedman, David, 209n5
furniture, 174n39

G

Garcia-Goyco v. Law Environmental Consultants, Inc. (2005), 201n7
Garcia-Goyco v. P.R. Highway Authority (2003), 206n23
Georgia
  Founding-Era copyright act, 181n13, 182n18, 183n25, 183n31
Gibson, James, 193n69
Ginsburg, Jane C., 179n1, 199n7
Goldstein, Paul, 182n16, 196n47, 200n20, 205n7, 206n15
Goldstein v. California (1973), 206n16
Gordon, Wendy J., 117, 189n20, 198n4
government. *See* federal government; state, definition; state copyright acts
Great Britain
  common-law protection of authors' works, 65–66

H

habeas corpus, writ of, 92, 189n25
Hadady Corp. v. Dean Witter Reynolds, Inc. (1990), 204n6
Hamilton, Alexander, 186n66
Hand, Learned, 23, 118
"Happy Birthday to You," 150, 208n17
Harper & Row, Publishers, Inc. v. Nation Enterprises (1985), 196n47
Harrison v. Sterry (1809), 189n25
Hayek, Friedrich A., 4, 60, 73, 197n51
Hogue, Arthur R., 34–35
Hohfeld, Wesley, 91, 189nn16–18
Hollywood film industry, 80–81, 82
Holmes, Oliver Wendell, 41

Hughes, Justin, 193n76
Hume, David, 73
Hylton, Keith N., 26

I

Illinois
  public performance protection, 177n110
In re Napster, Inc., 128–129, 202n23, 203n40
"information wants to be free," 113, 198nn1–2
infringement and infringing works
  abandonment defense, 205n7
  authors' attitude toward, 86–87
  Copyright Act (current), 27–29
  criminal sanctions, 29–30
  discouragement from, 44
  discouraging authorship, 49–50, *50*, 52
  economic costs to copyholders, 48–50
  economic costs to infringers, 48, 52, 179n18
  in everyday life, 79–83
  fair use defense, 25, 115, 119–120, 200n23
  general elements, 27–28
  import/export restrictions, 29, 175n58
  innocence defense, 23, 104, 207n4, 208n28
  marginal costs, 52–55, *55*, 180n21
  mass infringement, 53
  misuse defense, 124, 126, 201n7, 202n26, 203n33
  secondary liability, 28–29
  seizure and forfeiture, 29, 176n95, 196nn31–32, 196n37
  severe sanctions, 80, 81–83
  social norms, 82, 83, 84–85, 86, 97, 193n69, 193n75
  subtle forms, 27
  as theft, 86
  as unprotected works, 22, 174n42

See also remedies for infringement; unauthorized use
instrumentalist theory of property, 193nn71–72
intellectual privilege, copyright as, 90–92
intellectual property, 12, 31–34, *33*, *42*
intellectual property rights, 190n29, 193n76
International Motor Contest Association v. Staley (2006), 201n7
Internet service providers, 104
interstate commerce clause, 172n19
Irons, Edward S., 181n14
iTunes, 114, 116

J

Jay, John, 186n66
Jefferson, Thomas, 4, 6, 66–67, 184n42, 186n66
Johnson, Samuel, 146, 207n11
joint works, 24, 177n109, 191n49
Judge, Kathryn, 203n40

K

Kaiser Aetna v. United States (1979), 190n35
Kant, Immanuel, 59
Keane v. Fox Television Stations, Inc. (2005), 208n24
Kessler, Friedrich, 136, 204n4
Klerman, Daniel, 178n130
Kobak, James B., Jr., 202n21
Kreiss, Robert A., 191n50, 199n13, 205nn8–9, 205n11

L

labor-desert theory of property, 69–72
Landes, William M., 4, 23, 28, 53
language of copyright, 89–99
   copyright as "privilege," 89–92, 188n3

copyright as property, 89, 92–93, 188n1, 190n30
copyright *vs.* "property," 92–97
defending property, 97–98
importance of, 98–99
rhetorically rebalancing copyright, 98
Lanham Act, 153, 154, 208n21, 208nn24–25
Lasercomb America, Inc. v. Reynolds (1990), 126, 201n4, 202n18, 203n27
Leoni, Bruno, 4
Lessig, Lawrence, 23
Leval, Pierre N., 199n14
Levine, David K., 209n1
liberal, definition, 210n1
liberty, definition, 189nn16–19
libraries and archives, 196n44
Lichtman, Douglas, 28
literary works, 20, 32, 33
Litman, Jessica, 189n19
Locke, John
   labor-desert justification of property, 59, 68, 69–72
   Second Treatise of Government, 185n52, 188n8, 190n28
   theory of natural property rights, 75
   views of copyright, 69, 95, 185nn52–53, 192n52
Lofgren, Charles A., 184n44
Loren, Lydia Pallas, 191n50, 202n19
Lotus Development Corp. v. Borland Intern., Inc. (1995), 21, 173n35
Lycans, Andrew P., 193n69

M

Madison, James
   on copyright, 65–68
   copyright as nuisance, 62
   on monopolies, 66–67, 184n43
   natural rights and copyright, 64, 67
   original meaning of Constitution, 186n66

on property rights, 184n43
on state copyright laws, 65
on trial by jury, 189n25
marginal costs
of production, 45–47, *46*, 52–53,
147, 148, *148*, 150, 157, 160–
161
technology's impact on, 148, *149*
of unauthorized users, 48, 52–55,
54, *55*, 179n18, 180n21
market failure
copyright as response to, 41
remedies, 113, 117
See also economics of copyright
market growth
effect on copyright, 157, 158–161,
209n1
reducing costs of expressive
works, 165, 210n27
Marx, Karl, 49–50
Maryland
Declaration of Rights, 62–63
Founding-Era copyright act,
182nn18–19, 183n31
Massachusetts
Founding-Era copyright act, 63,
181n13, 182nn18–19, 183n31
Merrill, Thomas W., 190n35
*Metro-Goldwyn-Mayer, Inc. v.
Showcase Atlanta Cooperative
Productions, Inc.* (1981), 205n9
Mickey Mouse, 106, 151–154,
197n54
Micro Star v. Formgen (1998), 205n9
Mill, John Stuart, 145
Millar v. Taylor (1769), 65
misuse doctrine
antitrust law violations, 201n14
award of attorney's fees, 140, 206–
207nn23–25
codification, 123–132
codifying, 123–132
in the courts, 125–127, 201nn13–
14, 202nn16–19, 202–
203nn26–27, 203nn33–34,
203n40, 203n45

definition, 127–128
expansion, 202n19
as infringement defense, 124, 126,
201n7, 202n26, 203n33
legal effect, 128–129
limiting copyright privileges, 124
scope, 125, 130
section 107(b) as proposed,
127–130
section 107(b) in practice, 130–
132
monopolies
Founders' aversion to, 62–63,
181nn14–15
property rights defense against,
184n43
Mossoff, Adam, 92, 190n26,
190nn35–36, 192n61
Motion Picture Association of
America, 93
movie industry, 80–81, 82
musical works, 148, 198n60, 200n25
See also sound recordings

N

*National Cable Television Association
v. Broadcast Music, Inc.* (1991),
201n13
*National Comics Publications, Inc. v.
Fawcett Publications, Inc.* (1951),
204n6
natural law, slavery under, 178n132
natural rights
in absence of government, 75–76
as check on customs, 178n127
as check on positive law, 178n127
common law and, 37, 178n129,
180n10
in Constitution (US), 178n129,
185n52
constitutional principles and,
180n10
copyright as, 60–64, 71
copyright as violation of, 2, 77, 91
copyright in natural rights theory,
59–60, 68–76

definition, 188n8
enabling human social life, 73
existential view, 68
freedom of contract as, 72
justifications of, 60
modern day, 75
property rights as, 72–73, 74
safeguarded by civil rights, 92,
    190n28
special legal weight, 189n23
in state copyright acts, 62, 181n13
Negroponte, Nicholas, 210n19
Netanel, Neil, 12
Netherlands
perfume as copyrightable, 173n34
New Hampshire
Founding-Era copyright act, 63,
    181n13, 182nn18–19, 183n31
New Jersey
common-law copyright protec-
    tion, 177n116
Founding-Era copyright act,
    181n13, 182nn18–19, 183n31
New York
Founding-Era copyright act,
    181n13, 182n18, 183n25,
    183n31
sound recordings, 33–34, 177n114
unfixed expressive works, 32
Nimmer, David
on abandonment of copyright,
    205n9
on common-law copyright, 33,
    177n117
on misuse defense, 201n14,
    202n19
on patent infringement, 201n12
on supremacy clause, 206n15
Nimmer, Melville B.
on abandonment of copyright,
    205n9
on common-law copyright, 33,
    177n117
on misuse defense, 201n14,
    202n19
on patent infringement, 201n12

on supremacy clause, 206n15
"No Music Day," 198n60
nonprofit entities, 196n44
*Norfolk Redevelopment and Housing
    Authority v. Chesapeake &
    Potomac Telephone Co.* (1983),
    189n23
North Carolina
Declaration of Rights, 181n15
Founding-Era copyright act, 63,
    181n13, 182nn18–19, 183n25,
    183n31
novels, 18th-century, 16, 172n17

O

On Liberty (Mill), 145
open copyright. *See* uncopyright and
    open copyright
originalist Constitution, 60, 67, 71,
    186n66
originality requirement, 23
Origins of the Common Law (Hogue),
    34–35

P

Pacific & Southern Co. v. Duncan
    (1983), 204n6
packet-switched networks, 167–168
Paine, Thomas, 188n8, 190n28
Palmer, Tom G., 4, 6, 186n64
passing off, 83–84, 153, 187n12,
    208n24
patent
compensation for takings, 96,
    192n60
vs. copyright, 21–22, 23
as fundamental civil right, 92
misuse defense, 124, 125, 127,
    201n12, 202n21
novelty requirement, 23
as privilege, 92, 190n26
in public policy path, 42, 43
royalty payments for unpatented
    invention, 180n23
speed of process, 198n63
Patry, William F., 191n49

Patterson, L. Ray, 187n83, 199n14
Pennsylvania
    Founding-Era copyright act,
        182nn18–19, 183n31
performances, public. *See* public per-
    formance
perfumes, 21, 173n34
philosophy of copyright, 59–77
    Barnett's positivist account of
        natural rights, 72–73
    copyright's naturalness, 60–62
    copyright's unnatural origins,
        62–68
    Locke's labor-desert justification
        of property, 69–72
    Madison on copyright, 65–68
    natural rights, here and now,
        74–76
    natural rights theory, 68–76
    state copyright acts, 62–65
phone records, compulsory licens-
    ing, 175n65, 191n39
piracy. *See* infringement and infring-
    ing works; unauthorized use
politics of copyright, 101–109
    assessing copyright policy, 107–
        109
    copyright's balance, 45, 179n10
    copyright's complexity, 104
    copyright's imbalance, 101–105,
        179n10
    copyright's indelicacy, 105–107
    duration of copyright, 102, *103*,
        107
    economic considerations, 163–
        164
    lack of essential knowledge,
        197n51
    limits on copyright, 104–105
    power of copyright, 104
    scope of copyright, 102–104
    sound-recording rights, 25
Pollack, Malla, 16
positivism, 59–60, 72–73, 91
Posner, Richard A., 4, 23, 35, 53, 116
postage stamps, 195n25

Powell, H. Jefferson, 184n44
The Power of Sympathy (Brown), 16
*Practice Management Information
    Corp. v. American Medical
    Association* (1997), 203n34
*PRC Realty Systems, Inc. v. National
    Association of Realtors* (1992),
    203n33
*Princeton University Press v.
    Michigan Document Services, Inc.*
    (1996), 200n27
privilege, definitions, 90–91,
    189nn16–18
property and property rights
    acquisition, 95
    alienation, 94–95
    as bundle of rights, 93
    common-law protections, 38
    compensation for takings, 96
    vs. copyright, 24, 26, 71, 92–97,
        186n64
    defending, 97–98, 184n43
    definitions, 96, 190nn34–36
    instrumentalist theory, 193nn71–
        72
    labor-desert theory, 69–72
    law of, 171n4
    as natural rights, 60, 72–73, 74
    ownership's duration, 24
    preservation, 96
    right to exclude, 93–94
    termination power, 27, 175n70
    use, 94
    as web of relations, 93, 97
public broadcasting entities, 175n65,
    191n39
public choice theory, 105–106, 107
public display of a work, 25
public domain
    "blockheaded" authors, 146–150
    Creative Commons license, 207n9
    uncopyrighted works, 145–146
public goods, *42*, 43
public performance
    copyholder's rights, 25
    dynamic works, 25

"Happy Birthday to You," 150,
208n17
sound recordings, 25, 175n59,
175n61, 175n65, 191n39,
191n44
state laws, 32, 177n110
public policy, 41–57
intellectual property, *42*
optimizing copyright, 51–57
specter of copyism, 47–50
standard economic model, 45–47,
46
publicity, right of, 152
publishers, transfer rights, 26–27

R

radio stations, 25
Rakove, Jack N., 184n44
Rand, Ayn, 6, 69
"rational basis" test, 18
recipes, 173n33
Record Rental Amendment (1984),
197n47
Recording Industry Association of
America, 93
registration of copyright, 22–23, 63,
177n107
Reichman, J. H., 198n63
remedies for infringement
criminal punishment, 29–30,
196n37
definition, 22
expansion, 104
forfeiture, 29, 176n95, 196nn31–
32, 196n37
import/export restrictions, 29,
195n29
monetary relief, v, 29, 53
before registration, 22–23
retroactive, 129
reverse passing off, 153, 208n24
Rhode Island
Founding-Era copyright act, 63,
181n13, 182nn18–19, 183n31
*Rosemont Enterprises, Inc. v. Random
House, Inc.* (1996), 200n2

Rosen, Hilary, 93
*Rowe v. Golden West Television
Productions* (1982), 177n116

S

Sandefur, Timothy, 4
Scalia, Antonin, 186n66
Scott v. Sandford (1856), 184n39
Sears, Mary Helen, 181n14
secondary liability, 28–29, 176n84
secondary transmission, 104, 196n43
seizure and forfeiture, 29, 176n95,
196nn31–32, 196n37
ship designs, 30, 31, 104
Siwek, Steven E., 198n61
slavery, 178n132, 184n39
Smith, Adam, 82, 165, 210n26,
210n28
Smith, Eric H., 198n61
social benefits of copyright, 51, *51*,
54
software, 20, 28, 150, 196n44, 196n47
Sonny Bono Copyright Term
Extension Act, 18, *103*, 106,
194n9
*Sony Corp. v. Universal City Studios,
Inc.* (1984), 28–29, 199n13, 204n5
sound recordings
common-law copyright protection, 177n114
compulsory licensing, 175n65,
191n39
copyholder's rights, 25
copyright limitations, 196n43
digital audio transmission, 25
New York, 33–34
as property, 93
public performance, 25, 175n59,
175n61, 175n65, 191n39,
191n44
state laws, 177n114
unauthorized copying, 84–85
South Carolina
Founding-Era copyright act,
182n18, 183n25, 183n31
Spencer, Herbert, 6, 69

Spooner, Lysander, 6, 69
Sprigman, Christopher, 23
state, definition, 171n7
state copyright acts
  citizenship/residence of author, 63, 182n18
  common-law claims, 137–138
  duration of copyright, 182n17
  Founding Era, 61, 62–65, 183n25, 183n31
  influence on US Constitution, 64, 183n26
  pricing of copyrighted works, 63, 183n25
  publication date of works, 63
  registration requirements, 63
  unfixed expressive works, 32
  as utilitarian, 64, 183n31
  works covered, 63
Stationers' Company, 70–71
statist legal positivism, 171n6
Steamboat Willie (film), 106–107, *107*, 151–154, 197n58
Stipp, David, 198n1
Supreme Court, US
  Aronson v. Quick Point Pencil Co. (1979), 180n23
  award of attorney's fees, 140
  Campbell v. Acuff-Rose Music, Inc. (2005), 119
  common-law principles, 61
  copyright as content-neutral restriction, 134–135
  copyright description, 76–77
  Dastar Corp. v. Twentieth Century Fox Film Corp. (2003), 139, 153–154
  Eldred v. Ashcroft (2003), 18, 194n11
  Feist Publications, Inc. v. Rural Telephone Service Co., Inc. (1991), 19
  Fogerty v. Fantasy, Inc. (1996), 180n9
  misuse defense, 124, 201n4, 202n21

origins of copyright restrictions, 33
"progress" interpretation, 15, 171n9
property definition, 96
"rational basis" test, 18, 173n24
retroactive duration of copyright, 102, 194n11
Wheaton v. Peters (1834), 184n38
Zoltek Corp. v. United States (2006), 96

T
takings, compensation for, 96
Tamburo v. Calvin (1995), 203n33
tangible property. *See* property
tax code
  compared to Copyright Act, 85–86
  copyright tax code, 86–87
Tehranian, John, 79
Telecom Technical Services v. Rolm Co. (2004), 201n7
television programs, 92–93, 104, 204n6
termination rights
  co-owners, 191n49
  compensation, 26–27, 95
  duration, 191n46
  enforceability, 26–27, 175nn69–70, 191nn47–48
  limiting effectiveness of abandonment, 137, 191n50, 205nn10–11
  See also abandoned works; alienation
Thomson, Judith Jarvis, 189n18
321 Studios v. Metro-Goldwyn-Mayer Studios, Inc. (2004), 203n45
toll goods, *42, 43,* 126
trade secrets, 32, *42, 43*
trademark, 31, *33, 42,* 152–154
trademark and unfair competition law, 152–154
transfer rights, 26–27

trial by jury, as fundamental civil
    right, 92, 189n25
trusts, law of, 171n4
Twain, Mark, 96

U
unauthorized use
    discouraging authorship, *50*
    increasing consumer surplus, *51,*
        51–52
    marginal costs, 53–55, *54*
    morality of, 83–87
    noninfringing personal use, 93,
        190n38
    television programs, 92–93
    See also infringement and infring-
        ing works
unclean hands doctrine, 126, 200n2
uncopyright and open copyright,
    145–155
    blockheaded authorship, 146–150,
        148, 149
    composing for love, not money,
        150–151, *151*
    Steamboat Willie, 151–154
    toward an open copyright system,
        154–155
    uncopyright notice, 146, *146,*
        208n28
unfixed works
    common-law protections, 34,
        177n117
    indirectly encouraged by copy-
        right, 179n6
    joint ownership, 177n109
    state statutory restrictions, 32
    transfer of ownership, 177n109
United States v. Loew's, Inc. (1962),
    201n4
*United States v. Paramount Pictures,
    Inc.* (1948), 201n4
United States v. Texas (1993), 189n23
use rights, 94

V
Valenti, Jack, 93
*Video Pipeline, Inc. v. Buena Vista
    Home Entertainment, Inc.* (2003),
        202n17, 202n26
Virginia
    Founding-Era copyright act,
        182n18
visual arts
    authorship, 129, 203nn43–44
    copyholder's rights, 25
    Copyright Act (current), 24, 30
    exclusive rights, 24
    protected works, 103, 195n19

W
Walt Disney Company, 106–107,
    151–154
    See also Disney, Walt
Walterscheid, Edward C., 183n26
Warfel, Harry R., 182n16
"We Celebrate Your Birthday" (Bell),
    150–151, *151*
Weber, Max, 171n7
Webster, Noah, 63, 64, 182n16,
    183n26
Wheaton v. Peters (1834), 184n38
Williamson, Hugh, 64
works made for hire, 24
writings
    constitutional requirement, 19,
        102–103
    definition, 19

Y
Yoo, Christopher S., 46, 162, 179n10,
    179n14, 210n18

Z
Zoltek Corp. v. United States (2006),
    96, 192n60
Zywicki, Todd, 178n130

ABOUT THE AUTHOR

Tom W. Bell is a professor at Chapman University's Fowler School of Law and an adjunct fellow of the Cato Institute. His writings include *Regulator's Revenge: The Future of Telecommunications Deregulation* (Cato Institute), which he edited with Solveig Singleton; "Five Reforms for Copyright" in *Copyright Unbalanced: From Incentive to Excess*, edited by Jerry Brito (Mercatus Center at George Mason University); and many papers and articles. After earning a JD from the University of Chicago, Bell practiced law in Silicon Valley and Washington, DC. He began teaching in 1995, took a year's leave of absence to serve as the Cato Institute's director of telecommunications and technology studies, and joined Chapman University's Fowler School of Law in 1998. Bell and his family live in San Clemente, California.

ABOUT THE MERCATUS CENTER AT GEORGE MASON UNIVERSITY

The Mercatus Center at George Mason University is the world's premier university source for market-oriented ideas—bridging the gap between academic ideas and real-world problems.

A university-based research center, Mercatus advances knowledge about how markets work to improve people's lives by training graduate students, conducting research, and applying economics to offer solutions to society's most pressing problems.

Our mission is to generate knowledge and understanding of the institutions that affect the freedom to prosper and to find sustainable solutions that overcome the barriers preventing individuals from living free, prosperous, and peaceful lives.

Founded in 1980, the Mercatus Center is located on George Mason University's Arlington campus.

www.mercatus.org

Made in the USA
Charleston, SC
23 April 2014